BAD

AN UNPRECEDENTED INVESTIGATION INTO THE MICHAEL JACKSON COVER-UP

DYLAN HOWARD

Skyhorse Publishing

Skyhorse Publishing books may be purchased in bulk at special discounts for sales promotion, corporate gifts, fund-raising, or educational purposes. Special editions can also be created to specifications. For details, contact the Special Sales Department, Skyhorse Publishing, 307 West 36th Street, 11th Floor, New York, NY 10018 or info@skyhorsepublishing.com.

Skyhorse® and Skyhorse Publishing® are registered trademarks of Skyhorse Publishing, Inc.®, a Delaware corporation.

Visit our website at www.skyhorsepublishing.com.

10 9 8 7 6 5 4 3 2 1

Library of Congress Cataloging-in-Publication Data is available on file.

Jacket design by 5mediadesign
Jacket photo credits: Getty Images

Print ISBN: 978-1-5107-5509-3
Ebook ISBN: 978-1-5107-6327-2

Printed in the United States of America

OTHER BOOKS BY DYLAN HOWARD

Epstein: Dead Men Tell No Tales
Aaron Hernandez's Killing Fields
Diana: Case Solved
The Last Charles Manson Tapes: Evil Lives Beyond the Grave
Billion Dollar Hollywood Heist
Royals at War

PRAISE FOR DYLAN HOWARD

"Dylan Howard is the rare combination of cutting-edge journalist, true crime commentator, and relentless investigator."

—Dr. Phil McGraw, host of TV's #1 daytime talk show, *Dr. Phil*

"Renowned."

—Nancy Grace

"A wunderkind Hollywood gossip reporter."

—*Columbia Journalism Review*

"Big-name producer."

—*Vanity Fair*

"Howard is a throwback to an older age of journalism."

—Anne Helen Petersen, *BuzzFeed*

"One of my favorite people in American media."

—Anthony Scaramucci

"A tabloid prodigy."

—Jeffrey Toobin, staff writer at the *New Yorker*, CNN senior legal analyst, and *New York Times* bestselling author

"The king of Hollywood scoops."

—*Ad Week*

"The go-to guy for authoritative showbiz news and analysis on cable and over-the air television."

—*Los Angeles Press Club*

"When Dylan Howard focuses his attention to investigating a case, you can be sure he will uncover sensational new information that we, as readers, viewers or listeners, will find astonishing."

—Dr. Drew Pinsky, *New York Times* bestselling author and TV and radio personality

CONTENTS

AUTHOR'S NOTE

Bad is the untold, revelatory true story of the strange and larger-than-life career of Michael Jackson, the King of Pop. In the wake of the controversial film *Leaving Neverland*, a two-part documentary telling the stories of two young boys who were befriended by the singer and claimed they suffered years of agonizing abuse, I set out to investigate Jackson's life and death in unprecedented depth and determine if, as one lawyer suggested, the pop star I idolized growing up in Australia as a teenager ran "the most sophisticated child sexual abuse procurement and facilitation operation the world has known."

    Bad is a dramatic narrative account based on dozens of interviews, Jackson's own riveting personal journal, interviews with Jackson family members, multiple first-person sources—some of whom have asked to remain anonymous—and thousands of pages of court documents. I also acquired dozens of top-secret pages from Jackson's private investigator's files and case notes. What I uncovered in Michael Jackson is a man who was both naive and Machiavellian, unorthodox, a devoted father, a shrewd businessman, and a drug addict whose life was cut short but whose sound and style have influenced artists of various genres. Remarkably though, in death, there remain two portraits of Michael Jackson: the reigning King of Pop, and a pedophile whose pattern of abuse ruined his reputation. Fans and individuals alike will forever be asking if the insidious claims made about Michael were true. This is the new narrative and the sad legacy of one of the bestselling music artists of all time, who amassed sales of over 350 million records worldwide.

—Dylan Howard

PROLOGUE

If you think you know all there is to know about Michael Jackson . . . If you think you've heard every shocking detail about the King of Pop . . .

Think again.

The superstar has been dead for more than a decade. While there remain serious questions about the truthfulness of those who have accused him of the most heinous acts, there is absolutely no question that whatever his intentions, Michael lacked a sense of what was or was not appropriate for children to do—or see. Especially children that were not his own.

Perhaps no evidence—evidence, not hearsay—is more powerful than the disturbing files that have been found on Michael Jackson's personal electronic devices: private home videos that reveal a viscerally disturbing side of the superstar who died in 2009 from a drug overdose.

Was he a twisted adult or just a man-child, stunted in bad boy adolescence?

You decide.

The long, agonizing minutes of video footage—which has been circulating through the back street of Tinseltown for the last few years, and was obtained as part of the investigation for this book—features Michael engaged in aggressive, foul-mouthed role-playing sessions with young boys in his bed, without a chaperone, at a secluded resort. Michael was so unashamed that he personally recorded some of the clips.

This startling, previously unseen content seems, yet again, to cast very serious doubt over whether the legendary entertainer was truly innocent of being a child abuser.

However, it also reminds us that the private life of Michael Jackson may ultimately be like the Japanese film *Rashômon* from 1950. In that classic tale, the sexual assault of a bride and the slaying of her husband are told from the very different points-of-view of four participants or observers—including the ghost of the husband. Alas, we do not have that luxury with Michael. For many narratives, there can be no true resolution.

The Michael Jackson story may be one of those.

The scandalous videos in question were shot at the end of 1999 while Michael was at the posh Sun City resort, located in the mountains outside Johannesburg, South Africa. The forty-one-year-old singer was accompanied by two children, whose identities I have chosen not to reveal for the sake of their own privacy, given the video has never been released publicly.

A few years earlier, Michael had struck up a friendship with the children's parents. The star had visited their home several times and even attended one of the children's bar mitzvah.

He made the special trip to South Africa just to celebrate the occasion.

The week he recorded the home movies, Michael stayed in his usual King Suite at Sun City. The luxuriously furnished, 2,600-square-foot accommodations included two bedrooms with king-size beds and two massive bathrooms with a sauna and a Jacuzzi, an elegant living room, a cozy study, and a dining room, all featuring maple paneling on the walls. Each room was lined with two-story windows and lavish curtains.

All of Michael's private videos from that trip were made in the master bedroom. Most of them were shot at night. He had powerful lights rigged to the tops of two wooden posters at the head of his canopy bed. The illuminated area seemed more like a movie set than a bedroom. All of the footage takes place on this, akin to a Hollywood sound stage the likes of the famed Paramount lot, on Hollywood's Melrose Avenue.

The first recovered clip I watched provides a surprisingly wholesome glimpse into Michael's private life. It begins with Michael lounging on the far edge of the bed, facing the camera. He is resting above the covers, dressed in black pants, a black button-down shirt, and his shoulder-length hair is spindly and disheveled. His plastic surgery–riddled nose is covered in flesh-colored Band-Aids. Michael is holding his one-year-old daughter, Paris, while his two-year-old son, Michael Jr., and one of the young boys are pretending the bed is a wrestling ring. The other child is behind the camera capturing the scene.

Michael is speaking in a deeper tone as he clumsily adlibs dialogue as if he were a sports commentator:

> "And, um . . . they're doing very well! And, uh . . . having not spent too much time with their families, it's been like, uh, very much, well, training for this fight. But as you can see what's happening in the . . ."

Michael is interrupted by a doorbell. He knows exactly who is on the other side of the door: his longtime nanny Grace Rwaramba. She has arrived to take Paris away, presumably to bed.

"We've gotta take Yib-Yib back," Michael announces to the group of children, referring to Paris. He gives his daughter a loving embrace and a smooch on the cheek.

"I love you," the singer declares, holding his sleepy daughter against his chest.

"I love you," the toddler gently replies. "I love you, Da-Da."

Meanwhile, the wrestling match between the two boys is in full swing. Little Michael Jr. climbs up on the headboard and raises his arms like he's about to do a spectacular wrestling move. Child Number Two zooms in on the adorable contender.

Michael can be heard off-camera asking Paris to give the boys a kiss.

"She wants to give you a kiss, Doo-Doo," Michael announces to the cameraman.

The doorbell rings again. Michael reacts impatiently.

"Doo-Doo, you've got to open the door," he commands. "It's Grace . . . [redacted]?"

The child cameraman shuts the camera off as Michael starts issuing a ten-count to end the wrestling match.

The scene resumes after Grace has removed Paris from the suite. Michael Jr. and the first child are still battling on the bed and the second child is still behind the camera. Michael is lounging a bit deeper. He is leaning on his right side and has his head propped against the headboard. His eyes are very heavy and his speech is very lazy as he playfully argues with Michael Jr. about which character he's pretending to be from the videogame *Ready 2 Rumble Boxing*.

"Afro Thunder? Butcher Brown?" Michael says. "I'm Butcher Brown."

"No, I'm Butcher Brown," his son retorts.

The scene cuts out again.

When recording continues, Michael Jr. is no longer in the bedroom. Child One is sitting in Michael's previous spot on the bed. Child Two is on the other side of the bed. Both boys are now sporting Michael's Band-Aids on the tips of their noses.

The camera is on a tripod and facing the two boys. Michael is off camera, playing director.

"Now you blackmail him," Michael instructs Child One. "Blackmail him."

"Listen up, [redacted]," the young boy says, hoping to sound intimidating. "If you don't let me come in, I'll tell . . . I'll tell all your friends what you did."

"What you did to that girl," Michael prompts.

"What you did to that girl, huh?" Child One adds with a devilish smile.

The camera cuts out again, however, the next scene adds a little more context to the seemingly artificial gripe.

"When it was my friends coming over, you had to join in!" Child One whines, now wearing Michael's baseball cap, which he defiantly throws on the bed. "That's horse shit!"

"That's because I'm the older one," Child Two argues.

"So?" Child One presses in a typical brotherly fashion.

"I don't want you . . . just," Child Two trails off, shooing his brother away with a flick of his hand.

Following another break in the recording, Child One appears in frame using the hotel room phone.

"Hey, Weasel," the boy says to the undisclosed person on the call.

"Weasel!" Michael exclaims with child-like approval followed by cackling laughter. "That's so cute . . . Weasel."

While Child One continues the brief conversation, he compulsively presses on his nose bandage and playfully covers his mouth like what he's saying is a secret.

After speaking, he quickly hangs up and hands the phone to Child Two, who sets it aside. It's unclear if anyone was actually on the other end of the line.

"Do you want something to eat?" Michael asks the boys.

The kids both nod and he offers them watermelon. One of Michael's children can be heard crying out for him and he leaves the room. Child Two instructs Child One how to stop the camera.

When the next scene begins, there is a startling shift in tone.

Child One is standing on the headboard and he has his arms wrapped around the wooden canopy beam at the top of the bed. He is facing the camera. Michael is in frame, in the foreground, staring back at the boy. Child Two is once again behind the camera.

At first glance, it appears as though they are re-enacting the final moments of a martyr on the cross. Michael, wearing his baseball hat, has seemingly cast himself in the "Father" role.

"Okay, [redacted]," Michael says sternly. "You've been up here all day. Come down."

"So?" Child One flings back, then cranes his head towards Michael and quickly fires off a fierce "Fuck you!"

Michael stares menacingly at the boy, unmoved by the vulgar response.

"[Redacted], I said come down here," he demands more firmly.

The boy dramatically looks away, his face awash with a kind of demonic possession. Then he issues another resolute "Fuck you."

"I'm sorry I ever had you as a son," Michael quietly declares. "You're a worthless nothing."

Child One continues hanging onto the beam and begins slowly panting. His eyes roll back slightly.

"Now bring your short ass down," Michael mandates, like a gunslinger calling out an opponent.

"Read my lips, you motherfuck," Child One slowly grinds out between his teeth as Child Two zooms in on his brother's haunting face. "Fuck . . . you!

Michael lunges at Child One, ferociously exploding like the werewolf he becomes in "Thriller." He grabs the chest area of the boy's T-shirt with his right hand and twists the material, pulling the quasi-crucified Child One menacingly towards him.

"Say it to me like you mean it!" Michael shouts, using only the bass in his voice.

Although Child One is clearly caught off guard, the boy grins—either cocky smirking or anxious fear—and does not break character.

"Read my fuckin' lips," he says, pretending to spit on Michael, who doesn't flinch. "Fuck. You."

Michael dramatically turns and exits the frame. Child One appears exceedingly pleased with himself as Child Two ends the recording.

The unsettling level of foul language and simulated abuse in that section of the footage cannot be ignored. Although Michael and the kids were engaging in what are clearly over-the-top theatrics, their preferred subject matter was without a doubt age-inappropriate. While they were obviously reenacting a film or video game they had recently watched together, that too, if true, only increases the poor judgment displayed by Michael. Incredibly, the kids do not appear disturbed by the provocative episode.

When the camera comes on again, Child One is sitting up at the head of the bed. A pillow is covering his lower half. He and Michael are in the middle of conversation.

"You say there's wonderful children in this school," Child One says, his voice filled with doubt. "These kids bully me every break."

"Are you serious?" Michael asks off-screen.

"I'm shit serious," Child One remarks, the unnecessary curse word still lingering in the air as the camera again stops recording.

It was the final clip of the evening.

The footage picks up in the morning. One of the children is the center of attention and the canopy bed remains his playground. The boy is wearing fresh clothes—a blue T-shirt and black athletic shorts—and he is sitting on the top of the wooden canopy frame like Peter Pan. One knee is bent with a foot resting on the beam, the other dangles and swings below it.

Michael is behind the camera.

"I want milk!" Child One says, a smirk curling on his face. "Doo-Doo wants milk from Jesse, he told me."

It is unclear exactly who the "Jesse" is that Child One refers to, but the boy is obviously trying to embarrass his older brother, who does not make another appearance in the footage.

"You snitch," Michael whispers.

"Yeah?" Child One asks. He then squeezes his own pectoral area and pretends to suck milk from his nipple.

Michael keeps the camera rolling as he moves around the perimeter of the bed, then up onto the mattress to get a swooping close-up of the camera-friendly boy. Child One hops down onto the bed and repeats his previous taunt.

"Doo-Doo wants milk from Jesse. Fresh!"

"You do," Michael fires back. "How do you want your milk?"

"Fresh," the chipper boy responds. "Fresh from the 'grizzle,'" he adds, likely meaning the cow.

Michael, apparently looking for a more specific response, repeats his question, but Child One turns the question on him.

"How do you like your milk?" the boy teases while swinging a pillow at Michael. "Warm!"

"Huh?" Michael asks, still unsatisfied with the boy's answer.

"Doo-Doo likes his milk warm," Child One continues.

Finally, Michael feeds Child One the "correct" response. "No," the singer murmurs, as if the camera might not detect his voice. "From the bottle."

Child One stops swinging the pillow for a split second to process Michael's statement.

"No!" the boy contests.

"From the bottle," Michael repeats with more conviction.

"No, I don't want milk from a bottle," Child One repeats.

"So you . . . you want it from . . . ?" flustered Michael responds.

He shuts off the camera before he finishes his thought; their "guy time" concluded with that final exchange.

After his trip to Sun City in 1999, Michael returned to his Neverland Ranch in California. A new obsession had consumed the singer. Not a child, but a child's entertainment. Michael contacted the company who made the *Ready 2 Rumble Boxing* game.

"The team received a call from a fan who enjoyed the game so much that he wanted to be in it," the game developer recalled, admitting he didn't believe it was really Michael Jackson until they met at Neverland. "He talked about the fun he had with the first game and how much he wanted to be in the sequel. He refused to be paid for his participation."

When *Ready 2 Rumble Boxing: Round 2* hit shelves a year later, Michael had become a secret "unlockable" character in the game. It featured his likeness, his dance moves, and even his real voice.

Although Michael was an avid gamer who collected classic arcade games and owned every gaming system, his desire to become a boxing avatar in that particular game appears to have been inspired by the 1999 trip. Instead of kids arguing over who gets to be "Butcher Brown" or "Afro Thunder," did he secretly want them fighting over who gets to be "Michael Jackson" in the next matchup? Was inserting himself into the video game another ploy to get kids to lower their guard, much like doling out his nose bandages or encouraging cursing on camera did? And if so, to what end? For vanity? Or to be a violator?

Now adults, both Child One and Child Two have denied there was any wrongdoing by Michael while they were in his company. They recalled meeting up with him at least eight times over several years. The youngest, Child Two—who was rarely seen in the home videos—spent several months with Michael shortly before the superstar's untimely passing. He, too, denied ever being inappropriately touched by Michael.

Even if Michael and the boys were playing out some kind of intense-bordering-on-disgusting cinematic scene, perhaps a prisoner or prisoner of war scenario, the footage confirms that we cannot afford a rush to judgment where things about Michael are concerned. Yes, the words and the actions are inexcusable on a certain level, but, much like Michael, they are not always what they seem. Kids often say creepy and inappropriate things, sometimes with uncalled-for sexual undertones. They may not even know what anything they're saying means, exactly—only that it's forbidden or something to giggle over. Like Michael's use of "Doo-Doo" as someone's name. Those who knew Michael best tend to agree that he remained very much a child throughout his adult life.

In short, it is likely acting, no less—though perhaps a little too much more—than he did in the music videos for "Bad" and "Thriller."

This level of potential misunderstanding, the danger of first impressions is, of course, why our society has trials. But tragically, even absolution in the court of law wasn't enough to save a monstrous star like Michael Jackson, who privately held a burning desire to be "the greatest ever"—like his idols Charlie Chaplin, Michelangelo, and Walt Disney. (See Appendix II for his Personal Diary.)

CHAPTER ONE

THE CASE FOR AND AGAINST

When asked why he was always hanging around with children, Michael Jackson had two answers.

First: "What I love, kids happen to love, or the child that lives inside the adult happens to love."

Second: "Well, I was raised in a world of adults."

Those are truthful and self-aware answers. But where Michael Jackson is concerned, it seems there will always be a new video—or scandalous documentary—to warrant a new explanation. And with them will come fresh interpretations, as there inevitably seem to be about what *really* caused the break up of The Beatles. Even in the crazy world of pop music, we do not see that kind of scrutiny of the late Prince, John Lennon, Yoko Ono, or even Elvis.

With each new video or every new tell-all comes new allegations. But occasionally old allegations dressed in new clothes for specials arise, like the much-hyped HBO two-part presentation *Leaving Neverland*, in which the star is accused of having committed truly repugnant acts on underage boys, from masturbation to oral sex.

That special, which first aired on March 3 and March 4 of 2019—after having premiered to much sensationalism at the prestigious Sundance Film Festival on January 25—was followed on March 4 by *After Neverland*, in which Oprah Winfrey interviewed the two individuals at the center of the narrative, Wade Robson and James Safechuck, and director Dan Reed. That HBO show was taped before what was essentially a supportive audience comprised of victims of sexual abuse.

"This is a moment in time that allows us to see this society corruption," Oprah declared, adding that she herself believed the tales recounted by accusers.

She wasn't alone in her belief. For example, there was the renowned Professor David Wilson, head of criminology at Birmingham City University, England, who said of the accusers: "They came across as authentic, and they came across as being sincere in what it was they were sharing."

He added that the two seemed to be the products of a grooming process that occurred over time and that "it was perfectly consistent that it would have taken them some time to be able to overcome that grooming process and be able to share the information that they shared."

But there are several qualifiers in Wilson's assessment. "Came across" and "perfectly consistent" are not the same as actually being truthful. Certainly the Jackson family did not see things in that same light, and they were much closer to the situation than Oprah or Professor Wilson.

The Jacksons' first salvo was a statement from the entire family which read in part:

> "Michael always turned the other cheek, and we have always turned the other cheek when people have gone after members of our family – that is the Jackson way. But we can't just stand by while this public lynching goes on. . . . Michael is not here to defend himself, otherwise these allegations would not have been made."

There were also confident denials from individual family members, like Jackie, who said, "I know my brother. He's not like that."

Nephew Taj—son of Michael's brother Tito, and an ardent online voice in support of his uncle—added: "I think the fault on my uncle was he just, he didn't have that bone in his body to look at it the other way . . . and I think that was the thing, is that his naiveté was his downfall, in a way."

Then there was Michael's brother Marlon, who was more blunt: "I have no interest in watching something that has no validity to it," he said, stoking the fire. "They weren't interested in gathering any evidence that wouldn't corroborate what they're saying."

Brother Jermaine, perhaps the most outspoken defender of his brother since his death, was the harshest critic of accusers Robson and Safechuck. He said that the time alone with the boys "were slumber parties" and that he was "one thousand percent sure" his brother did not molest them.

Jermaine damned the media and celebrities like Oprah for "blindly taking *Leaving Neverland* at face value" and for "shaping a narrative uninterested in facts, proof, credibility." The pain in Jermaine's words, in his voice, in his heart is palpable.

Michael's daughter Paris Jackson had a relatively cool head, replying to an angry tweet with:

> "... so ... not love and peace and trying to carry that message out? tabloids and lies are the bigger picture? I'll pray for you."

Dan Reed, the man behind the documentary, speciously defended his decision not to include interviews with family members: "People with no direct knowledge of that story or of those events don't have a place in the film."

Jackie Jackson disagreed: "When you start throwing allegations out about someone, then you got to go back and say, 'Wait a minute, let me make sure I'm telling the right thing. Make sure they're not selling me a bunch of goods.' Which they were."

Moreover, Oprah wasn't there either, yet her thumbs-up on the accusations helped to sell the documentary and the credibility of the two men to the public. Perhaps Mary Wilson, of the superstar group The Supremes, said it best and most impartially. In an exclusive interview after *Leaving Neverland* aired, she admitted to one of the investigators who worked on *Bad*, "Entertainers are different" in being rascally and added, "You don't know what everyone does in their bedroom." However, she added this as well—and it is crucial—that her adopted son, Willie, "grew up with me and Michael."

"He and my son used to play together. That's the Michael I know," she said

In other words, a rambunctious young man—but not a molester.

Finally, however, a much stronger and quite specific and detailed response on behalf of Michael came in the form of a lawsuit filed on February 21 against HBO and other defendants.

In a powerful opening statement—which was released into the public domain—legendary and highly respected Hollywood attorney Howard Weitzman (who, in full disclosure, has previously represented this author in unrelated matters) wrote:

> Michael Jackson is innocent. Period. In 2005, Michael Jackson was subjected to a trial—where rules of evidence and law were applied before a neutral judge and jury and where both sides were heard—and he was exonerated by a sophisticated jury. Ten years after his passing, there are still those out to profit from his enormous worldwide success and take advantage of his eccentricities. Michael is an easy target because he is not here to defend himself, and the law does not protect the deceased from defamation, no matter how extreme the lies are. Michael may not have lived his life according to society's norms, but genius and eccentricity are not crimes.
>
> Nothing and no one can rewrite the facts which show that Michael Jackson is indeed innocent of the charges being levied at him by HBO in its "documentary," *Leaving Neverland*. No one-sided "documentary" can substitute for a real documentary, or for a trial where both sides are heard, competent evidence is presented, and witnesses are cross-examined.
>
> Those behind this posthumous character assassination are:
>
> HBO: A company, recently acquired by AT&T, so desperate for eyeballs that its growing irrelevance to the cord-cutting generation was crystallized when its chief rival bluntly stated in its January earnings report that it considers a popular online game to be a more serious competitor than HBO. In producing this fictional work, HBO ignored its contractual obligations to Michael and his companies by disparaging both him and the *Dangerous* world tour that HBO had previously profited from immensely.
>
> Wade Robson and James Safechuck: Two admitted perjurers, one of whom is a self-described "master of deception," whose litigations have played out in the courts as a failed melodrama for more than five years. With more holes in their stories than anyone can count, both view

Michael Jackson, the man who they previously swore was an inspiration and did nothing to them, as a lottery ticket through accusations never brought during Michael's life. They never brought these claims during Michael's life, because they knew Michael would have held them both legally accountable for their defamation, just as Michael had held the "reporter" Victor Gutierrez—who seems to be the true author of these two men's fictional tales—liable before a jury for millions of dollars when he falsely made similar claims about Jackson.

Dan Reed: The HBO-deployed "documentarian" and director of *Leaving Neverland* who violated every rule of responsible journalism and documentary filmmaking. He all but embedded himself with the accusers' legal team to the point where he refused to devote even one minute of a 240-minute film to any of the mountainous evidence showing that Robson and Safechuck are lying. He refused to offer any counterpoint to their fabrications, and refused to talk to anyone whose statements might not fit the storyline of the fictional film he was dead set on making from the outset. Dan Reed made no attempt to review the legal records from Robson's and Safechuck's litigations with the estate, where the judge found that Robson had lied under oath during the litigations on key issues; and where Robson was caught red-handed hiding crucial evidence from the court, from the Jackson estate, and even from his own lawyers. Reed even ignored the fact that these men are still pursuing claims against the Jackson estate for hundreds of millions of dollars, so they have hundreds of millions of reasons to lie.

While the conduct of the above participants speaks for itself, special emphasis must be placed on HBO. HBO refused to even meet with representatives of the Jackson Estate—the primary beneficiaries of which are Michael's three children—who made no threats but just asked for a meeting to discuss problems with the "documentary." HBO is not in search of the truth—only in search of "content" and "engagement," as its bosses at AT&T have publicly ordered.

The real victims here are the primary beneficiaries of the estate,

Michael's three children, who are forced to endure this attack on their father, ten years after they buried him, and when he has no chance to respond.

Michael Jackson can never be silenced. His music and artistry live, as does his innocence. They will long outlast false claims, gossip, and allegations spread by those who seek to make money off him. In the end, this "documentary" will say much more about HBO than it ever could about Michael Jackson.

Weitzman went on to further excoriate the men at the center of the film:

Wade Robson and James Safechuck are admitted perjurers. They previously testified that Jackson never touched them inappropriately in any manner whatsoever. By 2013 and 2014, they were in financial dire straits. Safechuck was in serious need of money, the failed dreams of a successful acting and music career having long since passed him by. For his part, Robson was at the end of his choreography career. He had burned so many bridges that the only thing he had left was his connection with Michael Jackson. But in 2011, the Jackson estate had turned him down for the lead choreography job in a Cirque du Soleil show, a job that he told Cirque he "wanted badly." By 2012, Robson's wife was threatening to divorce him because of his inability to work.

So, in 2013 and 2014, Robson and Safechuck changed their stories. No doubt reading reports from *Forbes* and others and seeing programs like *60 Minutes* that reported on the unprecedented success of the Jackson estate—stories that all ran in the year before these men changed their stories—Robson and Safechuck filed suits against the Jackson estate.

Having claimed to have perjured themselves repeatedly prior to filing their suits against the Jackson Estate—and claiming to want to now "speak only the truth"—Robson and Safechuck still could not keep their stories straight after filing suit. Robson, in particular, was caught committing perjury repeatedly in 2013 through 2017, in his litigations against the estate.

For just a few examples among many that the estate pointed out:

a. The trial judge in Robson's initial case against the Estate found one of Robson's lies—on the key issue in that case (i.e., when he learned about the estate for statute of limitations purposes)—so clear that the judge took the extraordinary step of disregarding Robson's sworn statements on a summary judgment motion. The judge found that no rational fact finder could possibly believe Robson's sworn statement (i.e., his lie under oath) given the unequivocal evidence to the contrary and issued judgment in the estate's favor as a result.

b. In another of the many, many lies in which Robson was caught during his litigations with the Jackson estate, he swore under oath in 2016 that he had but one written communication with anyone about his abuse allegations from May 2012 until the date of his sworn statement—another fabrication. Through third party discovery—largely from Robson's mother, Joey, and his sister Chantal—it was revealed that Robson had thousands of such communications, talking to anyone and everyone about his evolving story of "abuse" (many of the communications were inquiries to his mother where he told her he was asking her to help him reconstruct "my story with Michael"). In fact, Robson had even written a book about his supposed abuse by Jackson in the year before filing his lawsuit—which he hid from the Jackson estate and hid from his own attorneys. When shopping his book in late 2012 and early 2013, Robson communicated with numerous publishers about his supposed abuse (contrary to his lie under oath that he had had only one written communication about his "abuse"). Robson first met with his lawyers about filing a lawsuit against the Jackson estate in March 2013, just a few weeks after being told by his book agent that no one was interested in publishing Robson's ludicrous story. More precisely, no one was interested in publishing Robson's fabricated and internally inconsistent tale until HBO, Channel 4 (UK), and Dan Reed came along.

Prior to filing the lawsuit, on February 7, Weitzman wrote a long, detailed letter to Richard Plepler, the former chief executive officer of HBO, in which the attorney forcefully and unflinchingly targeted the motives and credibility of the two accusers:

> Robson's fabricated story, of course, is that Jackson's abuse caused him to have two self-described nervous breakdowns in 2011 and 2012. Those breakdowns, according to Robson, caused him to realize that he had been abused by Jackson decades before. But there is a much simpler explanation for Robson's breakdowns. He has a family history of suicidal, major depression on his father's side. Robson's father committed suicide in 2002.
>
> Robson's first cousin on his father's side committed suicide in 2012. Unfortunately, major depression is a very heritable disease. Thus, it is no surprise that Robson had these breakdowns. And it is even less surprising that he has continued to have breakdowns given that when Robson saw a psychiatrist in 2011 he was prescribed antidepressant medication. But he refused to ever take that medication. To be clear, we ascribe no "fault" or "weakness" whatsoever to those who suffer or who have suffered from clinical depression. That said, we must note Robson's mental illness, and his abject and stubborn refusal to get appropriate medical treatment for it, because Robson's claim is that his "nervous breakdowns" are strong evidence of his abuse by Jackson. But those breakdowns are much more easily explained by Robson's family history of major depression and his own (apparent) diagnosis of depression for which he stubbornly and irrationally refused to take the medication prescribed to him by a medical doctor to treat it.
>
> As for Safechuck, by his own admission, he did not "realize" that he had been abused until after he saw Robson on the *Today Show* in May 2013 being interviewed by Matt Lauer about Robson's newly concocted story of abuse. All of a sudden, Safechuck realized that he had been

abused. He then contacted Robson's lawyers and filed copycat lawsuits against the estate for millions of dollars. And like Robson, he too had testified under oath that Jackson never did anything inappropriate with him. His two cases against the estate were also dismissed.

The motives and methods of those in front of the camera—and also behind it—are for the courts to decide. The court of public opinion, however, is already divided, and the man at the center of it all is unable to shed much-needed light and clarity.

With the passing of the years, Michael remains as big a controversy—and as big a mystery—as when he was alive. There is no question that his music was, and is, brilliant and groundbreaking. His music videos elevated the medium to the level of cinematic art. His example of excellence, of perfectionism, or sheer musicality inspired generations of youth, especially African Americans.

Yet his enduring and lamentably tenacious legacy is that of a sexual predator of young boys. During his life he vigorously denied these allegations, in the press and at trial. Now, as more alleged victims have come forward to tell their tales of alleged abuse, portraying Michael as a master manipulator and sexual deviant, can we expect more?

Was he an abuser of helpless children, or was he a misunderstood Peter Pan–like character helping "lost boys" find their way?

With unprecedented research, exclusive new interviews, Michael's own words, and access to long-hidden files, the investigation of *Bad* throws light on what was undeniably the sad life of an increasingly lonely, self-destructive icon.

"When you're young and you're working, the world can seem awfully unfair," Michael once said.

He would know. The entertainer's childhood memories were actually just snapshots, a blur of vague recollections of singing and dancing, often past his bedtime, of relentless practice and a dizzying performance schedule, of the watchful glare and cruel hand of his father, Joe.

From an early age, the child prodigy often headed straight to rehearsals or the recording studio after school. Breaks were infrequent and the opportunity to play with children other than his siblings was nonexistent. And even downtime with his brothers was limited.

Michael's boyhood was also hijacked by tragic off-stage pressures: years of domestic abuse, unyielding isolation, and constant sexual disorientation.

"I received quite an education as a child," Michael once stated, alluding to the hotel rooms the minor shared with his sexually active older brothers, and the restroom peepholes he was encouraged to utilize during gigs at sleazy venues.

"Perhaps this freed me to concentrate on other aspects of my life as an adult," he once mused.

Freed him or imprisoned him? There is no telling how witnessing actions that radical, without context or understanding, affected him. He watched his brothers with abandon . . . and was then required to go on stage, as an adolescent, mimicking that bumping and grinding—and doing it better. Therein are the seeds of not just confusion but abuse: what could an untutored boy do with this information? Like Elvis before him, like Mick Jagger, like so many rock stars, he was making love to an audience . . . but as an uncomprehending boy!

Whether these early indecent exposures turned Michael off from sex—or made him insatiably hungry for more—the experiences formed his impressionable adolescent mind. They gave the future superstar dangerous physical and emotional boundaries, which plagued him publicly and privately throughout his increasingly reclusive adult life.

Tragically, Michael became the biggest victim—of his own success.

CHAPTER TWO

A CHILD SHALL LEAD THEM

The situation in which Michael found himself in the early 2000s was far different from the one twenty years before, when he was at the pinnacle of his worldwide domination of the entertainment industry.

Michael went to New York to sell his first autobiography. He succeeded in selling it for several million dollars, and, in a fitting touch, his editor was one of the most publicized women in history: none other than Jacqueline Kennedy Onassis. Michael and the former First Lady were utterly unalike in terms of their background and age and every other yardstick save one: like Michael, she was a superstar who could not go anywhere without being mobbed, photographed, scrutinized, and judged.

Stephen Davis, who ghostwrote the book for Michael, recalls: "She was the only person in America who could get him on the phone."

Davis went to Encino, California, and did hours of interviews with Michael at the superstar's home over eight months. In retrospect, perhaps the ghostwriter's most valuable contribution to the legacy of Michael was not what he wrote but what he saw. He said that there was always an adolescent boy around.

"It was like Batman and Robin," Davis said, adding that there were several of them. And while Davis did not doubt that the youths shared a bed with Michael, he adds, "I don't believe for a minute that he ever molested them or touched them or anything like that, or gave them alcohol."

They were just pals. Playmates. Regardless of whether that was "normal" behavior or an indicator of being psychologically stunted is almost beside the point.

Michael did not engage with them sexually.

Stephen was said to be have paid $300,000 for the memoir. And when he insisted, Michael got one more perk: the relentlessly private Jackie wrote a three-paragraph introduction to the book. (Years later, in 2009, when the book was reissued, Motown founder Berry Gordy wrote an introduction that preceded Jackie's. He concluded the lengthy preface with these heartfelt lines: "The more I think and talk about Michael Jackson, the more I feel the King of Pop was not big enough for him. I think he was simply 'The Greatest Entertainer Who Ever Lived.'")

Ultimately, the volume that emerged was a handsome package of fluff and puff. Dedicated to legendary film dancer Fred Astaire, it was called *Moonwalk*, after the dance step in which the performer seems to be walking forward but moves backward. Though Michael made the step famous on the *Motown 25: Yesterday, Today, Forever* special that aired on May 16, 1983, it had been around since the 1930s.

The book became a huge international bestseller. Fans simply had to have a copy, and they numbered in the millions worldwide. *Moonwalk* stayed atop the bestseller lists for months.

In terms of public relations spin, the book was masterful, presenting a fairytale image of Michael as a trouble-free young man possessed of talent at the level of genius. According to the book, his heart was larger than could be measured and his compassion index was inexhaustible. Where children were concerned, he was a veritable masked crusader, striving to set right every wrong.

Moonwalk outlined the Jackson legend. It recounted how the children of a large but economically challenged African American working-class family in Gary, Indiana, catapulted their way to international fame.

But it only told a very, very small part of the story.

The seventh child of Joe and Katherine Jackson, Michael Joseph Jackson was born on August 29, 1958. His father operated a crane at a steel mill in the gritty, industrial city of Gary, Indiana, just east of Chicago. His mother worked part-time at a department store and took care of their nine children: Michael, Rebbie, Jackie, Tito, Jermaine, La Toya, Marlon, then later Randy and Janet.

Joe played guitar in the Falcons, a rhythm-and-blues band that performed at clubs in the area and would sometimes practice at the Jackson home. The Jackson brothers were fascinated by the music their father listened to and played and would sneak his guitar into their room to practice. Tito strummed out the chords to top radio songs while the other boys backed him with doo-wop harmony. But taking that guitar was a dangerous stunt in a house with a father as stern and prone to violence as Joe. The sneaky boys were busted when one of the guitar strings snapped. Upon discovery, Joe was enraged, but the resourceful man also saw a business opportunity.

"These boys are going to take me out of the steel mill," he wrote in a letter to his younger brother, Lawrence.

Though the family was poor, Joe managed to buy the kids their own instruments and they began practicing together in their modest, two-bedroom home.

In 1962, eleven-year-old Jackie, nine-year-old Tito, eight-year-old Jermaine, and five-year-old Marlon formed a band. The three eldest Jackson boys all learned to sing and dance. Tito studied guitar and piano and Jermaine took up guitar and bass. Initially, Jermaine was the front man of the group.

Within the year, at just five years old, Michael joined the band as backup percussion. But the vibrant youngster didn't stay in the background for very long.

Unlike his siblings, Michael memorized the dance routines with relative ease and his moves appeared effortless. And although he didn't really understand the lyrics, Michael phonetically imitated his oldest brother and gradually took over vocal duty.

"I wasn't forced to be little Michael the lead singer," the superstar admitted. "I did it and I loved it."

As the group's manager, Joe kept honing the act and refining the group name, changing it from The Jackson Brothers to The Jackson Five Singing Group. He finally rebranded them—simply as The Jackson 5.

Joe drove his group—his sons—hard, rehearsing with them every day as soon as they got home from school.

"If you messed up you got hit," Michael once recalled of the music rehearsals overseen by his father.

Joe's ambitious career goals greatly exceeded his ability to effectively cope with the demanding process. The patriarch would wake the boys at 2 a.m. to practice their routines before school, sometimes appearing at their windows at night in a werewolf mask. He'd insensitively flaunt his out-of-wedlock second family to make his children feel replaceable.

Little Michael was told that there were people in the audience with guns who wanted to shoot him and that if he didn't move correctly onstage, they'd find their target.

One has to wonder if, then, Michael believed this and thought, "If I put on a sequined white glove, maybe they'll only shoot at my hand." The mind of a child, especially a frightened child, can go to strange places—and stay there.

For the Jackson boys, the effects were distressing.

Young Michael would throw things at his father, which earned him a brutal beating. But Michael continued fighting against what he saw as injustice or cruelty. Although he was not perceived to be as macho as his brothers, Michael was the only one who stood up to their father. Years later, when asked about this, Joe took issue with the wording, not the charge.

"I whipped him with a switch and a belt," he said. "I never beat him. You beat somebody with a stick."

Michael, however, remembered the haunting occasions differently.

"It was more than just a belt," the singer refuted. "Cords, whatever was around."

Michael lamented using his dynamic agility to outmaneuver his father, but whenever he was caught it was "really bad."

"He'd throw you up against the wall as hard as he could. I got it more than all my brothers combined."

Joe's customary punishment was ten "whips" with his belt.

Michael was not alone in declaring that his father crossed lines when it came to child-rearing. La Toya, Michael's elder sister, remembers being "very badly" sexually abused.

She wrote in her autobiography, "When your father gets out of bed with your mother and gets into bed with his daughter and you hear the mother saying, 'No, Joe, not tonight. Let her rest. Leave her alone, she's tired,' that makes you crazy."

La Toya also noted, "There wasn't just physical abuse, there was also mental abuse which is very disturbing, and also sexual abuse."

The abuse of La Toya must be factored into Michael's own sexual development. From his brothers, Michael had learned that sex was secretive, urgent but not necessarily loving. At the very least, suspecting that La Toya was on the receiving end of this treatment may well have made Michael feel ashamed. That's a lot for a prepubescent boy to overcome.

Although Michael clung to and adored his mother, unfortunately, he could not rely on the Jackson matriarch to thwart the abuse. Katherine was a fervent Jehovah's Witness who seemingly swept everything under the rug. What finally saved Michael was his talent—and not just as something to escape into. When the boy developed into the face of The Jackson 5, and his involvement became integral to the success of the group, he gained leverage over his domineering father. Michael started refusing to perform until the beatings stopped. Their ego-driven stalemate was usually resolved by the remaining siblings.

Years later, Michael expressed his feelings about his father in a handwritten note to his security guard, Bill Bray, on the occasion of Bray's retirement in 1992.

"Joseph never ever had time for me," Michael wrote. "He only saw me as a way for him to make money. And as you know, Mother was a perfect mother but I never was with her." He concluded by writing, "What I'm simply trying to say is thank you for being a father."

Newly carried by the infectious talents of young Michael, the family won a slew of talent contests in the Chicago area. For the next several years, the Jackson 5 performed carefully choreographed sets in clubs throughout the Midwest, where they became regional stars. Toward the end of 1967, the group signed a recording contract with local Indiana music label Steeltown Records. Their first two-sided single, "Big Boy" and "You've Changed," was pressed in January 1968. At first, the record was only available for purchase at The Jackson 5 shows. But within months, the single was picked up for distribution by Atco Records—the label that released early tracks for The Beatles, The Who, and Sonny and Cher. The Jackson 5 record eventually sold over ten thousand copies.

Encouraged by the group's modest success, Joe cut back to part-time at the mill and devoted most of his energy to managing the band. They took a regular gig as a house act at a Gary nightclub where they played six nights a week. To earn extra income, the group also performed at strip clubs. When they performed the song "Skinny Legs and All," Michael would head out into the audience and make a show of ducking under tables to look up women's skirts.

The audience ate it up!

By the summer of 1968, The Jackson 5 had opened for national music acts like Gladys Knight and the Pips, James Brown, and Etta James. Despite constantly being in the spotlight, Michael had become increasingly solitary. Unlike his older brothers, Michael was too young to explore each new city during his limited time off. Instead, the budding star habitually hung around backstage at each venue.

"I wanted to learn as much as I could," Michael said, acknowledging that he spent his free time trying to decode each legendary performer. "I'd stare at their feet, the way they held their arms, the way they gripped the microphone."

One performance at the Apollo Theater in Harlem, New York, made a huge impact on Michael's sense of theatrics. During a routine, a stripper—whom Michael described as giving a "great performance"—pulled off her wig, took two oranges out of the bra she was wearing—and revealed that she was in fact a man!

"That blew me away," Michael confessed of the androgynous man's performance.

"I was only a child and couldn't even conceive of anything like that."

After completing several engagements at the Apollo, The Jackson 5 traveled to Chicago, Illinois to perform as the opening act for Bobby Taylor & the Vancouvers. The successful Canadian soul band was signed to Gordy Records, a division of the influential Motown Records.

A year earlier, boss and music mogul Berry Gordy had passed on the Jackson 5 when Motown superstar Gladys Knight—of Gladys Knight and the Pips—had pitched the boys. Joe Jackson felt certain he could change the man's mind.

After sixteen consecutive nights of performances, Joe bundled the family into their van for the five-hour trip through the night to Detroit and the audition with Motown. Mother Katherine had packed them sandwiches for the journey. Father Joe was at the wheel. They got to Detroit, caught a quick catnap in a hotel, rose the next morning, and Bobby Taylor personally introduced Joe, Michael, and the gang to Motown executive Suzanne de Passe. Suzanne, in turn, encouraged Motown founder Berry Gordy to sign the group.

This time, it happened. The music mogul offered the Jacksons a contract in March 1969. The call came from Gordy himself.

"Little Michael's performance was way beyond his years," Gordy later said.

Almost overnight, the family's life changed. The Jacksons moved to Los Angeles, California and stayed with Gordy and Diana Ross of the Supremes, who at the time lived down the street from each other in Beverly Hills. The twenty-five-year-old front woman had seen Michael perform years earlier during a talent show at the Apollo and embraced the idea of giving the budding star a boost.

The legend that Diana discovered the Jacksons isn't true, but she did help them a great deal; especially Michael. She would take him to museums and encourage the child to paint and draw—a welcome change from his grueling schedule of school and music. To help the Jackson 5 gain national exposure, Diana suggested the boys open for her super-hot girl group.

"She was my mother, my lover, and my sister all combined in one amazing person," Michael said years later as an adult, another statement that hinted at sexual confusion.

In the final months of the 1960s, the exceptional five-brother musical group emerged on the national scene to carry Motown into a new decade. And for Michael, the transition from child star to pop star would begin.

CHAPTER THREE

JACKSONMANIA

Over a remarkable year-long period from the fall of 1969 through the fall of 1970, the first four singles The Jackson 5 released with Motown all hit number one on the Billboard Hot 100 chart.

"The pros have told us that no group had a better start than we did—ever," Michael later confirmed.

As promised, Diana helped promote The Jackson 5's first single, the spirited puppy love number, "I Want You Back." Released on October 7, 1969, the song debuted at number 90. The catchy track gained unstoppable momentum after the Jacksons made an appearance on the television series *The Hollywood Palace* on October 18. Diana guest-hosted the episode, which was also The Jackson 5's first nationally televised broadcast.

"It made us feel like we were getting somewhere," Tito later recalled.

That "somewhere" was all the way to the top of the charts, where The Jackson 5 remained for several weeks. In its first two months, "I Want You Back" sold over two million copies.

"There's nothing more exciting than to be number one with your very first record," said Jackie, at the time. "For me, the musical highlight of our entire career is "I Want You Back" because that's the one that put the flag in the ground."

Although the song put Michael and the Jackson gang on the map, it didn't quite fill their bank balances. The band only earned two cents for every album sold and, of course, that sum was divided among the family. However, their breakout hit did trigger what the tabloids—then a powerful force in the make-it-or-break-it world of Hollywood—dubbed "Jacksonmania."

Similar to the "Beatlemania" hoopla generated by the arrival of The Beatles in the United States in 1964, The Jackson 5 enjoyed a meteoric surge in popularity. Their fans clamored for every tidbit of information about Jackie, Tito, Jermaine, Marlon, and the youngest, lead singer Michael.

Like The Beatles eight years earlier, they were mobbed everywhere they went. Police escorted them to and from performance venues with lights flashing and sirens blaring. Hotels where they stayed had to add extra security. In particular, young female fans began clamoring for more. Each had their favorite Jackson and some tried desperately to get into their rooms using ruses or disguises.

"People always call me the leader because I was up front singing and dancing, but there was really no leader," Michael revealed one time, confessing he always deemed oldest brother Jackie to be the band leader. "We just let the audience choose what they think or what they like because it's for them."

Based on the success of "I Want You Back," Motown gave The Jackson 5 the royal treatment.

They hired stylists and costume designers to rebrand the group with vibrant costumes and trendy Afro hairdos; they secured the boys coveted television spots on hit shows like *American Bandstand*, *Soul Train*, and *The Tonight Show Starring Johnny Carson*; and they organized a national tour at major venues like the Boston Garden in Massachusetts and Madison Square Garden in New York City.

There was just one small catch: eleven-year-old Michael had to turn nine again.

Motown executives decided that keeping Michael "young" would bolster The Jackson 5 image, and ultimately increase sales. Undeterred, the Jacksons complied.

"I figured out at an early age that if someone said something about me that wasn't true, it was a lie," Michael explained, referring to music industry professionals. "But if someone said something about my image that wasn't true, then it was okay. Because then it wasn't a lie, it was public relations."

Like he would one day sing in "Billie Jean," "the lie becomes the truth."

Perhaps that age-related fib was the origin of the phrase Michael wrote.

The success of "I Want You Back" made Michael a celebrity before he was even a teenager, in an act that further deprived him of a normal childhood. Michael and his brothers had to be pulled out of school because they'd become too famous, so private tutors were hired for them and home-schooling and on-the-road-schooling became the new normal. Record executives also made sure the band was well-rehearsed, not only for the stage, but for interviews with the media.

The image put forth was that of a family devoted to each other and absolutely dedicated to hard work. Big topics of the time, such as civil rights, were nowhere to be found in these talks. The Jacksons were a big happy family, always pulling together, happiest when they were in each other's company. Their mother Katherine was portrayed accurately as a devout and incorruptible Jehovah's Witness whose faith was unshakable, despite her having been marked with a limp from a childhood bout with polio. Her closeness to God was portrayed as bedrock, a cornerstone for the entire family.

Motown wanted The Jackson 5 to be an uncontroversial group that appealed not just to the eyes and ears, but—perhaps more importantly—to the hearts of everyone, no matter if they were black or white.

"The Motown people would be standing by to help us out or monitor the questions if need be," Michael divulged. "I guess they were worried about the possibility of our sounding militant. Maybe they were worried after they gave us those Afros that they had created little Frankensteins."

But the Jackson brothers did have a mischievous streak. As they walked out of one interview in which a Motown rep had shot down a reporter's question about racial politics, the boys, to be funny, gave the interviewer a "black power" raised-fist salute. The kids also pulled countless "innocent" pranks, including dropping water balloons from balconies, propping buckets of water above doorways, and sending huge room service orders to random hotel guests.

"We were cramped up in these hotel rooms, unable to go anywhere because of the mobs of screaming girls outside, and we wanted to have some fun," Michael said.

When The Jackson 5 released their first LP, Michael and his brothers became household names. Again, Diana used her clout to help sell the record, lending her name to the twelve-track *Diana Ross Presents The Jackson 5*. The album released on December 18, four days after The Jackson 5 appeared on the legend-making television variety series, *The Ed Sullivan Show*. Their debut album reached an impressive number five on the Billboard chart and immediately went gold, selling over five hundred thousand copies during its initial release.

Months later, on February 24, 1970, the Jackson 5 launched their second hit single, the title track from their upcoming second LP, "ABC." The playful tune cemented the "bubblegum soul" genre The Jackson 5 created: a unique combination of soul and pop. The single dethroned The Beatles' number one song "Let It Be."

Their twelve-track sophomore album debuted on May 8 and landed at the number four spot on the charts. It sold an estimated 850,000 copies and spawned the group's third number one song, "The Love You Save." That summer, their eleven-track third album also hit number four and generated the group's final number one song, the stimulating ballad, "I'll Be There." The tune helped propel The Jackson 5 record sales into the millions and showed off Michael's unbelievable vocal versatility.

Incredibly, and to little public knowledge, none of Jackson boys had played a single instrument on their numerous studio recordings. Motown had used seasoned studio musicians to lay down the tracks. This presented a major issue for The Jackson 5 and their upcoming national tour. They anticipated an enormous fan backlash if the group appeared on stage sans instruments. To solve the problem the Jacksons worked overtime to learn how to play all of their songs.

Ultimately, their efforts were well-rewarded. The group earned a then-astounding $25,000 for each gig. But that price tag included some hefty baggage.

"As our fame spread, our fans transformed casual shopping trips into hand-to-hand combat," Michael recalled. "Being mobbed by near hysterical girls was one of the most terrifying experiences for me in those days."

The singer likened "a thousand hands grabbing at you" to the sensation of being suffocated or dismembered.

"I still wear the scars," he confessed.

In one instance, opposing fans grabbed the ends of Michael's scarf and both began pulling, strangling the heartthrob singer.

"He put his hand under the scarf so it wouldn't tighten up on his neck," Jermaine divulged.

Over the next few years, The Jackson 5 became more than a national sensation—they were a public obsession. They released nine studio albums, sixteen top 40 singles, a twenty-two-episode *The Jackson 5ive* animated series, and were featured on merchandise ranging from cereal boxes to board games.

But as Michael developed into a young man, his trademark youthful appearance changed. He sprouted to nearly six feet tall, his baby face matured, and he battled a severe case of acne. Internally, he felt as if his body had betrayed him. The performer admitted that his traumatizing skin issues heavily impacted his personality and mental well-being.

"I couldn't look at people when I talked to them," he said. "I'd look down or away. I felt I didn't have anything to be proud of and I didn't even want to go out."

According to Michael's former doctor, Joe forced his twelve-year-old son to get experimental hormone injections to combat his poor complexion. But the radical treatment had a second, more devious purpose: chemical castration. Joe had hoped to stop Michael's signature singing voice from changing during puberty.

"The fact that he was chemically castrated to maintain his high-pitched voice is beyond words," the family physician condemned.

Scientifically, castration is the surgical removal of the testicles. Doing so essentially stops the production of the male hormone testosterone. However, chemical castration uses progesterone—a female hormone—to counteract testosterone without the emasculating surgery. Besides having a higher voice, the telltale side effects include inhibited growth of body hair, a slight, frail figure, and a pronounced chest cavity; three very distinct aspects of Michael's physique, as the world would come to notice.

During his growth spurt, Michael started noticing something else when he stared into the mirror, something that haunted him more than his fleeting blemishes.

He looked like his father.

That same configuration, the same mouth, the same eyes of that raging taskmaster was right there.

"The biggest struggle I had to face during those teenage years did not involve the recording studios or my stage performance," Michael said. "It was right there in the mirror . . . once I came offstage, there was that mirror to face again."

Michael often retreated to the company of his youngest sister, Janet, whom he called "my best friend in the family." Growing up, Katherine would assign her the task of taking care of him, doing his laundry, and even cleaning his room. But despite the chores and the age difference—Michael was eight years older—the two siblings were extremely close, sharing in common three very similar traits: shyness, sensitivity, and self-esteem issues.

Janet binge ate—and, later, began physically abusing herself by banging her head against a wall—because she was so distraught about her appearance. Her brothers didn't help, teasing her about her weight and looks. She too found comfort in Michael's companionship.

"We used to spend every day, all day, together," she said, referring to her brother. "When we were kids we had so much fun."

Inevitably, Janet entered the family business in the 1970s, performing with her brothers.

Although The Jackson 5 was a groundbreaking act and the punchy group had been role models for millions of people worldwide, their box office draw began to decline heading into the second half of the decade. Motown executives shifted their attention to Michael and Jermaine, hoping to steer both into lucrative solo careers—as the label had successfully done by separating Diana Ross and the Supremes.

As fate would have it, thirteen-year-old Michael's debut single hit the shelves first.

CHAPTER FOUR

DATE WITH DESTINY

Throughout the 1960s and '70s, the Jackson family's biggest musical rival was the Osmond family, a family of musicians from Ogden, Utah. Like The Jackson 5, The Osmonds consisted of a quintet of teen idol siblings. In early 1971, when the youngest Osmond brother, Donny, released a pair of hit solo tracks, "Sweet and Innocent" and "Go Away Little Girl," Motown's Berry Gordy decided Michael should put out his own solo record. Gordy selected the tender tune "Got to Be There." Although originally intended for The Jackson 5, the song was revamped to showcase thirteen-year-old Michael's emerging star power.

The single released on October 7, 1971 and, although it didn't outsell Donny's record, it landed impressively in the top five of the Billboard Hot 100. But perhaps more importantly, the success of the song showed Michael he still had a promising future in the music business.

"I became one of the first people in a Motown group to really step out," Michael said. "It was wonderful working on that record and it became one of my favorites."

Despite his creative shift to solo artist, Michael continued recording and touring with The Jackson 5. But he still craved one luxury that had always eluded him: artistic freedom.

"I had a couple of disputes with a couple of producers at Motown," Michael recounted. "They think they own you. They think they made you."

The singer recalled a recording session where a producer wanted him to enunciate the lyrics. But Michael felt that over-pronouncing the words diminished the feeling of the song.

"When it was over, I was right," he said with a laugh. "I won."

And during a Jackson 5 concert tour in 1972, when "Got to Be There" was riding high on the charts, Michael was again stifled by those who believed his creative ideas were "childish and silly."

According to Michael, before singing "Got to Be There" at a show, he wanted to run offstage and grab the hat he wore on the album cover. He knew the audience would go nuts if he walked back on stage with it on. But a road manager shot the move down.

"He thought it was the most ridiculous idea he had ever heard," the singer said. "I felt good about my instincts."

Indeed, it was a star-making theatrical bit that a decade later helped launch Michael's career into the stratosphere.

As the year progressed, Michael scored his first number one hit as a solo artist with the theme song for the 1972 horror film, *Ben*. The sequel to the 1971 film *Willard* delved into the loving relationship between a boy and a killer rat named Ben. Michael's love-ballad version of the title track played over the final scene and closing credits.

"*Ben* meant a lot to me," Michael disclosed. "A lot of people thought the movie was a bit odd, but I was not one of them. People didn't understand this boy's love for this little creature."

The charming tune helped publicly transition Michael into mature young man; it also earned him a Golden Globe award for Best Original Song, as well as an Oscar nomination in the same category.

By the end of 1972, Jermaine too had gone it alone, and released his first solo record, "Daddy's Home." Although the track peaked at number nine on the Billboard Hot 100, his subsequent track, "You're in Good Hands," stalled out at 79. The eighteen-year-old didn't release another solo recording for three years.

Meanwhile, Michael continued producing a string of radio-friendly songs.

His 1973 single, "With a Child's Heart," broke into the top fifty on the charts. He released three more tunes that year: "Morning Glow," "Music and Me," and "Happy." The fifteen-year-old and his brothers also dropped five Jackson 5 tracks, including the hit "Get It Together."

The following year, the group released their trendsetting nine-track disco record *Dancing Machine*. The title song went all the way to number two and sold over one million copies in its first month. During an episode of *Soul Train*, Michael also popularized the limb-wrenching, mechanical-seeming dance, "the Robot."

"Within a few days it seemed that every kid in the United States was doing the Robot," the entertainer said. "I had never seen anything like it."

Behind the scenes, however, things had taken a drastic turn. The Jackson boys were increasingly at odds with their guider and mentor, Motown. Despite the jolt their latest record had provided their careers, the label still prohibited the group from creating or playing or even selecting their own songs.

"I was the one who had to say that we, the Jackson 5, were going to leave Motown," Michael later remembered. "I knew it was time for a change, so we followed our instincts, and we won when we decided to try for a fresh start with another label, Epic."

But the career move came at a price. Not only did Motown own and retain the name "The Jackson 5," but Jermaine had been married to Gordy's daughter, Hazel, for three years. He did not make the move with his brothers to Epic Records. The remaining members officially renamed themselves The Jacksons and their youngest brother, fourteen-year-old Randy, filled in as the new fifth man.

The Jackson family had negotiated for greater creative control over their music and careers, which included a short-lived 1976 variety show called *The Jacksons*, but Michael remained socially withdrawn.

"He's just more sensitive than the others," Katherine would tell friends at the time, though she later admitted that he had become "a loner."

"He didn't get along with other people his age," she said. "I was worried about him, but I hoped he would grow out of it, that it was a phase."

For Michael, being endowed with musical talent was also a curse. He felt "down and out" when he wasn't immersed in his music, but the music kept him eerily reclusive and detached from healthy "human" habits.

"When I'm not creating, I'm not as happy," Michael insisted.

Over the next three years, The Jacksons released three albums. Their self-titled debut album—their eleventh in total—was another hit record for the band. Released in November 1976, the ten-track *The Jacksons* spawned the hit single "Enjoy Yourself," which sailed to number six on the charts. The following October, the nine-track *Goin' Places* peaked at number thirty-six and fostered a European concert tour that included a performance for Queen Elizabeth II of England. And thanks to light-hearted songs like "Blame it on the Boogie" and "Shake Your Body (Down to the Ground)," the Jacksons' 1978 album *Destiny* was a hit. It was also the album over which the brothers had the most creative control, largely free from Joe's stifling presence. At one point while the band was recording, police showed up after an enraged Joe couldn't get into the locked studio. When an Epic executive went outside to see what the fuss was about, he told the police he had no idea who the angry man was. That executive had never liked Joe.

As the 1980s loomed and many of the brothers entered adulthood, the Jacksons appeared poised to reinvent themselves and enjoy new levels of success. Destiny, it seemed, was the perfect name for their album.

But Michael had other plans.

The nineteen-year-old starred in his first feature film as the Scarecrow in the big screen adaptation of the Tony award-winning Broadway musical *The Wiz*, itself a retelling of L. Frank Baum's 1900 children's novel, *The Wonderful Wizard of Oz*. The movie also featured thirty-eight-year-old Richard Pryor as The Wiz, and, rather controversially due to her age, thirty-three-year-old Diana Ross as Dorothy.

Released in October 1978, the film cost a staggering $30 million to make and flopped at the box office, making just $21 million in return. It was Diana Ross's last big screen performance and Michael Jackson's only major one.

Reviewers fell at both ends of the spectrum. The *New York Times* felt the film was "the last gasp of what had been a steadily expanding black presence in mainstream filmmaking." However, noted critic Rex Reed registered that, "Visually, *The Wiz* outdoes everything I've seen on the screen in decades."

Michael stated, "I don't think it could have been any better."

Around the same time, Michael became addicted to the idea of making another solo record—a record that was truly his own, without Joe, or the record label, or his brothers, or anyone else from the old days telling him what to do.

So, in December 1978, the same month that *Destiny* hit store shelves, Michael went into a Los Angeles recording studio and began making *Off the Wall*. First and foremost, he wanted his fifth solo album—and really, his first true solo album—to sound different than the records he'd been making with The Jacksons. But even though he craved creative control over the music he made, he knew he couldn't make it alone. He needed new blood in the studio with him. He needed Quincy Jones.

Though only forty-four years old, Quincy was already solidified as something of a legend. He'd worked as a musician, arranger, composer, and conductor with many of the world's greatest entertainers—Frank Sinatra, Count Basie, and Ray Charles. As a teenager, he played trumpet in bebop bands that toured the world. He studied classical music in Paris. He worked as a record executive and produced several 1960s pop hits. He scored major films like *In Cold Blood* (1967)—for which he earned an Oscar nomination—*Bob & Carol & Ted & Alice* (1969), and *They Call Me Mister Tibbs!* (1970). He'd pretty much done it all, and yet perhaps his greatest musical triumphs were still ahead of him. Because he had not yet worked with Michael.

The first track on the album, "Don't Stop 'Til You Get Enough," was the first song Michael ever recorded that he also wrote by himself. It opens with him talking over a baseline before letting out a yelp so suggestive that he had a hard time convincing his mother that the song wasn't about having sex. During recording, he overheard a rough groove that *Off the Wall* bassist Louis "Thunder Thumbs" Johnson had composed, intending to play it with his own successful band, The Brothers Johnson. But by the following day, Michael had used it to write "Get on the Floor." The ballad "She's Out of My Life" reduced Michael to tears after he recorded it. Paul McCartney wrote "Girlfriend" specifically for Michael—a fact Quincy didn't even know when he suggested Michael record the song for the album.

"Our underlying plan was to take disco out," Quincy said. "I just thought it had gone far enough."

Off the Wall was pure, un-distilled Michael in a way a Jackson's record could never be. And as he was touring with his brothers in the months before the release of the album in August of 1979—the same month he turned twenty-one—an increasingly frustrated Michael realized how vital having complete control was to his music . . . and his sanity.

It was in 1979 that Michael took his first small—yet not-so-small—step into changing the man in the mirror. He got his first nose job.

Around the same time, inspired by Jermaine, he became a vegetarian in an attempt to clear up his complexion, and as the already slender Michael burned calories with his relentless rehearsing and performing, his weight loss began to alarm people. Those around him noted how unhappy he seemed, and Michael himself acknowledged he was mentally depressed.

"I had very few close friends at the time and felt very isolated," he said. "I was so lonely that I used to walk through my neighborhood hoping I'd run into somebody I could talk to and perhaps become friends with. . . . I wanted to meet anybody in the neighborhood—the neighborhood kids, anybody."

Michael's mood worsened when the 1979 Grammy award nominations were announced. *Off the Wall*, one of the most critically acclaimed and popular albums of the year, garnered only a solitary nomination. Michael watched the ceremony on television, and despite the fact that he won for Best Male R&B Vocal Performance, all he could think of was putting together a new album that would be impossible for the Grammys to ignore. This album would be known as *Starlight Love*—for a little while, anyway. The name, of course, was eventually changed to *Thriller*.

CHAPTER FIVE

THRILLER NIGHT

In the 1980s, Michael's ambition to outdo himself finally created an insurmountable barrier between him and the rest of the world. A song about a wrongful paternity claim, a music video about horror movies, and a single sparkling glove helped Michael become the most famous pop star—and the most famous person—on the planet.

Why did he wear that glove? Explanations vary. Eccentricity? To hide skin blotching caused by vitiligo? So audiences could follow his rapid hand movements? (This was the same reason given years later to explain white tape or bandages he wore on his fingertips: so fans in the balcony could see the moves.) It did not really matter; it became iconic.

Living up to the success of *Off the Wall* was no easy task. The record had sold millions and spawned four Top Ten hits. And in the years since its release, technology like car stereos, cassette tapes, and the Walkman—which allowed fans to record songs off the radio and listen to music anywhere—had caused a dip in record sales. No one was expecting Michael's next album to overachieve. No one, that is, except Michael.

"Record companies never believe a new album will do considerably better than the last one you did," Michael said. "There were times during the *Thriller* project when I would get emotional and upset because I couldn't get the people working with me to see what I saw."

In the summer of 1982, Quincy listened to about six hundred song submissions to determine which nine would ultimately make up *Thriller*.

"The producer's main job is to find the right tunes," Quincy said. "It has to give you goosebumps."

Naturally, Michael's own musical creations were among the candidates. Quincy had even recalled that Michael had been "writing music like a machine."

He'd already worked out much of the duet "The Girl is Mine" with Paul McCartney, and he had written what would become the first song on the album, "Wanna Be Startin' Somethin'," years before during the *Off the Wall* sessions, though he'd been too shy to show it to Quincy at the time. During the *Thriller* sessions, he even delayed playing "Beat It" for Quincy for the same reason.

After Quincy selected the nine best songs, he customarily dropped the four weakest and replaced them with four more promising hit-making tracks. Those new songs on *Thriller* were "Pretty Young Thing," "Human Nature," "The Lady in My Life," and "Beat It."

Incredibly, when Michael listened to the first mix of the album he hated it—as did Quincy, who notoriously called it "twenty-four-karat sonic doo-doo." The record label was putting immense pressure on them to deliver the album because Christmas was approaching. In an age long before digital downloads, the label understandably wanted shoppers to have plenty of time to hear it on the radio and go to the store to buy it. But Michael stood firm.

"We put too much material on the record," Quincy explained. "You can ruin a great album in the mix. It's like taking a great movie and ruining it in the editing."

It was decided that the team would take several more days to remix every song on the record.

It worked wonders. *Thriller* was eventually released worldwide on the last day of November. The album was a monster hit. Selling over a million copies a week at its peak, *Thriller* spent nearly forty weeks as the number one record in the US and went number one in eight countries. It dug into the Top Ten for just shy of two years, produced seven top ten singles, and earned Michael eight Grammy awards, including album of the year and record of the year for "Beat It."

With total sales exceeding 66 million, *Thriller* also earned the Guinness World Record for "bestselling album."

For *Thriller*, Michael knew he had to unlock the full potential music videos had begun to offer pop stars. Although he had made videos for *Off the Wall*, it was before the advent of MTV. He was determined to change the understanding of what a music video could be.

Michael hired top-notch Hollywood talent to work on the videos—which he preferred to call "films"—and even shouldered some of the large financial cost to produce.

First, Michael filmed "Billie Jean." In the video he's being chased by a detective-looking photographer. As Michael dances along the sidewalk, the tiles light up beneath his feet. He ends up in Billie Jean's hotel room, but vanishes before getting caught by the seedy sleuth, who is apprehended by police.

Even though it took MTV months to actually play the video, in many ways it put the young cable television channel on the map. Many artists, from Rick James to David Bowie, accused the network at the time of avoiding the videos of black musicians. But they couldn't ignore Michael, who in turn paved the way for so many others. One critic even dubbed Michael "MTV's Jackie Robinson."

"Billie Jean" first aired on March 10, 1983. Michael's outfit in the video—a black leather suit, pink shirt, and red bow tie—instantly became trendy for school-aged children worldwide.

Next up was "Beat It." Taking a page out of *West Side Story*, Michael's music video centered on rival Los Angeles gang members. In addition to professional dancers, the singer hired dozens of actual L.A. gang members to be extras. For greater and almost exact authenticity, he filmed the video in L.A.'s notorious Skid Row.

"Beat It" first aired on March 31 and played more frequently than "Billie Jean." Again, Michael's wardrobe—this time a blazing red leather jacket—immediately became iconic.

It seemed Michael had attained the highest of heights, but his world—and our own—were about to change forever.

To celebrate Motown's 25th anniversary, Gordy put together a star-studded musical revue. Hosted by comedian Richard Pryor, *Motown 25: Yesterday, Today, Forever* was held on March 25 at the Pasadena Civic Auditorium in Pasadena, California. It included top Motown acts like Lionel Richie, Marvin Gaye, Stevie Wonder, and Diana Ross. The show was recorded with a live audience for a prime-time broadcast on NBC.

"I told you before this evening was going to contain a lot of wonderful surprises and I wasn't kidding," Pryor announced to the at-capacity crowd before introducing The Jackson 5.

After a film montage featuring the Jacksons, which included black and white footage of the boys auditioning for Motown, the original five members reunited on the stage. It was their first public performance in eight years. Michael stood front and center. The twenty-four-year-old wore a black sequined blazer and silver sequined shirt, his soon-to-be trademarked black pants, Florsheim Imperial black leather loafers with silver socks, and a single shimmering silver glove.

The amped-up audience was on their feet as Michael and his brothers sang portions of "I Want You Back," "The Love You Save," "Never Can Say Goodbye," and "I'll Be There." Upon finishing their set, the Jacksons all hugged and exited the stage—all, that is, except Michael.

"Those were magic moments with all my brothers. . . . I like those songs a lot," he delicately told the breathless crowd, some of whom were shouting "Billie Jean!"

"Especially, I like . . . the new songs."

Michael bent over, picked up a black fedora "spy" hat, and held it on the crown of his head. The dazzler assumed his crouched, panther-like profile pose and kicked his hips to the rhythmic intro of "Billie Jean." Michael's dramatic use of the hat made the crowd erupt, just as he had known they would. After twenty seconds of razor-sharp dance moves, Michael tossed the hat into the wings and started singing. His body, like liquid mercury, never stopped pulsing, moving, supercharging the audience in the venue. His characteristically bright-eyed face had been replaced by a dynamic scowl.

Michael Jackson, the pop icon, had arrived.

During a musical interlude, approximately two-and-a-half minutes into the intense performance, Michael spun, again turned sideways to the audience, tugged at his pants to expose his silver socks, and then glided backwards while appearing to walk forwards several steps. He finished the move with a triple twirl into a crouch that terminated on the tips of his toes.

For a moment, the audience was too stunned to process the mind-blowing, historic event.

A minute later Michael did the "moonwalk" move again, but more casually, showing the audience, and later the viewers, that it wasn't a camera trick or a fluke.

It was Michael's gravity-defying skills. All Michael.

The crowd didn't wait for the end of the song to start cheering. The response was so enormous it brought the taping of the television special to a standstill. People were crying, strangers were high-fiving, and all in all, everyone needed a minute to collect themselves. An announcer eventually begged the audience to be seated so the show could go on.

Backstage, it was a vastly different story.

Michael was disappointed because he didn't hold the toe move long enough. He blamed the "mistake" on a shortage of rehearsal time. "The night before taping, I still had no idea what I was going to do with my solo number," the star later confessed. "I hadn't had time because I was so busy rehearsing the group . . . I pretty much stood there and let the song tell me what to do."

But his awestruck siblings, who like the rest of the crowd watched the brilliant routine for the first time that night, assured their perfectionist brother that he was electrifying. Michael later called the event one of the "happiest and proudest moments of my life."

On May 16, 1983, over 30 million more people watched Michael's iconic performance on television. The following day, they were all trying to imitate his unforgettable dance moves. Legendary film star Fred Astaire, one of the greatest dancers in movie history and someone who Michael longed to follow in the footsteps of, called to personally tell Michael how blown away he was.

The entertainer had officially become a phenomenon.

Capitalizing on the skyrocketing sales of *Thriller*, Michael began working on a million dollar "Thriller" music video. On paper, Michael's idea for the video seemed ridiculous: a fourteen-minute short film where a charismatic singer on date turns into a cat-like werewolf, and then into a zombie who line-dances with ghouls. But for Michael, it all made sense. It was his childhood fantasy finally realized.

"It's just neat to become another thing, another person," Michael said, at the time. "Especially when you really believe it and it's not like you're acting. . . . I just like jumping into other people's lives and exploring."

Perhaps stemming from his father's penchant for scaring him and his brothers with Halloween masks, or Michael's own dark, suppressed persona, the singer was fascinated by fictional characters that had a secret gruesome side, like Dr. Jekyll and Mr. Hyde, Dorian Gray, and Count Dracula.

He was equally fond of real-life figures like Barnum & Bailey Circus founder

P. T. Barnum, whose freak show exhibits in the nineteenth century showcased biological oddities including the Swiss Bearded Lady, 30-inch man Commodore Nutt, and the nearly 8-foot giantess Anna Swan. In the 1980s, Michael even attempted to purchase the severely deformed skeleton of Joseph Merrick (a.k.a. The Elephant Man).

When his radical idea for "Thriller" was given the go-ahead, Michael hired Hollywood director John Landis—whose 1981 horror film *An American Werewolf in London* was the sleeper hit of the summer—and Academy award-winning makeup artist Rick Baker to cinematically tie all the loose ends together.

"It was amazing working with Michael at the time," Landis said, "because he was just ridiculously famous . . . people used to see him and go into hysterics."

The revolutionary combination of great filmmaking, top-notch special effects, an eerie voice-over performance by legendary actor Vincent Price, and, of course, Michael's spellbinding choreography not only worked, it revitalized the music industry and redefined a generation.

"He helped define the music video in terms of style, dance ensembles, and overall performances," Quincy admitted.

And once again, Michael's unique costume reshaped the world's sense of fashion. His angular red leather jacket with the black "V" was designed by the director's wife, Deborah, who also created the heroic brown leather jacket for the 1981 film *Raiders of the Lost Ark*. The single piece of wardrobe is considered the holy grail of rock and roll memorabilia and recently sold at auction for nearly $2 million.

On December 2, 1983, a year after the release of the album, the "Thriller" music video debuted on television. Literally overnight, MTV ratings jumped tenfold and *Thriller* record sales tripled.

A seventy-minute *The Making of Thriller* documentary was released later that month on VHS and sold over a million copies, making it the best-selling videotape in history.

Michael's spectacular career seemed to have no brakes and no speed limit.

But within the blink of an eye, a horrible accident a month later would cause the superstar to spend the rest of his life in a prison—of pain and drug addiction.

CHAPTER SIX

SMOKE & MIRRORS

Michael Jackson was used to being at the center of attention. But by 1984, the scale of his fame was incalculable, even for the seasoned entertainer. Around the world, his music played non-stop on the radio and television, he was on the covers of countless magazines—including two issues of *Rolling Stone* in a four-month period—and his likeness adorned every conceivable type of merchandise. Almost everyone, it seemed, wanted a piece of him.

Certainly, Michael had given his fans ample reasons to worship him. The twenty-five-year-old was incredibly talented, beyond charismatic, and his groundbreaking music grabbed people in every demographic. But despite the endless media coverage of the superstar, the public was still confused about who their idol really was.

Although Michael had grown up slowly in the spotlight, as an adult he was rapidly transforming himself in the shadows. His bewilderingly androgynous appearance and delicate voice was in great contrast with his macho military-style clothing. And his unconventional adult relationships with Hollywood stars like twelve-year-old Oscar-winning *Paper Moon* actress Tatum O'Neal and twelve-year-old Webster actor Emmanuel Lewis further complicated the singer's public image. As a result, an unfathomable mystique engulfed the performer. His ambiguity became a smokescreen so impenetrable that even Michael lost sight of himself. Though admittedly, he preferred it that way.

"I love to forget," Michael confessed at the time, referring specifically to his identity.

The singer noted that he stopped short of substance abuse to alter his personality.

"I'm certainly no angel, and I may have my own bad habits, but drugs aren't among them," he insisted.

But that changed on January 27, 1984.

Pepsi had paid Michael a then-unheard-of $5 million to star in a series of commercials for the soda company. Despite the hefty payday and maintaining control over how he was portrayed, Michael still had reservations about doing the gig.

"I feel it's wrong to endorse something you don't believe in," the star said after inking the deal. "I think it's a bad omen . . . I still don't have a good feeling about it."

The first of two ads aired in 1983 and featured children in the street imitating the star. Michael made a brief onscreen appearance to show his approval. He also reworked the lyrics to "Billie Jean" to sing Pepsi's praises as the "thrill of today." Naturally, that year, Pepsi sales skyrocketed.

Michael filmed the second commercial on that fateful Friday in January. The singer teamed up with his brothers to stage a flashy rock concert at the Shrine Auditorium in Los Angeles, California. The venue was packed with fake concert goers and lucky fans.

The cameras captured the Jackson gang "backstage" drinking Pepsi and then followed them onto the stage to perform the adapted "Billie Jean" jingle. At the climax of the sixty-second commercial, a pyrotechnic eruption silhouettes Michael during his dance-filled path down a set of stairs leading to the stage. At least, that was the original plan.

During the infamous sixth take of the scene, Michael—who was rather foolishly instructed to remain posing at top of the stairway until after the fireworks went off—was within feet of the explosion; close enough for sparks to splash on his head and ignite his heavily styled hair. During his ten-second descent, Michael still had no idea that he was on fire. The commercial crew converged on the singer, who began involuntarily spinning, hoping to put out the roaring flames. Several people used their jackets to help snuff the blaze. His brothers, confused by the pandemonium, thought he had been assassinated.

When Michael finally stood up, the center of his scalp was hairless. He grabbed the singed, bald area with his silver gloved right hand and was rushed off stage. After getting bandaged, Michael was put on a gurney. He requested to exit the arena through the crowd, not out a back door. He wanted everyone to know that he would be okay. Michael even kept his glove on.

"I just remember we were all abruptly excused for the day," said actress Kathy Griffin, who was an extra in the audience that day. "The last thing a production would do following an accident like this would be to announce to hundreds, if not thousands, of extras something like, 'There's been a horrible accident. Everybody go home!'"

Michael was taken to Cedars-Sinai Medical Center. His plastic surgeon, Doctor Steven Hoefflin, reported that the star was "quite shaken up" and had a "palm-sized area" second-degree burn and a small, quarter-sized third-degree burn. He believed the hair in the affected area would grow back. Michael was treated with antiseptic cream and was prescribed several drugs to ease the pain and help him relax.

Later that day, the performer was transferred to Dr. Hoefflin's Brotman Memorial Hospital where, after taking a sleeping pill and watching a late-night movie, he was finally able to rest.

The next morning, the Pepsi "scandal" was front page news around the globe. Michael received a tsunami-sized outpouring of well-wishes. Meanwhile, inside the hospital, the patient was doing fine and was even overheard singing in the shower. Michael was discharged from Brotman that afternoon.

After watching footage of the incident and seeing how close he came to losing his life, Michael was hell-bent on getting revenge on the cola company, who he deemed woefully negligent for the incident. He wanted the burn video plastered all over the news. Pepsi, of course, did not.

Though they denied any wrongdoing, the company agreed to pay the star a $1.5 million settlement, which Michael used to finance the Michael Jackson Burn Center at Brotman.

Although his head wound was a relatively minor injury, it led to Michael initiating a series of cosmetic surgeries. These superficial operations ultimately forced his deepest psychological issues to surface.

Privately, Michael's desire to feel better began to consume him.

Without his rowdy brothers to romp around with or to keep him grounded, Michael tried desperately to come up with new ways to relieve tension and elevate his increasingly somber mood.

To conceal his scarred head from fans and paparazzi, the star began wearing wigs. Michael found these costume accessories also helped him "play" himself in public, to get into character like he was the leading role in his own fairy tale.

He also leaned heavily on his love of cartoons as a form of "escapism." They were fun, of course, but they also took him back to a more innocent time—1971, to be exact, when he and his brothers were depicted in that one-season ABC cartoon series, *The Jackson 5ive*. Though Michael and his brothers were too busy—and expensive—to participate directly in the show (they were portrayed by voice actors), Michael had gotten a real, satisfying kick seeing himself depicted in such an innocent format. He also appreciated the fact that his own voice was created by an actor very appropriately named Fullilove. Donald Fullilove. He never forgot that joy.

Now, though, it was Disney animation he craved.

"It's like the world is happening now in a faraway city," he said of his experience watching old Disney movies and animated shorts. "It's like everything's all right."

Michael's work ethic also provided the escape he craved. When the star—who was a devout Jehovah's Witness from age five—religiously fasted on Sundays, he would dance in his studio to the point of physical and mental exhaustion. For Michael, it was an acceptable and legal way to get high.

"It just empties you out," the singer divulged. "I am caught up in a trance with it all."

All of his life, Michael had relied on the rigid rules of his faith to keep himself in check. As a Jehovah's Witness, he was raised to believe that the world would soon end and those who best served God would survive the apocalypse. That meant shunning earthly indulgences like sex and money.

Although his generous donations to the religion were accepted, as well as the attention he brought to it, Michael's celebrity status was frowned upon by Kingdom Hall elders. They claimed it caused others to worship him as a false idol. The leaders also took issue with Michael's sexually charged dance moves and the "pagan" content of his "Thriller" music video. As a result, Michael demanded this disclaimer get added to the beginning of the film:

> "Due to my strong personal convictions, I wish to stress that this film in no way endorses a belief in the occult."

At the height of his fame, Michael still went door-to-door several days a week spreading the word for the Jehovah's Witness, though he frequently wore disguises. But by 1987, Michael was fed up with the endless stream of commands passed down from the Witness elders. It became impossible for him to live in accordance with the religious tenets while maintaining his historic career. So that June, Michael issued a press release excusing himself from the holy organization.

"I was not required to shun my son," Katherine said, referring to the rule that forbids a Witness from speaking to ex-members. "But we can't talk about matters of faith any longer, which is a shame."

In his decision to leave his faith behind, Michael not only lost the support of his mother, but he removed a crucial horizon line. For the first time in his life, the star was free to be himself and to do things that were previously off limits.

He began regularly using prescribed narcotics to cope with migraines, which he felt stemmed from his burn injury. Undoubtedly, the drugs also gave him the edge on his age-old insecurities, which were triggering full-blown panic attacks.

Being a celebrity no longer fulfilled Michael as it once had. And with the insane success of *Thriller*, he finally began to mourn the loss of his anonymity. Michael was unexpectedly frustrated that people were unable to treat him normally.

"They see me differently," he lamented. "They won't talk to me like they will a next-door neighbor."

It was yet another internal conflict that worsened as his success increased. Michael likened his debilitating "vulnerable feelings" to "a hemophiliac who can't afford to be scratched."

To avoid unnecessary heartache, Michael "got off" on being surrounded by unconditional love, sources told me.

"My best friends in the whole world are children and animals," the star, perhaps sadly, admitted. "They're the ones who tell the truth and love you openly without reservation."

Both to ensure an ample supply of such affection and to avoid dealing with the real world, Michael started creating his own kingdom: a place he would call Neverland.

CHAPTER SEVEN

A WORLD APART

Back in 1983, when Michael and Paul McCartney were filming the music video for their hit song "Say, Say, Say," the former Beatle stayed at an expansive property on the edge of Los Padres National Forest in Santa Barbara County, California. Then known as Sycamore Valley Ranch, the sprawling 2700-acre estate also served as a backdrop for portions of the video. At the time, Michael told his sister La Toya—a costar on the shoot—that he'd one day purchase the ranch.

Nearly five years later, he did. Michael finalized the deal in March 1988 while he toured the country with *Bad*, his blockbuster follow-up album to *Thriller*. Although the press reported that the twenty-nine-year-old paid about $30 million for the homestead, the price was actually closer to $20 million.

Michael's first order of business was to change the name of the property. He officially called it Neverland Ranch—Neverland, for short—after the mythical island home of Peter Pan, the boy who never grew up. Peter was a character to whom Michael famously compared himself. In fact, Michael's Hollywood manager once talked him out of starring as Peter Pan in a movie.

"Michael is already Peter Pan," the representative later said. "He didn't need to play him."

Several weeks after settling into Neverland, Michael hosted a housewarming gathering for his closest friends and relatives. Quite contentiously, his parents weren't on the guest list.

"We'd seen a lot from that boy, but this was really something we couldn't figure out," said Joe. "I don't know why he would be so hurtful to us, and especially to Kate."

Put simply, Michael didn't want to tell his parents, with whom he had always lived. He didn't want them to talk him out of his extravagant relocation. He didn't want to lose his newfound freedom. Michael was so secretive about the purchase that Joe and Katherine learned about Neverland from a news report, which Michael claimed to them was false.

But as slighted as Katherine felt, she was far more concerned for her son. Due to the remote location of the ranch—a winding 100 miles north of the Jackson home in Encino—and the considerable isolation Neverland afforded the singer, Katherine feared that Michael, left unchecked, would get crushed under the weight of his own career and his already overtaxed weaknesses would intensify.

Sadly, she wasn't wrong.

With no concern for cost, the entertainer quickly spent millions of dollars turning his real estate into his unreal estate.

"I wanted to have a place that I could create everything that I never had as a child," Michael once said. "Everything that I love is behind those gates."

The property featured a 12,600-foot Tudor-style home that spanned fifty acres. The main residence included five bedrooms and eight bathrooms. The view from Michael's master bedroom was a tranquil four-acre lake with a stone bridge. To ensure his privacy, Michael had multiple deadbolt locks added to his bedroom door. It even had an old-fashioned sliding bolt that only a person within the room could unlock.

In case of an emergency, Michael also had a secret safe room installed in his massive walk-in closet.

Michael's primary office was a cluttered treasure trove of mannequins and life-sized superhero statues huddled together, rows of showcases filled with personal memorabilia, a television on every wall, comfy chairs, and a desk in total disarray. Nothing in the room seemed to have a permanent place.

His home also had five fireplaces, a wine cellar, eighteenth-century French oak parquet flooring, and was heavily furnished with antiques, artwork, and collectibles amassed by Michael during his extensive worldwide travels. One of his prized possessions was the Best Picture Oscar from the 1939 film *Gone With The Wind*, for which Michael paid $1.5 million at auction. He also displayed an array of commissioned paintings featuring himself as royalty, with children, and with historical figures, such as Abraham Lincoln and Albert Einstein. Michael was always in the center of the depicted scene.

The Neverland grounds had several guesthouses, each with two suites, a fifty-seat movie theater and a video store, a recording studio and a dance studio, a lagoon-style pool and pool house, a tennis court, a barbecue area, and a private outdoor garden. And bronze statues of children accented every corner of the stunning property.

Over ninety employees made Neverland "tick." It was estimated that Michael spent $4 million each year on upkeep alone. The full-time staff included gardeners, ranch hands, maids, and chefs. Michael also retained an on-site Neverland Valley Fire Department service in case of an emergency, and he ruled the homestead with an iron fist. If a staff member didn't smile enough, or seemed otherwise unhappy, Michael would relieve them of their duties. His ranch also had a maintenance shop and separate staff facilities. Michael even hired a "deer chaser" to keep unwanted flower-chewing creatures off his beautifully manicured landscape.

In an effort to entertain his guests, Michael had an entire amusement park installed. The complex boasted all of the classic fair rides, including a Ferris wheel, a carousel, a roller coaster, bumper cars, and a swinging pirate ship.

"I can't go into a park, I can't go to Disneyland, as myself," the star said, justifying the extravagant additions. "I was always on tour, traveling, and I never got a chance to do those things."

It was ironic: Jackson was in the Disney theme parks from 1986–1996, and sporadically thereafter, in the blockbuster seventeen-minute, $30 million 3D movie *Captain EO*, a character named after Eos, the Greek goddess of the dawn.

The science fiction extravaganza—complete with in-theater laser effects—a family of musicians from Ogden, Utah was written by *Star Wars* creator George Lucas and directed by Francis Ford Coppola of *The Godfather* and *Apocalypse Now* fame. In it, Jackson plays spaceship commander who bears a gift for the Supreme Leader (Anjelica Huston). Reaching her world, the crew is arrested and earmarked for imprisonment and torture. However, EO knows there is good in the woman and sings his gift, the song, "We Are Here to Change the World." Robots become instruments, guards are transformed into dancers, and all seems well until the ruler sends her dread Whip Warriors to stop EO. But he mutates them as well, and finally works his magic on the Supreme Leader. On the heels of the song "Another Part of Me," the hero and his team joyously depart.

In every meaningful way, *Captain EO* and Michael were the same. He tried to remake his own world as he did the planet of the Supreme Leader.

In addition to the rides at Neverland, there were two railroads and a train station on his compound. The three-foot narrow-gauge Neverland Valley Railroad had two cars pulled by a steam locomotive that he named Katherine. The other train was a two-foot narrow-gauge replica of a C. P. Huntington locomotive. The fully functional train station contained an eye-popping candy counter so guests could stock up on treats before riding directly to the movie theater.

When he wanted to travel more freely around the facility, Michael usually drove a customized black Batmobile golf cart, which he sometimes equipped with high-powered water pistols. Impromptu water fights frequently broke out at the ranch.

To indulge his love of animals, Michael had a zoo built on the premises. Some of the animal tenants included a sixteen-foot tall giraffe named Jabbar, the thirty-five-ton elephant Gypsy, and Kimba the lion. His reptile house contained several rare species such as a pure white king cobra and a twelve-foot albino python. Michael even owned a donkey and zebra hybrid called a zebroid.

"We have busloads of kids who don't get to see those things," Michael said. "They come up and enjoy it in a pure, loving, fun way."

Over the years, Michael's personal pets included several chimpanzees; Bubbles was the most famous. Purchased by the singer from a Texas animal testing facility in mid-1980s, Bubbles lived with the pop star at Neverland. He ate at the dinner table, slept in a crib in Michael's master bedroom, and even used the same bathroom as the singer. He often joined Michael in the movie theater and helped himself to snacks at the candy counter.

"I come home to my chimps and I can hug them," the singer said. "They run around and help me clean the room."

The same could not be said of his boa constrictor, Muscles. However, the giant snake came to be emblematic of Michael's generosity. Michael's manager was Frank DiLeo, and DiLeo's son wanted to bring Muscles to his school for show-and-tell. Michael freely gave his permission, but DiLeo was terrified of handling the snake. So Michael brought it to the boy's school himself. DiLeo was humbled, stunned, and eternally grateful.

Neverland was also rumored to have one "uninvited" resident. Michael was convinced his property was haunted by a ghost that he'd nicknamed George.

"I was skeptical about George at first, but I did see him several times," a long-time employee told me, confirming that Michael also "had experiences with George."

Michael insisted the specter emerged from the nearby Zaca Lake, where the ancient Chumash Indians conducted tribal rites. He believed the ghoul turned lights on and off at the carnival rides and sweets stands, and he was convinced it set off alarms outside his bedroom. Whether or not George was a real issue, the situation fueled Michael's mounting paranoia.

As intended, Neverland was most frequently visited by children. Besides allowing them to take advantage of the rides and the zoo, Michael encouraged kids to bounce on his giant in-ground trampoline and have full-force water balloon fights. He even allowed them to drive the golf carts. He treated them like adults but joined in their childish games. Michael often sprinted across his property to outmatch them in an athletic competition. He'd laugh whenever he got pushed in the pool, even if still fully clothed. He rocketed down his "super slide" face-first on a burlap bag, hoping to cross the finish line before them, but was quick to give advice on their technique.

After leaving his religion behind, Michael began hosting his own annual Easter egg hunt, which he voraciously participated in with the children. And always, without so much as a flinch, he let the kids plunder the eggs from his basket. The singer even allowed them to crack real eggs over his head, after which he casually put his black hat back on and continued having fun.

Michael was great with kids.

But the casual, line-blurring relationships he had with numerous boys would ultimately turn his fairy tale into a horror story.

CHAPTER EIGHT

DANGEROUS LIAISONS

The first half of Michael's solo career was filled with hits. During the second half, he just kept taking them.

It didn't matter that he used his stardom as a positive force. In 1985, he cowrote the smash "We Are the World" with superstar singer Lionel Richie. The charity record to combat famine was produced by Quincy Jones for United Support of Artists. Joining those two for the January superstar jam were Stevie Wonder, Paul Simon, Kenny Rogers, Tina Turner, Diana Ross, Billy Joel, Dionne Warwick, Willie Nelson, Bruce Springsteen, Huey Lewis, Cyndi Lauper, Bob Dylan, Ray Charles, Harry Belafonte, Waylon Jennings, Bette Midler, several Jackson siblings, and a host of other music legends. Released on March 7, the single—which ran more than seven minutes—sold over 20 million copies around the globe. An album, which included music by Prince, sold over three million copies. The project raised in excess of $63 million for humanitarian aid.

It is arguable that anyone but Michael could have pulled such a massive project off so fast and so effectively.

But in a way, it was followed by a rapid slide from the heights of achievement.

After making three hugely successful albums with Quincy, Michael cut ties with the producer for his eighth studio album, *Dangerous*. Instead, the singer teamed up with a range of producers in a variety of studios. The ambitious undertaking was expensive, even for Michael, who personally contributed $10 million toward his two-year project.

At the end of 1991, *Dangerous* debuted at number one and remained in the top ten for over a year. It had one chart-topping single, "Black or White," and the lone Grammy it received was not for Michael, but for the audio engineers. For most artists those results would be impressive, but not for the man Elizabeth Taylor had newly anointed the "King of Pop."

Michael navigated his life by attempting to prove he was bigger than Elvis and The Beatles. It's one of the reasons he spent $47.5 million to own The Beatles song catalogue in 1985. His most monumental decisions were driven by a desire to be "the biggest" entertainer and cultural messiah on earth. In an almost psychopathic way, he even wanted to be bigger than himself. For that eighth album, Michael had written twelve of the fourteen tracks. He viewed anything less than *Thriller*-level sales as a personal failure.

Ultimately, *Dangerous* "only" sold 30 million records, about a third of the copies *Thriller* had moved.

"He's very competitive," confirmed the singer's twenty-five-year-old sister Janet, whose own music career in the early nineties had transformed her into one of the biggest stars in the world.

Meanwhile, rumors swirled about Michael's personal life and staggeringly altered appearance—both his obvious cosmetic surgery and his ever-lightening complexion. And the arrival of "grunge" represented a sea change in popular music, which appeared to be moving in nearly the opposite direction of Michael's ultra-polished pop. The album that replaced *Dangerous* at number one was Nirvana's *Nevermind*.

For the first time in his life, Michael was in need of an image adjustment.

Making an extremely bold move, the pop star agreed to do a concert during the 1993 Super Bowl halftime at the Rose Bowl in Pasadena, California. While that may sound unremarkable now, Michael was the first to "play" the famous NFL event. His ten-minute show began with a loudspeaker introduction by actor James Earl Jones followed by a solid minute of cheering from the crowd. Michael played a medley of *Dangerous* songs with "Billie Jean" slipped in the mix and ended with "Heal the World" while surrounded on the field and stage by thousands of children.

The inspired performance was generally well-received.

And then, ten days later, Michael sat down with Oprah Winfrey for a ninety-minute primetime interview that aired live from Neverland. When Oprah inevitably asked him about his lightening skin, he spoke guardedly about his vitiligo, a disease that alters skin pigment. The question of whether it was the disease or skin-bleaching—or both—that had lightened Michael's skin would dog him for the rest of his life.

Sadly, it was the autopsy that finally answered the question.

Though there were many who doubted him, Michael was telling the truth. The coroner's report described "patches of light and dark pigmented areas" on the skin, with vitiligo as the diagnosis. Among Michael's medicines was Benoquin (monobenzone) 20 percent cream for vitiligo, a tube of BQ/KA/RA—consisting of Benoquin 8 percent, Kojic acid 1 percent, and retinoic acid 0.025 percent—hydroquinone 8 percent lotion to lighten pigment, and UVA Anthelios XL sunscreen to protect depigmented skin.

Incredibly, more than half of all US televisions being watched that night were tuned in to see Michael, and while he didn't exactly come off as "normal," he managed to humanize himself.

***

With his major media appearances and the ongoing success of the *Dangerous* world tour, 1993 appeared to be getting off to a good start. But just days after the Oprah interview, Michael, perhaps in a celebratory mood, invited another person to the ranch who would also play a big role in ultimately shaping the public's perception of him: an adolescent named Jordan Chandler.

Jordan was born on January 11, 1980. His parents were divorced in 1985. Both parents had remarried. June, his mother, had wed car dealer David Schwartz. Father Evan Chandler, a dentist, lived with his new wife Nathalie, and their son and daughter, in Beverly Hills, California. Evan dreamed of becoming a screenwriter.

Remarkably, Michael had first spoken to Jordan in May 1992 at a car rental agency owned by the child's stepfather. The singer had needed a car after his Jeep had broken down on Wilshire Boulevard in Beverly Hills, California.

"My stepfather called me and told me that Michael Jackson was at Rent-a-Wreck and that I should come down and see him," recalled Jordan, then an avid fan of the music icon.

He and his mother June raced to the shop to catch the superstar.

Even more bizarre, it wasn't the first time Jordan had met Michael. When the boy was five years old, he had a star struck encounter with Michael in a Los Angeles health food restaurant. The chance meeting had kicked off Jordan's intense fandom.

Aware of Jordan's affinity for the celebrity, David didn't charge Michael for the rental, and June took things a step further.

"I said, 'If you would like to see Jordie or if you'd like to speak to him, here is our number," the well-intentioned mother admitted telling Michael during that 1992 meeting.

Unpredictably, the thirty-four-year-old superstar actually followed up a month later.

For the next eight months, while Michael was on his *Dangerous* tour, the pair kept in regular contact over the phone. Their conversations progressively got longer and more frequent, sometimes lasting several hours, several times a day.

"He was excited to hear from him," June recalled. "They were talking about things that interested Jordie."

Childish things, like video games and water fights. The videogames would have included *Michael Jackson's Moonwalker*, which was released for various systems beginning in 1989. Each edition featured some variation of Michael saving abducted children from the villainous Mr. Big, all of it accompanied by techno versions of the superstar's songs. The game was inspired by the 1988 film *Moonwalker*, a collection of short movies, and music videos from *Bad*. It must have been surreal for kids to play as the character Michael Jackson with the real Michael Jackson giving them pointers.

Michael also treated the boy to stories about famous people and, of course, Neverland.

The star also put Jordan in touch with another boy: a ten-year-old from Australia named Brett Barnes, whom Michael claimed was a "cousin." Brett had been traveling with the pop star during the world tour.

Michael eventually asked if Jordan would like to visit Neverland when he was done touring. Naturally, getting the invite entranced young Jordan.

"He said that Neverland was a place where kids had the right-of-way, they had the dominance," Jordan remembered Michael explaining to him during one encounter. "You could have what you want when you want it."

In February 1993, Michael made good on his offer. June, Jordan, and his seven-year-old stepsister Lily all spent the weekend at Neverland, where the Chandlers slept in the guesthouse.

"We went on jet skis, played videogames, and went on golf cart rides," Jordan said, recalling that one evening the pop star initiated an after-hours trip to Toys "Я" Us for him and his sister. "We were allowed to get anything we wanted."

A couple of weeks later, Michael picked the family up in his limo and brought them back to Neverland. This time, young Brett was included in the weekend getaway. The trip concluded with a trip Disneyland in Anaheim, California.

The weekend after, the family returned to Neverland. This time, Jordan begged his mother to let him sleep in Michael's bedroom like the other boys. She denied his request, however. Still, Jordan rarely returned to their guest cottage before 11 p.m.

The following month, the three Chandlers joined Michael for several nights in Las Vegas.

Jordan and his family were all booked to stay in the same suite at the Mirage Hotel; however, that's not exactly how the sleeping arrangements panned out.

"After my mom and Lily went to sleep, we went to watch the movie *The Exorcist*," Jordan said of their first night together. "We were in his room, in his bed. And when it was over I was scared, and he said, 'Why don't you just stay in here?' And I did and nothing happened."

The following morning, Jordan came clean to his mother about the sleepover.

She desperately told him not to do it again.

Later that day, when Jordan informed Michael, the star threw a fit.

"He burst out in tears and said, 'She can't set up barricades like that,'" Jordan stated. "'It's just a simple slumber party. . . . There's nothing wrong with it!'"

That night, at approximately 11:30 p.m.—when Michael and Jordan were supposed to be attending a performance of Cirque du Soleil—the two showed up at the hotel suite. When June opened the door, the star was still in hysterics.

"We're a family," she recalled the singer saying through a waterfall of tears.

"Why can't he sleep in my bed? There's nothing wrong . . . Don't you trust me?'"

Although she initially protested, June ultimately gave in. And the next day Michael gave her an expensive Cartier bracelet and took the family to see David Copperfield's magic show.

There had been no inappropriate physical contact between Michael and Jordan in Vegas. But, according to the boy, that soon changed.

In the subsequent months, Jordan's trips to Neverland occurred more frequently and June and Lily did not always accompany him. Michael and Jordan routinely slept in the same bed everywhere, from Disney World to Europe and even in Jordan's own home.

"He was just with Michael the whole time," June noted. "He started dressing like Michael. He started acting withdrawn, sort of smart-alecky. He just didn't want to be with us."

Jordan claimed that the abuse began with getting hugged in bed and being told, "I love you." The boy alleged that, over a short period, Michael started kissing him on the cheek, which developed into kisses on the lips, and then Michael began using his tongue.

"I told him I did not like that," Jordan divulged.

When the boy objected and asked the star to stop, Michael again started to cry and said, "Just because most people believe something is wrong doesn't make it so."

Whenever Jordan was tentative about Michael's sexual advances, the singer told him that Brett had already done it with him.

When that didn't relax the boy, Michael would deliver a low psychological blow.

"If I didn't do it, then I didn't love him as much as Brett did," Jordan said, reiterating that Michael's haunting words had ultimately persuaded him to surrender. "Michael Jackson rubbed up against me in bed. We would lie on top of each other with erections."

But the worst was still to come.

Allegedly, Michael gradually ramped up the nature of the abuse from hugging and kissing to masturbation and oral sex.

In May 1993, Jordan and his family flew with Michael to the World Music Awards in Monaco. During the four-day trip, Michael, who was allegedly battling the flu, sent June and Lily on a shopping trip with his credit card. The singer remained at the hotel all day—as did Jordan.

"That's when the whole thing really got out of hand," Jordan said in a legal declaration, claiming the pair took a bath together. "This was the first time that we had seen each other naked.

"Michael finished taking off my shirt," the boy claimed. "When I was left only in my underwear, he pulled them down and took them off with his teeth." When they got in the tub, Jordan said that he sat on Michael's lap where the King of Pop washed his hair, kissed his neck, "and gave me goosebumps." He alleges that Michael urged him to wash and touch the singer's genitals.

After that, the two were shower buddies, which Jordan said was Michael's preferred venue for sex.

Frighteningly, the thirteen-year-old said Michael masturbated in front of him and climaxed while the two were in bed.

"He kept on saying, 'Tell me when you're ready and I'll do it for you,'" Jordan claimed. "One time he just reached over and said, 'Okay, just tell me how this feels.'"

Michael allegedly proceeded to fondle the teenager above his shorts, then, after receiving a favorable response, continued beneath his clothing until both were satisfied.

Another time, "Michael Jackson had me suck one nipple and twist the other nipple while Michael Jackson masturbated," he reported in the declaration. "On one occasion when Michael Jackson and I were in bed together Michael Jackson grabbed my buttock and kissed me while he put his tongue in my ear. I told him I didn't like that. Michael Jackson started to cry."

The upshot, according to the document, was that, "Michael Jackson told me that I should not tell anyone what happened." Jordan added that Michael told him people wouldn't understand their special connection. "He said that we had a little box, and this was a secret . . . and nobody can know about what's in the box but him and me."

The star also listed off other boys who had kept the same secret, including Brett, Macaulay Culkin, Wade Robson, and "a boy who went on the Bad tour" named James Safechuck. (Culkin has long denied Michael ever sexually assaulted him.)

After that trip, Michael completely stopped playing with Jordan in that conventional sense. Although he helped the boy with school assignments, the star used the opportunity to take advantage of Jordan.

"From that point, till the end of our relationship, he masturbated me with his mouth," Jordan claimed, but noted "that was as far as it went."

During a lengthy trip to France, he reportedly molested Jordan every day. And at the boy's home, Michael allegedly slept in the boy's bed over thirty times in three months. During the five-month period from March to July in 1993, Michael had spent at least seventy nights with the child, including at the Disney theme park in Paris.

Fortunately, there was one person who was removed enough from the situation to notice that something terrible was happening to young Jordan: his own father.

Evan believed that his son Jordan had been sexually abused by Michael.

So, too, did Michael's sister La Toya, who said he was "definitely" guilty and that she "cannot, and will not, be a silent collaborator of his crimes against small, innocent children." She subsequently retracted those remarks in an interview with me for the Australian magazine *Woman's Day* after Michael's 2009 death, claiming that she was pressured into making them by her then-husband Jack Gordon, an entertainment manager who handled her burgeoning career among others.

In any case, La Toya's remarks were counterbalanced by all the other siblings.

That left the forty-nine-year-old dentist-to-the-stars lacking both inside support and undeniable proof. He vowed to use whatever means necessary to extract the information from his brainwashed son.

But Jordan wasn't the only one keeping secrets.

CHAPTER NINE

DOCTOR'S ORDERS

Before Michael Jackson entered his life, Evan Chandler had several brushes with fame—and a long trail of controversies.

In the 1960s, Evan was a member of the upbeat New York City band The Fugitives, except back then, the swarthy musician was known by his birth name, Evan Charmatz. The twenty-two-year-old co-wrote their 1966 song "Your Girl's a Woman," which landed in the top 40 that summer.

By the end of the decade, Evan had switched gears and enrolled in dental school. In 1971, he met June Wong at a city clinic and two years later the lovers moved to West Palm Beach, Florida, where Evan started practicing dentistry. He also changed his last name to Chandler, he said, to avoid sounding too ethnic.

But according to FBI files obtained as part of this book's investigation, it's possible Evan had a pressing legal reason to switch identities. Someone with the same name was flagged for violating the Federal Reserve Act. Such crimes could include bank fraud, embezzling, handling stolen government property, and even domestic conspiracy; however, no charges were ever brought against him.

Evan and June married in 1974 and, three years later, the Chandlers relocated to Los Angeles. Evan had dreams of being a Hollywood screenwriter; instead, in 1978, he opened his own dental practice.

Jordan was born on January 11, 1980. The celebration was short-lived. A month later, Evan was under investigation by the dental board for shoddy dental services. One of his patients reported that he'd worked on a dozen of her teeth in a single visit, and many were fractured and decaying. Evan was fined, suspended from practicing for three months, put on five-year probation, and ordered back to dental school.

He filed an appeal, claiming that the board's decision made it impossible for him "to obtain professional malpractice insurance because of the restrictions placed on his license."

His request was denied.

During the summer of 1981, the thirty-seven-year-old rode out his suspension in New York, where he hoped to sell a screenplay. Unsuccessful, Evan returned to Los Angeles and resumed his dental career without the safety net provided by insurance. His probation was eventually lifted in the final months of 1983.

Jordan was only five years old when his parents divorced in 1985. June obtained sole custody of the boy. Evan was ordered to pay $500 per month in child support and was granted visitation rights. That same year, June married David.

Evan married a law student, Nathalie, two years later and opened a practice in Beverly Hills, where he became a moderately successful "dentist to the stars."

In 1992, Evan co-wrote the comedic film, *Robin Hood: Men in Tights.*

Incredibly, Jordan actually came up with the idea. Mel Brooks, who directed the film, recalled the eleven-year-old turning to his father at the dentist office and saying, "'You know what would be a great thing? A spoof of Robin Hood!"

Brooks loved the idea and slated it as his next production.

Evan even agreed to pay his son $5,000 for his invaluable suggestion, although he never honored the promise.

When Evan first heard about Jordan's newfound friendship with legendary pop star Michael Jackson, he believed that June had been the one selfishly forging the alliance. After all, it was June who had been trying to meet the entertainer for several years.

In 1984, June had written and hand-delivered a letter to Michael's bodyguard at Brotman Hospital while the singer was recovering from his Pepsi accident. The "get well" note, seemingly from Jordan, also included a photo of the boy and her telephone number. It was the same move she pulled eight years later at David's car rental agency.

But by April 1993, even though he had never seen them together, Evan realized that it was actually Jordan who had developed a special bond with Michael. But there was a lurking question in his mind: Was it vice versa? Evan was aware that the pair had started sharing a bed and he relied on June's opinion that their son was not in jeopardy. The doctor even bragged to the late *Star Wars* actress Carrie Fisher, a longtime patient, about his "very good looking" son's potential to bewitch Michael.

"This man was letting me know that he had this valuable thing that he assumed Michael Jackson wanted, and it happened to be his son," Carrie, who died in 2016, revealed. "When this first started happening, the good doctor saw no problem with this odd bunking."

Neither did Carrie—more or less.

"I never thought that Michael's whole thing with kids was sexual. Never. As in Neverland. Granted, it was miles from appropriate, but just because it wasn't normal doesn't mean that it had to be perverse. Those aren't the only two choices for what can happen between an adult and an unrelated child hanging out together."

Although the tasteless exchange was more "locker room talk" than perverse optimism, Evan was, at that time, clearly comfortable with the social arrangement.

"I felt that June should just divorce Dave, since they were having problems, and maybe hook up with Michael," Evan admitted.

"After all, they were having a good time, even if I had some reservations about it."

On May 20, Evan dropped by his ex-wife's home to see Jordan. He was startled to find Michael sitting on the floor in Jordan's room. It was the first time the two adults were meeting. After shaking hands, Evan grilled Michael about the nature of the friendship between him and his son. Deeply embarrassed but warm and responsive, Michael quickly won over the concerned father; at least temporarily. Evan's outlook on Michael changed—as did most people's—when the world's most notorious tabloid, *The National Enquirer*, published a screaming headline and tell-all article on May 25, 1993 that read as follows:

> **Michael Jackson's secret family—a millionaire's wife and her two kids**
> Michael Jackson has developed a bizarre obsession with a woman and her two children—and turned them into his secret family!
>
> The superstar has grown incredibly attached to June Chandler

Schwartz, her 13-year-old son Jordie and 5-year-old daughter Lily. Since meeting the mom and her children early this year, Michael has:

- Brought them to his ranch nearly every weekend.
- Phoned them as many as four times each day.
- Shared a suite with them during a Las Vegas vacation.
- Spent $1,500 on Jordie during one trip to Toys "Я" Us.

"I consider you my own family," he told June. "And I'll look after you as if you were."

June, 40, is the wife of Dave Schwartz, who went from rags to riches by starting Rent A Wreck and turning it into a $100 million a year car rental company.

Michael "adopted" June and her two children soon after he first met them at a Los Angeles Rent A Wreck office, said an insider.

"Michael rents cars from Rent A Wreck to make himself less conspicuous. He was in the office when June stopped by with her kids so that they could see their dad."

"Michael struck up a conversation with Jordie and the family was on cloud nine over the encounter."

After that meeting, Michael began calling the family every day, said the insider. "He had long conversations with Jordie and became fascinated by June, a beautiful Oriental woman.

"Michael was calling three or four times a day."

June and the children made their first trip to his Neverland Valley ranch a few months ago.

The group had such a good time that Michael, in disguise, took the family to Disneyland several times. "The more they enjoyed it, the more I did—and the closer we became," he told the insider. Added the insider, "Michael began hosting them at Neverland nearly every weekend."

His special treat was to take the children to Toys "Я" Us on Saturday mornings.

"One morning, he bought Jordie $1,500 worth of toys!"

Michael recently took June and the children on a five-day vacation to

Las Vegas, where they all stayed in his private three-bedroom villa at The Mirage hotel, said a source.

"When they arrived, Michael gave the children and their mother a tour of the place. The next day he took the boy shopping, then to the hotel arcade."

John Miklie, who runs the arcade, said Michael couldn't stay long "because too many kids crowded around him."

That night, Michael and Jordie swam with dolphins in the hotel's dolphin pool, said the source.

The next day, they went shopping again and Michael took Jordie and Lily to the "Siegfried & Roy" show. "When Michael walked back to his villa holding their hands, he was smiling like a proud papa," said an eyewitness.

The day after that, Michael and Jordie ate dinner at the Mirage's Chinese restaurant.

"They talked in whispers and laughed like a father and son," said waiter Chad Jahn, who served them.

Later that night, the two went to the hotel's circus-type show, called *Cirque Du Soleil*.

"They sat in section 206, row CC," said the eyewitness. "When the show was over, Michael bought the boy a *Cirque Du Soleil* sweatshirt."

When the group left Las Vegas, they headed to Michael's ranch, said the insider.

Since then, the singer has also taken "his family" on vacation to Disney World in Florida. And last week they all went to Monte Carlo, where Michael attended the World Music Awards.

"He's infatuated and obsessed with June, Jordie and Lily," said the insider. "He has adopted this family as his own."

"Michael told me, 'I'm enjoying having June, Jordie and Lily with me.

"The four of us are like a little family. We all have so much fun together that it's ecstasy.'"

After reading the tabloid tale that painted June as the fairy tale princess, Evan called his ex-wife and demanded she cut ties with the entertainer. The father-of-two was mostly concerned for the welfare of his children, fearing they had become obvious prey for kidnappers. But he also couldn't overlook Michael and Jordan's "romantic" dinners and dates the editorial mentioned. David—who was publicly humiliated by the scandalous exposure—agreed with Evan. It was time for the family to leave Neverland.

But June refused, calling them "selfish." And Michael reassured the distraught mother that she was making the right decision.

"Grownups don't trust each other, and that's the real problem here," he asserted. "It's such a shame that this kind of stuff happens."

Determined to personally assess the outlandish situation, Evan invited Jordan and Michael to spend Memorial Day weekend at his house. Michael accepted.

Arguably the most famous person on the planet was unconditionally spending his days with a little boy and his nights sleeping on a cot in the little boy's room. The superstar never let Jordan stray too far; everywhere the boy went, Michael followed. For days, they whispered secrets, had inside jokes, and Evan noticed Michael's eyes were often fixed on his son. Michael had explained that their relationship was "cosmic," but Evan wondered if it was actually caustic.

Before going their separate ways, Evan and Michael agreed to keep the lines of communication open. Over the next several weeks, Jordan continued spending his summer with Michael, who was about to kick off his *Dangerous* world tour. Meanwhile, most of Evan's calls went suspiciously unanswered.

Feeling slighted and duped by mega-millionaire Michael, the doctor decided it was time to order a surgical strike.

CHAPTER TEN

CIRCLING THE DREAM

On July 7, 1993, June was riding alone in Michael's limo when she used his car phone to check her home answering machine. There was a message from Evan. Her ex-husband was on the warpath.

"June, make sure you play this message for Michael and Jordie," he said on the recording. "All three of you are responsible for what is going on. No one is a neutral party. Since Jordie has repeatedly refused to return my phone calls, this will be my last voluntary attempt to communicate. I will be at your house at San Lorenzo this Friday, July 9 at 8:30 in the morning. Take my word for it, there is nothing else any of you has to do that is more important than being at this meeting."

Unsure of how to handle Evan's threats, June called David. She begged her husband to call her ex and convince him to back off. David agreed to handle it.

In the meantime, Evan and his attorney, Barry Rothman—a patient of Evan's with a sordid legal track record—requested that the courts revise the custody agreement between Evan and June. Evan wanted Michael out of Jordan's life, which meant he had to take the boy from June.

Rothman, according to his legal secretary at the time, Geraldine Hughes, claimed Jackson was framed by her boss. Speaking to journalist Roger Friedman in 2003, Hughes said she kept a daily-annotated calendar during her time with Rothman, and among her revelations that called into question Rothman's judgment was a story of a memo between the attorney and Chandler.

"Rothman advised the father how to report child abuse via a third party rather than going directly to the police," she said. "If it were any other case, you'd just pick up the phone and call the police."

In her own book, *Redemption: The Truth Behind the Michael Jackson Child Molestation Allegations*, released in 2004, Hughes extrapolated on her time working for Rothman, who ultimately fired her.

> My best description of an encounter with Mr. Rothman is a real-life encounter with a real-life demon straight out of the pits of hell. . . . Mr. Rothman ran his office like a concentration camp. His goal was always to inflict pain, humiliate and render you worthless so he could feel more superior. In his eyes, there were only two classes of people, boss and employees. Even his associate attorneys fell under the employee classification because he treated them no differently. He would rant and rave and humiliate them publicly just like the clerical staff. We were all equally abused.

The following evening, David audio recorded a series of phone calls between himself and Evan. The men spoke at length about how Evan planned to separate Michael and Jordan. At first, David tried to talk him out of the Friday meeting.

"You're not going to get anywhere," David cautioned.

"I'm worried about my kid," Evan responded, unaware that the conversations were being taped. "I don't know what's going on with you people and Michael Jackson."

For several minutes, Evan candidly explained the situation from his perspective.

"The message was very harsh, and it was very true," Evan professed. "It was to let them know that I am not kidding around."

For both men, the primary concern was protecting Jordan. But Evan revealed that he would stop at nothing to ensure it.

"This will damage him for the rest of his life," he said. "I've tried to talk to [June] about that and she's not willing to talk to me about it. She doesn't even want to hear what might be harming him."

Generally, David felt Evan was overreacting and was going to cause more trouble than if he simply let Michael and Jordan's relationship "run its course."

"I would be a negligent father if I did not do what I am now doing," Evan said. "It's gone way too far. Jordie is never going to be the same person he was. . . .

Something has happened inside of him and in his life that is now making him respond to me in a totally different way. . . . This is life and death for my son. I have to get their attention."

Still hoping to change Evan's aggressive approach, David argued that they should meet privately before dragging Michael into the conflict.

"I don't want to hurt anybody," Evan argued. "I want them to hear my concerns. Let them just tell me why I'm wrong. Let them just tell me that.

"As long as they don't want to talk to me, I can't tell them what my concerns are, so I have to go step by step, each time escalating the attention-getting mechanism."

David asked for Evan's opinion of Michael. The doctor blasted the singer for being "an evil guy."

"He's worse than bad," Evan vented. "He broke up the family. He was put on notice . . . the first sentence out of my mouth was, 'Michael, I think you're really a great guy. You're welcome into the family, as long as you are who you seem to be.'

"Michael is using his age and experience and his money and his power to great advantage with Jordie. He's also harming him, greatly harming him, for his own selfish reasons. He's not the altruistic, kind human being that he appears to be. . . . If Michael Jackson were just some thirty-four-year-old person would this be happening? No. He's got power, he's got money, he's got seduction."

David continued to probe the angry accuser, inquiring what Evan would do if Michael and June didn't show up to the 8:30 a.m. meeting the following morning.

"They will be destroyed," Evan said point blank. "June is gonna lose Jordie. She will have no right to ever see him again. Michael's career will be over . . . June is harming him, and Michael is harming him. I can prove that, and I will prove that. And if they force me to go to court about it, I will . . . . This man is gonna be humiliated beyond belief. He will not believe what's going to happen to him. Beyond his worst nightmares."

Although David understood where Evan was coming from, he theorized that perhaps Michael was actually more into June than Jordan.

"He has no interest in her whatsoever," Evan said. "The fact is he doesn't even care about her. He doesn't even like her. He told me he doesn't. He can't stand her. He told me that when he was in my house."

Still dead set on having the meeting, Evan insisted that his radical strategy was coming from a place of love, not hate.

"I think what's going on now is bad for Jordie, and therefore any alternative is better," he said. "Jordie's my life. Period. I love him so much that I'm willing to destroy my own life to protect him—to do what I think is the best thing to do."

Toward the end of their final phone call, David asked Evan if he felt Michael and Jordan were sexually intimate.

"I don't know, I have no idea," he said. "There's no reason why they would have to cut me out unless they need me to be away so they can do certain things which I don't think are good to be doing.

"They don't like you, and they don't like me, and they don't like her. They don't want anybody coming between them. In fact, when he talks to Michael on the telephone, he goes in another room because I'm not allowed to hear what they're talking about."

Evan knew he was going to be viewed as the villain and that Jordan would be heartbroken. "I'm taking Michael away from him," he admitted. "All I care about is what happens to him in the long run . . . June's not gonna save him. Who's gonna save him? Gotta be me."

Evan promised that he would keep things simple at the meeting. "I don't want to say anything that could be used against me. My whole part is going to take two or three minutes, and I'm going to turn around and leave, and they're going to have a decision to make."

Evan made one final guarantee before the men hung up: "By the way, they're going on tour on August 15. They're going to be out of the country for four months. . . . If they don't show up tomorrow, they're definitely not going."

At the meeting the next day, Evan was the only one who showed up. The irate father called his ex-wife and informed her that the story would be all over the news media. June was unmoved by Evan's threats. Her attorney, Michael Freeman, decided, "If he really believed Jordie was being abused, why would he not go to the police instead of the press?"

That afternoon, David and June played the recorded conversations for Michael's private investigator, the notorious (and later jailed) Anthony Pellicano, and Michael's high-powered lawyer, Bertram Fields.

When Michael heard the tape, he dismissed the matter as "extortion."

"People are always trying to get money out of me," Michael said. "I didn't do anything wrong . . . tell Evan that Michael Jackson said, 'go to hell.'"

Taking the matter more seriously, Pellicano asked for June's permission to question Jordan. The investigator needed to be certain that Michael hadn't made any inappropriate advances toward him.

"I decided to be straight with the kid," Pellicano said of their hour-long interrogation. "There was no time to be delicate."

Jordan claimed Michael was innocent.

On July 11, Jordan spent the day with his father. Evan had insisted that one of the boy's teeth needed immediate medical attention. Despite the turmoil, June consented.

Michael, however, was furious.

He had organized a lavish birthday party for Lily at Neverland. Naturally, he wanted Jordan to attend. June—shocked by Michael's volatility—excused herself and her kids from the event. Michael immediately shut the party down.

That afternoon, Michael unequivocally cut ties with the family. His attorney demanded he not see—or speak—with any of the Chandlers. And for the first time June began to side with Evan's assessment of the superstar.

Meanwhile, Evan made a "final offer" to settle the matter with Michael—one on one.

"Evan's pissed off at me because I have the kind of relationship he wishes he had with Jordie," Michael told Pellicano. "I'm not meeting with the guy and giving him more ammunition to use against me."

The next day, Evan and his attorney met with June to restructure their custody agreement. Evan refused to return Jordan if she didn't agree to his terms. Fearing legal repercussions, June signed a new arrangement that prevented Jordan from seeing Michael, stopped her from taking the boy out of Los Angeles, and excused the nearly $70,000 Evan had owed her in unpaid child support.

That day, June still went home without Jordan. Evan had no intention of letting him go—then, or anytime soon.

For the next couple of weeks, Evan continued building his case against Michael. He and Rothman secured written testimony from Dr. Mathis Abrams, a Beverly Hills psychiatrist, that it was "reasonable" to assume that "sexual abuse may have occurred" between Michael and Jordan.

The problem: Dr. Abrams hadn't actually met with either party and relied solely on Evan's version of the events.

The police, too, were aggressively pursuing the case and it was almost as if the lyrics from "Billie Jean" had come to life: "For forty days and for forty nights, the law was on her side." They interviewed over forty children who had been around Michael at Neverland Ranch . . . not one of whom corroborated the Chandler story. The lack of evidence, and tactics, were so overwhelming that attorney Fields, long considered one of the most ruthless lawyers in Tinseltown, was prompted to write to Los Angeles Police Department chief Willie Williams (The letter has since been released into the public domain):

Dear Chief Williams:

I represent Michael Jackson. All my adult life I have been a staunch supporter of the LAPD. For years, I represented Jack Webb. Working with Jack, on *Dragnet* and *Adam-12*, I met many officers for whom my respect and admiration continues to this day. Your comparative handful of officers who risk their lives every day to protect the rest of us deserve our unqualified appreciation. Sometimes, however, even a dedicated police officer, when engaged in a significant investigation, loses sight of the importance of fairness and respecting the rights of the accused. In the current investigation of Michael Jackson, that has occurred, officers investigating the matter have entered the homes of minors and have subjected them to high-pressure interrogation, sometimes in the absence of their parents. I am advised that your officers have told frightened youngsters outrageous lies, such as "we have nude photos of you" in order to push them into making accusations against Mr. Jackson. There are, of course, no such photos of these youngsters and they have no truthful accusations to make. But your officers appear ready to employ any device to generate potential evidence against Mr. Jackson. In addition, your officers have told parents that their children have been molested, even though the children in question have unequivocally denied this. They have also referred to Mr. Jackson as a "pedophile," even though he has not been charged, much less convicted. And harassing minors and their parents is not all. The search conducted at Mr. Jackson's residence resulted in the removal of many items of his personal property, including his address book, which includes the names and addresses of potential witnesses. We have asked for either the return of such records or that they be copied at our expense. This has been refused, in order to hamper the defense in conducting its own investigations of the case. These tactics are not merely inappropriate, they are disgraceful. . . .

Even the New York police, not known for their gentility, refrained from conducting this kind of overzealous campaign against Woody Allen, who was accused of a similar offense. Why is the LAPD not according Michael Jackson the same degree of balance and fairness?

I urge you to put an end to these abuses. Investigate these accusations as thoroughly as possible, but do it in a manner consistent with honest, common decency, and the high standards that once made me proud of the LAPD.

Sincerely,
Bertram Fields

Jordan himself still maintained Michael's innocence. But the boy was about to change his tune in the most dramatic of fashion.

On August 2, while having a tooth extracted by his father, Jordan was allegedly given an intravenous dose of the sedative sodium amytal—a so-called "truth serum." Jordan was still in a hypnotic and very impressionable state after the surgery. Evan used the opportunity in an attempt to get to the bottom of his son's relationship with Michael.

Evan approached the difficult issue from several angles.

He tried pressuring Jordan to confess that Michael sexually violated him, but Jordan rebuffed his father. Evan pretended to already know the truth, but again, his child wasn't buying it. Ultimately, he convinced Jordan that coming clean was the only way to save his friend Michael from global embarrassment.

Jordan gave in. He admitted that Michael had touched his private parts.

At that moment, Evan sympathetically hugged his defeated son, who returned the embrace.

"We never talked about it again," Evan said. "The prison walls had cracked, and I was confident the rest would take care of itself."

Armed with a new arsenal, Evan sought a meeting and Michael and his private eye Pellicano agreed to meet the pair two days later at the Westwood Marquis Hotel. Michael knew it was foolish, but he couldn't persuade his heart otherwise. He needed to see Jordan. The star wanted to assure the boy that everything would be okay.

Their reunion was bittersweet. Both Michael and Jordan managed an "I've missed you" before Evan sobered up the situation, sources said.

"I believe that Michael has acted inappropriately toward Jordie," Evan told Pellicano, who considered the father's carefully chosen words.

Michael surveyed the sullen face of the young boy, who reacted with an affirmative nod. Evan handed Michael the report from Dr. Abrams and read him an excerpt.

"These circumstances create the possibility that there exists negligence toward the child, even as far as prostitution."

Somewhat confused, Michael asked Evan to clarify his accusation.

"It means the doctor thinks you had sex with my kid," the father snapped.

"Be a man. Admit it!"

Humiliated, Michael called the claim "preposterous" and further denied knowing Dr. Abrams. Pellicano concurred, abruptly cut the meeting short, and told the Chandlers to "get out" of the hotel suite. But Evan contested. He read another line from the report:

"A thirty-four-year-old man constantly sleeping with a thirteen-year-old boy when other beds are available constitutes perverse and lewd conduct."

Pellicano repeated his previous instruction and announced that they were now at "war."

Still resisting, Evan demanded that Michael take a polygraph test to prove his innocence. "If it comes back that he didn't do it I'll be out of your lives forever," the father bargained. "He can take Jordie on tour with him and I won't have a thing to say about it."

Pellicano continued speaking on Michael's behalf, calling the accusation and the lie-detector demand "an insult."

"I'll see you in court," Evan told Michael emphatically. "I'm going to ruin you. You're going down."

Michael was silent as Jordan and his father left the suite. After the door closed, Michael stood, stared out the window, and started crying.

"Oh my God," the singer exhaled, and repeated the phrase several more times.

Although Pellicano tried to reassure the frazzled star, Michael realized he might lose his two most precious resources; his loved one and his career. But something far more dangerous than Evan Chandler had finally caught up to the superstar—his addiction to painkillers.

CHAPTER ELEVEN

HEAD CASE

Michael wanted the Chandler situation wrapped up before his *Dangerous* tour in Asia began on August 24, 1993. He directed Pellicano to resolve the increasingly explosive issue.

Over the next few weeks, Pellicano attempted to negotiate a fair resolution with Rothman.

Initially, Rothman demanded $20 million for Evan and Jordan to go away and effectively disappear. The large sum would pay for Jordan's schooling, the boy's extensive psychiatric care, and it would permit Evan to retire and spend quality time with his son.

But Pellicano had an entirely different approach to the settlement.

Since Michael was in the process of setting up several production companies at the time, Pellicano countered with a $350,000 "screenplay deal." The infamous Hollywood fixer-to-the-stars figured it was a win-win for both parties; the deal would disguise Michael's payoff as a business expense and simultaneously appeal to Evan's Hollywood aspirations.

Rothman wasn't going for it and rebuffed the offer.

At Michael's request, Pellicano returned with a $1 million, multi-picture deal. Rothman came back with $15 million.

"It's never going to happen," Pellicano responded.

"We'll have a trial and see how that goes," Evan noted through his lawyer.

With negotiations stalling out, Evan used another legal battle as leverage.

On August 17, the court threw out the flimsy custody agreement Evan had made with June and ordered the thirty-nine-year-old father to hand Jordan back to her. Evan asked for, and was granted, a brief extension. He was buying time for

Jordan to meet with Dr. Abrams. Evan knew exactly what would go down when they did. Jordan would officially confess to the psychiatrist about having been molested by Michael, Dr. Abrams would be legally obligated to report the accusation to the Department of Children's Protective Services, and the welfare agency would have to notify the authorities of the alleged charges against Michael. Evan hoped the strategy would allow him to maintain custody of his son.

During Jordan's three-hour psychiatric session with the doctor, the boy shared several tales that portrayed Michael as a sexual deviant who used childish code words like "lights" (erection) and "duck butter" (semen) to woo him.

Although Dr. Abrams admittedly didn't have the opportunity to fully scrutinize the veracity of Jordan's shocking claims, the doctor believed the information was actionable and he alerted the welfare department.

Almost immediately, Jordan was assigned a caseworker who promptly met with the child. The worker created an eleven-page report based on their interview.

"Minor said Mr. Jackson tried to make him hate his mother and father so that he could only go with Mr. Jackson," the investigator wrote in the report, a copy of which was obtained as part of our investigation, describing Jordan's illicit relationship with Michael from beginning to end. "Minor also said Mr. Jackson told him about other boys he had done this with."

In the report, Jordan blamed his mother for being seduced by the trappings of fame. He also stated he wished to remain with his dad.

Within days, the Los Angeles Police Department's Sexually Exploited Child Unit opened a criminal investigation. Evan and Jordan also filed a lawsuit against the singer.

Michael was preparing to travel overseas when Fields and Pellicano updated him on the alarming situation.

"Is my life over?" the fearful star asked the two men.

They assured Michael that they would defend him and he would come out on top.

"All my life I've been working so hard," Michael said, the strain of the circumstance evident in his fragile voice. "I can't lose it all now."

Michael left the country just as the scandal broke on every major news outlet across the globe.

Additionally, the LAPD and the Santa Barbara County Sheriff's Office were granted search warrants that gave them complete and unfettered access to Neverland and Michael's residence in Century City, California. Their objective was to find evidence that supported Jordan's claim that Michael was a pedophile.

Aided by a locksmith, numerous investigators went through every room on Michael's properties. All safes were opened, every VHS and computer were seized and examined, and the entire residence was photographed to corroborate details of Jordan's story. The officers carted out boxes of potential evidence, including pictures, diaries, linens, makeup, and magazines.

Within days, police served additional search warrants for Michael's Las Vegas suite at The Mirage and the Jackson home in Encino, California. Even though Michael had prepared for such a scenario, the singer was understandably thrown into a state of shock.

"Imagine having a stranger reading your most private thoughts," he said, referring to his volumes of journals, "someone going through all of your stuff while you're a million miles away!"

On August 24, the severity of the situation finally caught up with the entertainer.

Michael barely completed his first show in Bangkok, Thailand. In between songs, the star ran offstage where he was administered breathing treatments via an oxygen tank.

"I can hardly take a deep breath," Michael said to his handlers. "I'm sick. I think I'm dehydrated."

The troubled pop star bowed out of his second scheduled date in the city.

It was the first of many missed performances as the scandal began to mount.

In Los Angeles, Jordan complied with criminal investigators and provided a detailed description of Jackson's private anatomy, including his unusual skin tones, minimal groin hair, and a substantial dark spot at the base of his genitals. According to handwritten notes made during the investigation, Jordan specifically noted the singer's "cow-blotchy-pink/brown (not white but pink)" genitals and a "brown patch on ass/left glut."

He also mentioned that Michael had a "body oil stink."

Officials asked Jordan if Michael was circumcised. Jordan insisted that the singer was. He also drew a rudimentary picture of Michael's penis. The sketch was a step above generic.

Shortly after interviewing Jordan, investigators raided the offices of Michael's dermatologist and his plastic surgeon, looking for Michael's medical records. They believed it was likely that he had his "telltale" traits surgically altered to throw off Jordan's testimony.

But Michael's files were inexplicably missing from both offices.

Extensive interviews were also conducted with Michael's active and previous employees.

"My job was to hide all of Michael's women's perfumes," admitted his house-keeper, who was present during the Neverland raid. "He only used female fragrances, and I guess they thought that might look bad."

Unbeknownst to Michael, the Sexually Exploited Child Unit of the LAPD had also contacted the FBI to ask if the agency "would be interested in working a possible federal violation against Jackson concerning the transportation of a minor across state lines for immoral purposes." They believed Michael had violated the Mann Act. Also known as the Slave Traffic Act, the law was designed to stop the transportation of adults or kids for "prostitution, debauchery, or any other immoral purpose."

This hefty accusation against Michael wasn't entirely unwarranted.

According to secret FBI files, a year earlier, a Canadian couple reported their suspicions to authorities that Michael had smuggled one of his child abuse victims across America by train. The pair—who both worked in child services—said a boy aged about twelve or thirteen was identified as Michael's "cousin" to anyone who asked and travelled with the singer in a neighboring compartment. They said Michael was "very possessive of the boy at night" and added they "heard questionable noises" during the train ride. Incredibly, the situation was never fully investigated.

Concerning the Chandler case, a US Attorney decided they were "not interested in prosecuting Michael Jackson for a violation" of the law. But the FBI did decide "to assist the LAPD and Santa Barbara Sheriff's Office under a Domestic Police Cooperation matter."

With the global press turning on the iconic performer, Michael and his camp kicked into overdrive. Besides adamantly denying the molestation charge, Michael very actively—and very publicly—agreed to cooperate with the investigators.

"I am confident the department will conduct a fair and thorough investigation and that its results will demonstrate that there was no wrongdoing on my part," Michael said in an official statement issued to the press.

He also assured fans: "I intend to continue with my world tour."

Continuing his offensive pushback, Michael filed extortion charges against the Chandlers. The legal tactic was such a power play move that Rothman quit representing Evan and Jordan. The frazzled family hastily replaced him with famed civil rights attorney, Gloria Allred.

"My client wants the truth to come out," Allred said in her first press conference, promising to focus on the "real issues" in Jordan's case. "Why is Michael Jackson, an adult, repeatedly sleeping in the same bed as a young boy?

"There has been a concerted effort to deflect attention from what really happened."

But only a week later, she too was replaced by another hard-nosed Hollywood attorney, Larry Feldman. The Chandlers weren't interested in a lengthy, layered trial like Gloria was crusading for. They just wanted a swift and lucrative conclusion with minimal anguish. The Chandlers felt Feldman was their best chance at an easy multi-million-dollar payday.

As the *Dangerous* tour rolled through South America, additional concert dates were cut from the itinerary as headline after headline took the focus off the music and placed it to the minors he was often seen in company with. The allegations continued churning up a media storm for Michael and the press in each new country portrayed him as guilty.

Michael had become increasingly reliant on a lethal combination of anxiety meds, painkillers, and sleeping pills. He stopped eating and his health rapidly deteriorated.

By November, nearly a third of the thirty-stop leg of the tour had been canceled. A rep for the singer stated that Michael was "barely able to function adequately."

Due to Michael's weakened condition, the last eight cities on the tour schedule were scrapped. The singer released an unusually candid video-recorded statement about his drug problem.

"The pressure resulting from these false allegations coupled with the incredible energy necessary for me to perform caused so much distress that it left me physically and emotionally exhausted," Michael said. "I became increasingly more dependent on the painkillers to get me through the days of the tour."

After learning about the cancelation, Feldman encouraged Michael to promptly return to Los Angeles.

"Allow us to try this case in court in an expeditious manner rather than running away from this matter," he challenged the pop star.

But instead, Michael was flown from his final tour stop in Mexico City to London, England, where he checked into rehab for his addiction. His longtime friend Elizabeth Taylor had orchestrated the life-saving—and lawsuit-delaying—move.

"I can't think of anything worse a human being could go through than what he's going through now," the sixty-one-year-old Oscar-winning actress told the press. "I believe he will be vindicated.

One of the most incredible, and ultimately poignant account, of how Michael busied and distracted himself during the period from 1989 to 1996 comes from Ray Robledo, manager of Neverland. Michael had generously hired the man, who had lost his position on a game preserve.

When Robledo arrived, Michael had just successfully bred a donkey and a zebra to create a "zonkey." Though the new hire was amazed, the creature—better known as a "zebroid"—is the result of any crossbreeding matching equine creature with a zebra.

However, Robledo claims Michael was also trying to mix other breeds, including his lion Kimba, the giraffe Jabbar—no doubt "honoring" basketball great Kareem Abdul-Jabbar—and various iguanas and snakes, including a white king cobra.

The manager also said that Michael insisted on hiring a person who did nothing but prevent free-ranging animals from eating the estate's many roses.

These were odd but engaging times and Robledo said they ended with the accusations from Jordan Chandler.

"When Michael did show up at the ranch there were no more train rides or carefree conversations with him," the man recalled.

Robledo tried to give him encouragement, reminding him that there were those around him he could trust and how, in time, hardship passes. Michael seemed lost, however. He asked Robledo to play the Yes song "Owner of a Lonely Heart" throughout the grounds.

He was trying to figure out what actually mattered in life, Robledo recalls.

Part of Michael's withdrawal, even at home, was not unwarranted. Later, other Neverland employees were apparently not as concerned . . . or taciturn.

Maid Adrian Marie McManus would later testify at the 2005 child molestation trial that she witnessed Jackson touching boys inappropriately.

Married cooks, Philippe and Stella LeMarque, would testify that their employer took "sexual advantage of young guests," Philippe saying that he actually witnessed Jackson putting his hands in the underpants of eleven-year-old *Home Alone* star Macauley Culkin in the small hours of the morning in 1991.

During the trial that would ensue, Culkin adamantly denied the charges:

Q: You heard about some of the allegations about whether or not Mr. Jackson improperly ever touched you, right?
A: Yes.

Q: Did Mr. Jackson ever molest you?
A: Never.

Q: Did Mr. Jackson ever improperly touch you?
A: Absolutely not.

Q: Has Mr. Jackson ever touched you in any sexual type of way?
A: No.

Q: Has he ever touched you in any offensive way?
A: No.

Q: What do you think of these allegations?
A: I think they're absolutely ridiculous.

Q: When did you first learn that these prosecutors were claiming that you were improperly touched?

A: When did I first learn that?

Q: Yes.

A: I—somebody called me up and said, "You should probably check out CNN, because they're saying something about you."

Q: And did you check it out?

A: Yes, I did.

Q: And what did you learn?

A: I learned that it was a former cook had done something to me, and there was something about a maid or something like that. It was just one of those things where I just couldn't believe it. I couldn't believe that, first of all, these people were saying these things or—let alone that it was out there and people were thinking that kind of thing about me. And at the same time it was amazing to me that they—that nobody approached me and even asked me whether or not the allegations were true. They kind of just were—threw it out there just like—they didn't even—they didn't even double-check it basically. I mean, even if they assumed that they knew the answer, what got me was that they didn't even ask.

Q: Now, are you saying these prosecutors never tried to reach you to ask you your position on this?

A: No, they didn't.

Q: Do you know if any police officer from Santa Barbara has ever tried to call you to see what the truth is?

A: No.

Culkin's steadfast denials were subsequently reiterated—not on the stand, but in interviews—by Michael's friend Emmanuel Lewis, the star of TV's *Webster*.

"We just had the best times, you know? He's always been nothing but a great friend, not just to me but to my whole family."

At the same time as things were heating up legally, Michael's professional commitments and business dealings were quickly drying up. *Dangerous* tour sponsor Pepsi cut ties with the entertainer, permanently ending his lucrative partnership with the brand. A scheduled primetime NBC special called the *Jackson Family Honors* was suspended indefinitely. And Michael was originally slated to provide the theme song and a music video for the 1993 film *Addams Family Values*. Not only was he dropped from the feature, he became the punchline of a scene in the film (fourteen-year-old actor David Krumholtz screams when he sees Michael Jackson posters on a cabin wall).

When Michael emerged from rehab on December 10, he stoically returned to Los Angeles where police subjected the thirty-five-year-old to a thirty-minute strip search that involved photographing his nude body.

"It was the most humiliating ordeal of my life, one that no person should ever have to suffer," Jackson recalled. "But if this is what I have to endure to prove my innocence . . . so be it."

Michael stood on a platform in the middle of a room at Neverland while several people examined his fully exposed extremities. Although much of Jordan's description loosely matched Michael's anatomy, the boy had gotten one crucial detail wrong. The King of Pop wasn't circumcised.

Other rumors were also squashed too.

Chief among them was a report that Michael's flaccid genitals had the letters "WOOH" tattooed on them. His come-on line was reportedly, "If you want to see it say 'WINNIE THE POOH,' rub it."

Santa Barbara district attorney, Tom Sneddon, the man tasked with prosecuting Michael, tried to make a big point of a little spot that he said matched a drawing the boy made:

> The photographs reveal a mark on the right side of Defendant's penis at
> about the same relative location as the dark blemish located by Jordan

> Chandler on his drawing of Defendant's erect penis. I believe the discoloration Chandler identified in his drawing was not something he could have or would have guessed about, or could have seen accidentally. I believe Chandler's graphic representation of the discolored area on Defendant's penis is substantially corroborated by the photographs taken by Santa Barbara Sheriff's detectives at a later time.

However, other law enforcement disputed that there was any similarity.

Meanwhile, another party was heard from. According to FBI files, by September 1993, the Bureau had accumulated reports from the British press about another boy who claimed to have had unsolicited sexual encounters with the King of Pop—before he became music royalty.

The accuser was British disc jockey Terry George and he claimed that in 1979, when he was just thirteen years old, Michael called him to describe, graphically, his own sexual activities, and to ask the boy about his own. The two had met when the Yorkshire lad was a devoted autograph collector and took to waiting at theaters and hotels. Terry was said to have tracked Michael in February 1979 to the Dragonara Hotel after a concert in Leeds. In the lobby, the plucky boy eavesdropped hotel workers to learn the star's room number. Heading to the suite, Terry claimed he knocked on the door and was admitted for an exclusive interview.

Terry remembered Michael making him feel special, like a friend. Telephone numbers were exchanged.

As he followed the scandal unfolding in California, Terry—now twenty-eight—told the press: "I can believe that the allegations are true because of what happened to me."

According to Terry, "He just came straight out with his questions. I just giggled. I felt embarrassed and awkward. I didn't really understand what he was talking about."

Terry said he tried to change the subject, at which point Jackson reportedly made the topic more immediate by asking, "Do you believe I'm doing it now?"

In all, the calls said to have lasted a quarter of an hour of which "five minutes or so" were "devoted to sex."

Why didn't the boy hang up the phone? Because, he said, Michael was a superstar and Terry was flattered by the attention. Terry claimed that Michael lost interest in him when he was no longer a child.

Upon receiving this information, the FBI investigated, including involving the Office of the Legal Attaché at the American Embassy in London with a "priority" request for additional information. There was travel to Santa Barbara to meet with Assistant District Attorney Ron Zonen and members of the Santa Barbara County investigation and prosecution teams.

According to internal FBI correspondence notes, obtained as part of this investigation, on September 7, 1993, the FBI and the LAPD Sexually Exploited Child Unit jointly got involved in an exploration of "possible federal violation against Jackson concerning the transportation of a minor across state lines for immoral purposes (MANN ACT)."

A meeting was scheduled for September 10 at the office of the Los Angeles district attorney.

Though forces were massed, and resources deployed across the globe, the bottom line, according to an internal FBI letter, was that the Los Angeles Division ultimately decided to "take no action on this matter."

Los Angeles law enforcement was equally unsuccessful in amassing compelling evidence.

But a court of law and the court of public opinion are—as history has proven—two vastly different things.

Although investigators uncovered no incriminating testimony from dozens of children and his legions of employees, and despite having no other witness besides Jordan, Michael and his legal team decided to pay the Chandlers off.

Innocent or not, Michael simply did not want to endure a lengthy trial.

"I wanted to go on with my life," he later confessed.

On January 25, 1994, Michael settled out of court for $22 million. Of that sum, $20 million ($15.3 million after the substantial attorney fees) was put in a trust fund for Jordan. Evan and June each received $1 million. The payout also stipulated that Michael was in no way admitting to any guilt.

"In all my private stuff, there wasn't one piece of evidence to prove I had done anything wrong," Michael stated, further lamenting that he never got a lot of his confiscated possessions back. "It makes me want to cry when I think about it."

After leaving his legal woes behind, Michael turned his full-attention, and the attention of the world, to another pressing legal matter: his marriage to Elvis Presley's daughter, Lisa Marie.

CHAPTER TWELVE
CHILDHOOD SWEETHEART

Behind the scenes, Michael Jackson had very little in common with his debonair stage persona.

"It's all just fantasy, really," Michael admitted. "I think it's fun that girls think I'm sexy. I like to make my fans happy, so I might pose or dance in a way that makes them think I'm romantic. But really, I guess I'm not that way."

In private, Michael was timid around women and had very few romantic encounters with the opposite sex. Those who knew him best in the 1980s could only recall him going on a handful of dates and none of them were serious relationships.

The first girl Michael was reportedly "into" was child star Tatum O'Neal, the daughter of television and movie star Ryan. The pair met in 1975 at a lavish Paul McCartney party. At seventeen years old, Michael was five years older than Tatum. The young actress recalled being smitten with the Jackson 5 star, but noted that, at that time, she was not ready for a "mature" relationship.

"Michael, who was sweating profusely, seemed as intimidated as I was," she later recalled.

Over the next few years, the two kept in close contact.

"We'd talk on the phone all the time," Tatum said. "Michael used to come to my house when I was living with my dad, and I remember him being so shy. Once he came into my bedroom and he wouldn't even sit on my bed."

On one occasion, the two held hands at a club on the famous Sunset Strip in Los Angeles.

"It was the most magical thing," Michael cooed. "It was better than kissing her. It was better than anything."

Although Michael claimed the starlet "wanted to do everything" and that he "didn't want to have sex at all," Tatum politely denied the assertion.

"I have a great deal of respect for Michael Jackson as an artist and as a person," she said. "However, he has a very vivid imagination."

But by the end of 1978, Michael had moved on from Tatum.

"He asked me to go to the premiere of *The Wiz* with him," Tatum recalled, though she declined the invite. "He never talked to me after that."

That same year, Michael met thirteen-year-old model Brooke Shields at a party in Manhattan, New York. Although their encounter was brief, Michael made a lasting impression on the girl.

"Nothing was jaded about him," Brooke recalled. "I just was so impressed by his sweetness."

In 1981, Michael ran into Brooke at the 53rd Annual Academy Awards, which he attended with Diana Ross. Brooke was scheduled to present an award at the event.

"She just came up to me and said, 'Hi, I'm Brooke Shields. Are you going to the after-party?'" Michael recalled of their second encounter. "I said 'Yeah' and I just melted. I thought, 'Does, she know that photographs of her are all over my room?'"

Michael, wearing his *Off the Wall* black tux with a black bow, put his arm around Brooke and the two posed for the paparazzi. At the after party, the pair lit up the dance floor.

"I was up all night, spinning around in my room, just so happy," Michael said of the evening. "She was classy."

The two exchanged numbers and soon discovered that they had a lot in common. Brooke's overbearing mother was also her manager and notoriously pushed her daughter to the limit, much like Michael's father had done with him. Both Michael and Brooke had grown up quickly and had successfully transitioned from child stars to adult superstars. They were also both steadfast virgins who preferred sharing laughs instead of sharing beds.

Michael was taken by Brooke's warmth and genuine kindness.

"We just felt safe with each other," Brooke said. "We watched movies and ate candy and laughed at the craziness around us."

While she admitted that they loved each other, she insisted "it was not at all romantic."

"It was easy for him to be a friend to me, because I was the most celebrated virgin ever," she stated. "You saw women who were more sexual, who wanted to throw themselves at him and feel like they were going to teach him . . . we didn't have to deal with our sexuality."

For years, Brooke became Michael's go-to date for awards shows, beginning with the 1984 Grammys.

"Michael always knew he could count on me to support him or be his date," Brooke said. "We would have fun no matter where we were."

On several occasions, Michael asked Brooke to marry him and begged her to adopt children with him. But Brooke persuaded him to reconsider.

"I'm going to go on and do my own life and have my own marriage and my own kids," she told Michael, reassuring the sensitive man that he'd always have her.

In 1991, Brooke was Michael's "plus one" to Elizabeth Taylor's eighth wedding, which was held at Neverland. It was the last time they saw each other.

"Brooke Shields was one of the loves of my life," Michael said, still regretting that he "chickened out" one frisky evening together.

"I shouldn't have," he said.

Earlier that year, Michael surprised the public as pop star Madonna's date to the 63rd Academy Awards. Even Michael was surprised by the invite. He had asked the Oscar-nominated singer who she was attending the event with and Madonna responded, "You wanna go?"

At the March 25 show, both looked flawless in their complementary white glittery attire. Michael wore a more dazzling version of his trademark black pants. Aided in part by her Oscar win that night for "Sooner or Later" from the film *Dick Tracy*, Madonna dubbed it her "best date ever."

"Yes, he took me home," Madonna dished, then famously added, "You wanna know what happened after that? I'm not gonna tell you."

Madonna would later divulge that she and Michael made out that night.

"Tongue-in-mouth kissing," she boasted. "I did get him to sort of loosen up with a glass of chardonnay. And it worked wonders. . . . He was a willing accomplice."

Over the next couple of months, the King and Queen of Pop wined and dined a few times and decided to record the duet "In the Closet." Madonna also wanted to give Michael a complete makeover, including a contemporary hair style and trendier wardrobe, but he refused.

"I said, 'Look Michael, if you want to do something with me, you have to be willing to go all the way or I'm not going to do it,'" Madonna said.

He wasn't. So Michael recorded a solo version of the song and released it on the album, *Dangerous.*

Late in 1992, Michael was attending a private dinner party when he had a chance encounter with twenty-four-year-old Lisa Marie Presley. The two had met several times in Las Vegas during the 1970s. Elvis Presley used to take his then six-year-old daughter to see the family friendly Jackson 5 shows. Michael was sixteen at the time.

"She would sit right in the front and bodyguards would be right there," said Michael. "Afterwards, she would be escorted backstage and I would meet her and we would talk. This happened quite often."

After getting reacquainted at the dinner party, Lisa Marie admitted she was trying to break into the music business, but feared being compared to her famous father.

"Things always got too wild when people found out that Elvis' daughter wanted to sing," she said.

Listening to her demo tape, Michael agreed to help Lisa Marie launch a music career.

"You have real talent," he said. "You could be a star."

Lisa Marie was married at the time to rocker Danny Keough, with whom she had two children. But the aspiring singer was very drawn to Michael.

He opened up to Lisa Marie. They regularly spoke on the phone, connected over having spent their youth in the spotlight, and enjoyed comparing Neverland to Elvis' famous Graceland home in Memphis, Tennessee. They realized, in many ways, they were uniquely suited to understand each other.

"I know you have heard a lot of things about me, but most of it isn't true," Michael reassured her. "And the stuff that is true you shouldn't hold against me."

"I thought to myself, 'Wow, this is a real guy,'" Lisa Marie recalled. "I told him, 'If people knew who the hell you really are, they would be so surprised . . . that you sit around and you drink and you curse and you're fucking funny and you don't have that high voice all the time.'"

She also recognized the demons Michael was battling. They were the same ones that had taken her forty-two-year-old father on August 16, 1977, when she was only nine years old.

"I was aware of the drug use," Lisa Marie said of her dad. "He tried to hide it from me as best he could. I felt sort of helpless. It hurt. It still hurts."

She was also present when the lifeless body of her father was discovered in Graceland. With Michael, Lisa Marie was determined not to make the same fatal oversight.

"I wanted to save him," she later admitted. "I don't know the psychology of it and what it had to do with my father. . . . I felt that I could do it."

And Michael certainly needed taking care of. He and Lisa Marie had been casually dating when the Jordan Chandler battle broke out. She stood by him through the devastating ordeal.

"I believed that he didn't do anything wrong and that he was being wrongly accused," she said.

When Michael was overseas on the *Dangerous* tour, Lisa Marie sensed that he had started abusing medications. He sounded "off" when they spoke on the phone. Realizing that he needed a lifeline, she encouraged the singer to settle with the boy's family—but perhaps more importantly, to check into a rehab clinic. And, in an era before cell phones, she made sure he had phone numbers to every place she could be staying.

One evening, while sequestered in a hotel, Michael made a life-changing phone call.

"If I asked you to marry me, would you?" he questioned Lisa Marie, who was still married at the time. "Of course!" she immediately replied.

After a long pause, Michael professed his love to his secret fiancée.

Then, he made it official when he returned to Neverland.

In February 1994, with the Chandler lawsuit squared away, Michael and Lisa Marie became inseparable. They played at Neverland and took trips to Las Vegas and to Donald Trump's Mar-A-Lago estate in Palm Beach, Florida.

"It was romantic," the future President of the United States recalled. "Later, I asked Michael how things were going, and he said, 'Great. I just got to kiss the most beautiful girl in the world. I hope I'm worthy of her.'"

Michael gushingly added, "I've never known a person like her."

A friend of Lisa's confirmed that they had become lovers during the trip.

On May 26, 1994, less than three weeks after her divorce from Keough had been finalized, Lisa Marie married Michael in the Dominican Republic. They exchanged simple gold rings during the brief ceremony. Very few people, including the Jackson family and Lisa Marie's mother, Priscilla, were even aware of the intended marriage. Incredibly, the couple managed to keep it a secret for two months.

When word seeped out, Lisa Marie said, "I am very much in love with Michael, I dedicate my life to being his wife. I understand and support him. We both look forward to raising a family and living happy, healthy lives together. We hope friends and fans will understand and respect our privacy."

The newlyweds honeymooned in Budapest, Hungary—where Michael was shooting a promotional film for his ninth studio album *HIStory*. The power couple also spent time at a local children's hospital where they gave away toys to the underprivileged.

"I never met anybody who cared so much about children the way I do," Michael stated at the time. "I get real emotional about children. Lisa Marie is the exact same way."

Although Michael had been referring to other people's children, the thirty-five-year-old desperately wanted to start his own family.

"I want children so badly," he confessed to Lisa Marie. "I want more children than my father."

But privately, Lisa Marie wasn't convinced that having a baby with Michael Jackson was a smart move.

CHAPTER THIRTEEN

LOVE ME TRUE

Michael and Lisa Marie hadn't slept together while they were in the Dominican Republic. They were in separate beds—and even in separate houses. Michael slept in a multi-million-dollar oceanfront home that belonged to the owners of the Casa de Campo resort, while Lisa Marie stayed in a villa several miles away from her new husband.

Although Michael and his public relations juggernaut tried hard to make everything about the marriage look real, insiders suggested the marriage was a sham. Fixing Michael's corrupted image would become another logistical nightmare for the singer, who had broken the basic taboos of behavior in American culture.

The world had not yet invented fire control and damage control systems that could handle, let alone repair or restore, the injury to Michael's "brand." He had gone from being the world's most famous entertainer to the world's most notorious freak—and there wasn't a Band-Aid or a surgeon's scalpel in the world big enough to cover the wound Michael had inflicted on himself.

That is not to say that Michael's public relations team wouldn't try to recreate the megastar in the light they wanted him to be perceived.

The National Enquirer, then the highest-selling weekly tabloid in the world, published an eight-page spread in its August 23, 1994 issue featuring exclusive photos of the newlyweds. The photos were taken on the back half of their honeymoon while the couple was staying in their Trump Tower penthouse in New York City. They invited top celebrity photographer Dick Zimmerman to join them there and photograph them for the entire world to see. Zimmerman was the same photographer who snapped the shots of Michael used on the front cover and inside spread of the *Thriller* album.

They wanted their "secret" marriage officially publicized across the universe. Just one day before the photo session, Lisa Marie ended the "are they or aren't they married" speculation by announcing that she and Michael Jackson were indeed man and wife.

But newspapers around the world were already having a field day describing how abnormal the wedding ceremony had been, and how cavalierly Michael responded when presiding Judge Hugo Francisco Alvarez asked, "Do you take this woman, Lisa Marie Presley, to be your lawfully wedded wife?"

According to sources, Michael flippantly replied: "Why not?"

It's the little things that always give one away, and this response showed exactly where Michael's head was at the time. He didn't take his own marriage seriously and neither did anyone else. This move was perceived by many as a ploy to distract from things far deeper and more sinister.

"Michael looked like a little boy lost," Judge Alvarez told the media. "He stared at the floor throughout the ceremony. And when I pronounced him and Lisa Marie man and wife, he was reluctant to kiss her."

The judge revealed other aspects of the wedding that were unusual: "There were no tears of happiness, no joy, no laughter. The ceremony had a somber tone. It was bizarre."

He said that Michael, a perpetual Peter Pan fan, originally wanted to be married up in the air, while flying around. He wanted the judge to perform the ceremony while Michael's private plane circled the island. But the judge could not honor the odd request, as he explained to Michael's representatives. His authority to marry people was only valid on the soil of the Dominican Republic. If the wedding had been performed in an airborne plane, it would have been invalid, so Michael and Lisa Marie went to the judge's private home in La Vega.

And during the ceremony, Michael was apparently more fascinated with the tie Judge Alvarez wore than he was in his new bride. Of course, the tie showed a cartoon character, Fred Flintstone. The judge had bought the tie at Universal Studios in Florida. He said that Michael told him: "It's a great tie. I love Fred Flintstone!"

Remarkably, the judge noted a paradox: "But I never heard him say he loved Lisa Marie."

Another unusual note to this whole nuptial proceeding was that although this was a wedding between two people inextricably linked with musical fame, the ceremony didn't include any music. The entire ceremony was performed in stony silence.

But in the article accompanying the photos in *The National Enquirer,* Zimmerman insisted that the couple was "madly in love!"

"It's a real marriage, not a hoax," he said. "Lisa Marie has two children and they're going to be part of a normal family with her and Michael."

He explained how he came to have the assignment; to officially photograph the happy couple.

"Lisa's secretary called me and then Lisa got on the phone. She just told me, 'You're the one. We'd like you to do it.'"

There was a whole clutch of photographers from all over the world camped outside Trump Tower, hoping to get a quick shot of Michael and Lisa Marie, but it was Zimmerman who landed the official gig.

In the article, Zimmerman explained:

On August 2, I smuggled photographic equipment into the Trump Tower right under the eyes of the paparazzi outside. Michael and Lisa Marie were waiting to greet me. While I was setting up my equipment in their living room, Lisa Marie and Michael were being made up by makeup artists hired for the occasion. I left the choice of clothes to them. Michael selected a black military-style jacket with gold leaf embroidery and tassels. His makeup made him look very light skinned. Lisa Marie wore black pants and a matching long black jacket. For the first shot, I told them to stand close to each other and relax. They immediately put their arms around each other, and Lisa Marie cuddled right up to Michael. Then I told them to change into casual outfits. Michael chose a red military style shirt with a blue-striped collar. Lisa Marie changed into a white blouse, black jacket and blue jeans with the knees out. They both had their makeup touched up. For the second photo, Michael sat on the floor. Lisa Marie put her arm around his neck and nestled her face lovingly into his hair. Michael broke into a beautiful, spontaneous smile. Then I told Lisa Marie to sit in a chair and Michael to kneel beside her. He put his arm around her and pulled her head into his chest, while Lisa Marie tenderly took hold of his hand. Between shots, they were whispering and giggling to each other, enjoying little jokes.

During the photo session Zimmerman eventually decided he wanted to set up for an "artistic mood shot, with light and shade." He told Michael and Lisa Marie "to put their heads together and Lisa Marie to put both her arms around Michael, hugging him tight. Normally, a photographer has to manipulate people into what he wants. But in this case, they were so happy and natural it was almost difficult to keep their attention on the camera. They were so much into each other."

In an inset in the editorial spread, there was a close-up of Lisa Marie's hand with her wedding ring; a gold ring with an enormous diamond on it. In some of the shots Zimmerman took, Lisa Marie wore the ring on her left hand. In other shots she wore it on her right hand. Said Zimmerman: "That was never explained to me. All I know is that Lisa wanted to show off her wedding ring."

The celebrated photographer did elaborate about how he viewed the new married couple and their relationship: "Clearly they wanted to show off to the world how happy they are with each other. They didn't put it into words for me. They didn't have to. The pictures show it."

Others weren't buying it. There were rumors that Lisa Marie was pregnant by Michael. Zimmerman added: "They didn't say anything to me about it. But I'd be very happy for them if Lisa was pregnant. And I'd be delighted to take the baby pictures!"

In the photos, Michael and Lisa Marie were draped all over each other, but Michael's eyes were always focused on the camera. He played exclusively to the lens. He touched Lisa Marie when she was hanging all over him, but he did it lightly and tentatively. She, on the other hand, was obviously into it. She touched Michael with real enthusiasm. She threw herself toward him. He merely leaned into her, holding back, and was often watching the camera. This was Michael hard at work. Hard at work to prove that he was a "regular guy."

Michael also disclosed how he officially proposed to Lisa Marie at Neverland. Here is his account of the proposal in his own words:

"Lisa Marie and I were in the living room having a glass of wine. We had just finished watching *All About Eve*, starring Bette Davis. We both love that movie. I just walked over to her, reached into my pocket and pulled out a huge diamond ring. "So, what do you think?" I asked her. "You wanna?" I never even officially popped the question . . . It just sort of happened."

Of a prenuptial agreement, Michael said, "I would never ask Lisa Marie to sign a prenuptial agreement. What kind of marriage would that be?"

At the time, Michael was estimated to be worth just under half a billion dollars. Lisa Marie was worth about $9 million. But in a matter of a few years she was slated to come into another sum estimated somewhere between $80 and $200 million. Her mother had cleverly and spectacularly enhanced the value of Elvis's estate over the years, which Lisa Marie would soon control.

Michael went on to explain the nature of his relationship to new wife: "This is love. I swear it. I love Lisa Marie. Why won't people believe that? Why won't the public let me be happy? I don't get it."

He said that he understood that some of the problems people had in believing his marriage to Lisa Marie stemmed from his strange behavior at the wedding ceremony in the Dominican Republic. He explained that he was merely nervous at their wedding ceremony, and that he never meant to be disrespectful. It was unfortunate that a lot of people perceived him as being nonchalant and dismissive about something as serious as being married.

Later, Michael addressed the subject of having children.

"Yes, we want to have children," he said. "Yes, we will have children. But, no, she is not expecting right now. Don't rush me."

That September, Michael and Lisa Marie made the front pages of newspapers around the world when he kissed her on stage at the 1994 MTV Video Music Awards in Manhattan. If that wasn't proof enough of the validity of their marriage, Michael didn't know what to do to convince skeptics.

"Really, this is not a hoax," he concluded. "I swear it's not, and I don't care what people think. I really don't. All I want people to know is that I wouldn't marry someone just for publicity. That's just not me. I love her. This is serious. I hope people believe it. If not, then hey, too bad for them."

But years later Lisa Marie would reveal in an interview that the MTV kiss had been the idea of Michael's manager.

"I thought it was stupid," she said. "All of a sudden I became part of a PR machine."

For Lisa Marie, it was a sign that the marriage was in trouble immediately and would likely be short-lived. But over the next few months, articles appeared that showed Michael and Lisa Marie as lovebirds. Other articles turned up saying Michael wanted to move into Graceland and that he wanted to perform in some of Elvis's old outfits, altered, of course, to fit his slender physique.

According to the Hollywood rumor mill, Priscilla was not crazy about her new son-in-law. She was said to have been angered when informed from others that her only daughter and heir Lisa Marie had married Michael. Later, news reports claimed that Priscilla, shortly after being informed of the marriage, insisted that Michael and Lisa Marie sign a binding agreement forever keeping their respective fortunes separate. The Neverland fortune and the Graceland fortune were thereby assured of remaining in separate hands; Neverland in Michael's and Graceland in Lisa Marie's.

But the public was not convinced by all of the spin Michael was putting on his life as husband and stepfather—and ardent lover of Lisa Marie Presley. Far from it.

Jokes abounded about the marriage. The late-night television comedy shows continued to draw rich material from Michael, as they had since the seventies and eighties, when Joan Rivers especially never lost an opportunity to make sport of Michael and to mock him roundly.

One cartoon that appeared in print said it all. In the background of the cartoon, Michael, in his signature black fedora and sunglasses, stood naked in the doorway of his and Lisa Marie's bedroom. In the foreground, Lisa Marie sat naked on their bed, her leg crooked so that it discreetly covered Michael's groin from the viewer's gaze as he stood in the doorway in the distance. A dialogue bubble over Lisa's head said, "So that's where you keep your other glove."

A cartoon is a small thing, but somehow this cartoon made a big statement. And that statement was simply that the public was not buying into the new recreated version of Michael Jackson.

CHAPTER FOURTEEN
SEPARATION ANXIETY

On Flag Day, June 14, 1995, Diane Sawyer interviewed Michael and Lisa Marie on ABC's *Primetime Live*. More than 60 million people watched the tell-all. It proved to be entertaining, controversial, and damaging to most, if not all, of the participants.

As far as the entertainment factor goes, Lisa Marie and Michael declared their love was real, and to answer the persistent doubts so many people had about Michael's sexual preference, Lisa Marie emphatically declared to the word that "yes" they did have sex.

But not everyone found the show entertaining. After the show aired, Evan Chandler resurfaced and filed a lawsuit against Michael, Diane, and ABC over the content of the broadcast. He contended the show was a whitewash on behalf of Michael. In this respect, Michael had not done himself any favors with this exchange.

"What is a thirty-six-year-old man doing sleeping with a twelve-year-old boy—or a series of them?" Sawyer asked Jackson.

He replied, apparently sincere: "I've never invited anyone into my bed—ever. Children love me; they follow me."

Sawyer followed up with the obvious question: "Would you let your son, when he's twelve years old, do that?"

Lisa Marie replied, "If I didn't know Michael, no way." But she added, unhelpfully: "I know that he has a thing for children."

Evan maintained that Michael was allowed to promulgate lies on the show because Diane was journalistically negligent in her responsibilities to point out falsehoods laid out by Jackson in this interview that she knew to be untrue.

Sawyer was not only taken to court by the alleged victim's father but she was also taken to task by other journalists, who criticized her performance and line of questioning. These critics felt that she had let Michael use her as a public relations flack who was afraid to challenge him, the way a tougher and more trenchant journalist would have.

Santa Barbara district attorney Tom Sneddon told individuals he believed that Michael had actually lied during the television show when he said that there were no identifying marks on his genitals to link him to the accusations of sexual abuse made.

The worst aspect of Sawyer's interview, in the view of D. A. Sneddon, was that she got the facts in the case completely wrong. She announced that Michael had been "cleared of all the charges . . . we want to make that clear." Not so, according to Sneddon.

He stated: "Michael Jackson has not been cleared. The state of the investigation is in suspension until somebody comes forward."

Sneddon went on to state that Michael had pretty much lied to Sawyer when he stated that police had not found incriminating evidence against him in their searches of his various residences.

"The idea that there are not any photos or pictures, or anything, is pure poppy-cock," Sneddon insisted. "In the search, Jackson said they didn't find anything unless it was 'something somebody sent me.' That is not true."

Police found a book of naked young boys at play—something that is often found in the possession of pedophiles. They also confiscated a picture of a naked young boy wrapped in a sheet in Michael's bedroom, according to files obtained in the investigation of this book.

Dr. Doe Lang, a psychologist who taught communications skills at the New School in Manhattan, commented on the body language of Michael and Lisa Marie while they were on camera.

She noted that Michael took every opportunity to distance himself during the interview, though Lisa Marie was just the opposite, trying at all times to unite them.

Michael also constantly used the pronoun "I" instead of "we." What's more, Michael's body language established that he was definitely the boss in their marriage, and that Lisa Marie took a submissive role toward him.

Dr. Lang also noted that Michael displayed an attitude that said he was pretty much the king, to be obeyed and venerated. Lisa Marie got very little consideration from him as his wife. She acted as if she was totally in awe of him.

Although some people thought Diane went soft on Michael, Lisa Marie felt that she was far too hard on him throughout the interview.

Ever and again, it was clear to the public that Michael was in denial to the point of self-delusion. And he believed he could convince others to join him in his sorry state of mental fantasy.

But the interview didn't work. The public had given up seeing and believing Michael the way he wanted to be seen. No tricks could fix his damaged image, and nothing was ever going to set it straight. Especially not a flaky marriage that was about to fall apart.

Right after the interview, everything for Michael and Lisa Marie seemed rosy. In newspaper articles, they proclaimed their happiness and the joy of their sex life together. They shared how Lisa Marie was poised and ready to fulfill her aspirations as an actress and how they planned to have children.

But behind-the-scenes, insiders said that trouble loomed. A news story broke that Michael was preparing to build a new house on the grounds of the Neverland Ranch for his special friend, actor Macaulay Culkin.

Michael was reported to have been obsessed by his "beautiful thick red lips," according to Jordan Chandler, who once recalled Michael's fixation.

That's not all Michael was obsessed with, according to his maid from 1990–1994, Adrian McManus.

In a 2019 interview, she reported that it made her uncomfortable cleaning up after her employer. She said she would find underwear belonging to little boys "on the floor with Michael's, or they were in the jacuzzi." But what Michael really seemed to have a lot of was Vaseline, she said.

McManus insisted, "Sometimes it was found in the golf carts when Mr. Jackson would take off with the boys." She added, "and there was a lot of Vaseline in Michael's bedroom. It was actually all over the ranch."

She said she never went public with claims because she had been warned.

"They told me if I ever came up on TV that they could hire a hitman to take me out, slice my neck, wouldn't ever find my body," McManus said.

Most of the household staff disputed this claim, as did Karen Faye who had been Michael's makeup artist for roughly thirty years. On February 25, 2019, before *Leaving Neverland* aired, she reiterated her sentiments by tweeting:

> Michael Jackson's name, art, and legacy will live on forever. The accusers and con artists will disappear into obscurity when we stop saying their names.

Michael had started devoting most of his free time to helping Culkin, which ultimately took attention away from Lisa Marie.

The blushing bride felt ignored. She was quoted as fuming that her husband "seems to think that little brat needs him more than his own wife."

It was further revealed that Lisa Marie and Michael did not sleep in the same room because she could not tolerate him snoring. She also could not abide the way he played mind games. She particularly resented the way he'd say they were going out for a ride, then she'd find herself at the airport jetting off to some distant place with him.

"We were really on shaky ground," Lisa Marie later professed. "There would be periods of time where I had no idea where he was. . . . He would just disappear."

There were reports that when Michael and Lisa Marie were together, they had especially bad arguments over Michael's constant temper tantrums. One instance involved Lisa Marie's son Benjamin pulling Michael's new wig off while the two were horsing around at the Santa Ynez ranch. After the fracas, Michael flew off in a snit to sulk in France while Lisa Marie languished alone, 7,000 miles away.

On another occasion, Lisa Marie revealed she was furious when Michael lied in an interview, claiming that she had told him Elvis once had a nose job. She said she read it and threw it across her kitchen and screamed at him, "I told you what?"

During the marriage, Michael also left his bride to spend a huge chunk of time with the Cascio brothers, two New Jersey boys that he'd palled around with on his ill-fated *Dangerous* tour. He flaunted his relationship with fifteen-year-old Frank and eleven-year-old Eddie in late summer and all through the fall of 1993, even in the midst of the molestation accusation and its scandal.

In December 1994, the two brothers were reportedly set to spend Christmas at the Neverland Ranch with Michael, who was showering the boys with gifts and dressing them in expensive designer outfits. The Cascio family also received lots of benefits from the two sons hanging out with Michael. Their father went from working at the Helmsley Palace Hotel, where he first met Michael and introduced him to his handsome sons, to owning two restaurants. In addition, the Cascio family moved from a small bungalow in a shabby neighborhood to a five-bedroom hilltop house in an upscale section of Franklin Lakes, New Jersey. This new house even had a swimming pool and a tennis court.

According to the Cascio's neighbors, Michael would suddenly show up and sweep the boys into a limousine and take them on trips or to Neverland. These same neighbors testified that Michael was interfering with the boys' natural friendships with children their own age.

One neighbor said, "I think it's really very selfish of Michael to take two young boys out of their neighborhood, away from their friends of the same age, just so he'll have someone to keep him company."

Then, right after Christmas, Michael collapsed at the Beacon Theater on Manhattan's West Side while rehearsing for a comeback concert. He spent six days in the intensive care unit at New York's Beth Israel North Medical Center. While he was in the hospital, Lisa Marie stayed at his bedside. But as soon as doctors released Michael, he flew off to Paris and proceeded straight to Euro-Disney, where he ensconced himself in the $500-a-night Sleeping Beauty suite at the Disney Hotel. He then played for days with French children, while he ignored his own stepchildren who were back at home with Lisa Marie.

These were just some of the cracks in a marriage that was quickly destabilizing beyond repair. It came as no surprise when Lisa Marie filed for divorce from Michael early in the new year of 1996.

The Jackson-Presley divorce was shaping up to be among Hollywood's most complex and costly. One article held that Lisa Marie had filed for divorce at her mother Priscilla's encouragement because Lisa Marie was due to come into her inheritance and she should take a dramatic step to protect her new assets from her husband.

And before anyone could whisper the phrase "confidentiality agreement," another ex-bodyguard of Michael's filed suit against him in Los Angeles Superior

Court. Jerome Johnson asserted that he had been fired after he complained about his colleagues having to lie on behalf of Michael to help him dispel charges of child molestation against him.

The suit also held that Michael's drug dependency had been only a ploy for him to stay abroad while avoiding the authorities in the US looking into the charges. Mr. Johnson also stated that Michael had frequently had young boys spend the night with him while he was on the *Dangerous* tour. And, even after Mr. Johnson had been fired, he said that Michael's lawyers tried to pressure him to sign a document full of lies to protect the superstar from the grand jury investigation underway in Santa Barbara.

There were also reports on the divorce that alleged that Michael's income had fallen sharply. Sales of his *HIStory* album in 1995 had tumbled from the top 20 within two months. And his collapse a few weeks before Lisa Marie filed for divorce placed Michael's projected tour to promote the *HIStory* album in jeopardy.

The great experiment in spin control following the 1993 molestation affair had ended in ruin.

But Michael couldn't accept failure. The star still believed he could come back, bigger, bolder, and badder than ever. And although he had a good idea of how to do it, he just needed a willing accomplice.

CHAPTER FIFTEEN
KID GLOVES

As he had done in the past, Michael again relied on his wealth to resolve his legal troubles.

He managed to work out a divorce settlement with Lisa Marie that paid her, according to reports, a settlement of $15 million. If true, the financial gain ensured her friendship and her continued silence about their relationship and marriage—especially about Michael's involvement with young children while they were together.

"I was delusionary," Lisa Marie pointedly said years later about her time married to Michael. "I got some romantic idea in my head that I could save him, and [together] we could save the world. . . . I can tell you my intentions; I can't tell you what his were."

Asked whether she thought Michael did, in fact, sexually molest the boy who accused him in 1993, she grimly explained: "I don't know. I still don't know. I wasn't there."

When their marriage broke up, Lisa Marie was left angry and reeling.

Michael had strung her along, raised her hopes and expectations, then dropped her like a stone as soon as he could resume his games with his special friends, the young boys he so favored over her.

Lisa Marie told a friend that her feelings about her marriage to Michael really amounted to a sense of having brought shame on herself and her family. Said one of Lisa Marie's confidants, "Right now, Lisa Marie is trying to sort out her mind."

Michael had no such problem with his mind. He did not seem bothered that he left Lisa Marie distraught. During their marriage, he'd upset her by cavorting with young boys while he was away from her. A video even surfaced that showed

Michael romping on the amusement rides and the swings and monkey bars at Neverland with three handsome, pre-adolescent boys. Not only that, but during his marriage to Lisa Marie another scandal emerged in the tabloids: the mother of another thirteen-year-old boy said she had shown Michael a compromising video of the superstar acting inappropriately in a sexual manner with her son.

At the time, it was claimed that Michael paid the woman off for the video and to secure her silence. If true, this was a wise move on the part of Jackson, since the cases against him for child molestation were still open in Los Angeles and in Santa Barbara. The statute of limitations on these charges would not expire until the year 2000, so Jackson had to be careful not to end up in court and, from there, if convicted, in jail.

That he involved Lisa Marie in a lawsuit did not seem to bother Michael either. As a result of her marriage to Michael, Lisa Marie was named as a defendant Evan Chandler sued after the *Primetime Live* interview. The lawsuit upset Lisa Marie greatly, and she was highly relieved when the judge on the case dismissed her of any liability.

But Michael didn't seem to care a bit about involving his ex-wife in something so potentially embarrassing. He had new plans and schemes. He had decided to have children of his own. This possibility was bandied about while he was married to Lisa Marie, but the two never had a child. This, in retrospect, must have been a big relief for Lisa Marie when the doomed marriage fell apart.

In any event, Michael moved forward with his paternal plans. He even picked out the mother-to-be, the medical assistant he had known for years in the office of his Beverly Hills dermatologist, Dr. Arnold Klein.

Her name was Debbie Rowe. The thirty-seven-year-old had previously been married to a computer whiz, but that hadn't worked out. She was living alone in an inexpensive apartment in Van Nuys, California and had been commuting to work in Beverly Hills. She fancied herself as a very special woman to Michael. She had known him for fifteen years and is reported to have boasted to friends that she was the only woman alive to have seen Michael Jackson naked, with the exception of his mother. That is, until Michael allegedly broke her heart by marrying Lisa Marie.

Debbie claimed that when Jackson married Lisa Marie, she was shattered by it, since she was said to have had a major crush on him for years.

When Debbie and Michael first became an item, reports stated that Debbie had built a veritable shrine to Michael in her small apartment. She had posters of him and backstage passes to all of his concerts around the world fastened to her walls. When Michael visited Dr. Klein for treatments, Debbie was supposedly the only person allowed to touch him other than the dermatologist himself.

Michael and Debbie reportedly fell madly in love even while Michael was still married to Lisa Marie. Debbie stated that Michael was distraught that he and Lisa Marie were not able to have a child. She said that he called her one night and told her how lonely he was. She volunteered to come and relieve his loneliness and he sent a limo for her. When she arrived at Neverland, they were soon in an embrace that was quickly followed by a passionate trip to the bedroom, where they made mad love.

Debbie claimed, as they hugged and kissed, she whispered: "Michael, I could give you a child. Let me try to get pregnant."

His response, according to her: "Tears of joy were streaming down his face as we went to his bedroom and started to make love."

Debbie went on to say that Michael was a fantastic lover; however, he had to dress up to get turned on. Once he had dressed up in a suit of armor so he could play a knight conquering a peasant girl, the peasant girl played of course by the pliant Debbie. Another time Michael dressed as a pirate. Debbie told a friend: "He explained he had to dress up to get turned on. It made him feel romantic." She also said Michael was quite the cavalier and considerate lover at other times. For instance, he scattered rose petals on the bed. He burned candles and incense and filled the room with erotic fragrances.

Of course, he went the other way too, becoming raucous and dramatic. Once the lights in the bedroom started flashing and the music from *Thriller* began blaring from the sound system. Next, Michael appeared wearing one of his patented costumes, the ones reputed to turn him on like a latter-day Valentino.

Few could believe this rigmarole when subsequent events were factored into the equation. Debbie was an intelligent and well-paid shill, and yet another sexual beard, but this one assigned the role of breeder as well.

When she was six months into her pregnancy, Debbie reportedly demanded that Michael marry her and legitimize their child.

This Michael duly did while he was on tour in Australia. A judge married the couple in a civil ceremony minutes past midnight in a suite at the Hotel Sheraton Grand Sydney Hyde Park on November 15, 1996. Debbie was angry within mere minutes. She told a friend, "Here I was marrying my idol whose baby kicked inside me, and it seemed he wanted to gallop through the ceremony in double-time."

Although Michael gave her a platinum two and a half carat diamond ring, he didn't want a ring from her. And when the judge pronounced them man and wife in the hotel suite, Debbie said, "I turned to Michael expecting a big kiss, but all I got was a little peck on the cheek."

She was instantly in for a bigger shock. He also didn't want to sleep with her in the same bed on their wedding night—or even in the same room. That night in the Sheraton, Debbie Rowe slept alone in a $3,000-a-night suite, where it was reported that she cried herself to sleep. She told friends back home, "My honeymoon night with Michael was the most disappointing night of my life."

The next night wasn't much better.

Michael spent lots of time with a new special friend, an eight-year-old boy named Anthony. Michael claimed the boy was his nephew, but of course Michael Jackson has no such nephew. It was an all too familiar pattern.

Michael was scheduled that night to attend the opening of his short film *Ghosts*. Debbie thought she would be his escort. She thought wrong. He told her to stay at the hotel. He said the crowds might jostle her unborn child. Instead, he attended the premiere with Anthony and was widely photographed with the boy beside him.

The following day, Debbie again hoped for some face time with her new husband, but it was not to be. He had other plans. He took Anthony and visited Sydney's famous Taronga Zoo.

Debbie told a close friend, "I think I may have made the biggest mistake of my life, and the only way out of it is divorce." Bear in mind that this insight on Debbie's part is alleged to have occurred to her a scant seventy-two hours after her wedding ceremony. If this account of her wedding is all true—and it appears to be—it makes his first bare-bones wedding ceremony with Lisa Marie in the Dominican Republic look like a royal wedding by comparison.

But something was not right with the entire Debbie Rowe affair.

It was revealed that Debbie had been a biker chick who roared around Los Angeles clad in leather outfits on a Harley-Davidson and wanted to be a Hell's Angel. She was alleged to have shocked even hardcore bikers with her foul language, and she used to love to swill beer and tequila and then intimidate men with her vulgar, in-your-face challenges (she even named her golden retriever Cuervo, after the Mexican tequila). A friend told *People* in 1996 that Rowe's first husband, Richard Edelman, then a thirty-year-old teacher at Hollywood High, was "too quiet" for Rowe, a woman who, he fondly notes, "used language like a trooper but was always very pleasant." Her use of profanity is interesting in that Michael is on record as saying he loathed the use of foul language, yet another legacy of his Jehovah's Witness past.

So, Debbie was either a devoted groupie who was blinded by Michael's stardom—or she was a clever businesswoman willing to exchange breeding privileges for several million dollars.

As always with Michael, getting to the truth is difficult.

On February 13, 1997, Debbie gave birth to a boy and made Michael a father. Michael named his son Michael Joseph Jackson Jr., after his grandfather and great-grandfather.

But as soon as the baby had been delivered, Michael personally issued a warning to the newly promoted mother.

"Don't get too attached to him, Debbie," Michael mandated.

For Debbie, "the wife," it was clear what Michael's warning strongly implied: don't get too attached to him, either.

CHAPTER SIXTEEN

SEPARATED AT BIRTH

Stories swiftly appeared relating how heartbroken Debbie was that father Michael took the baby from her immediately. Michael was set on raising his son by himself, and mostly in France, if reports were to be believed.

Headlines screamed that Michael had stolen the baby from Debbie, but these stories were countered by reports that Debbie had a marriage contract with Michael that was closer to an employment contract than anything to do with a conjugal arrangement as it would usually be structured.

According to these reports, Debbie received a million dollars for having Michael's son. Plus, she was to receive an additional million dollars if she had a second child.

There were also escalators in the deal that would pay Debbie more money the longer she stayed married to Michael.

Yet there were accounts of how distressed Debbie became over the treatment Michael accorded her. He took the baby boy from her immediately after his birth and traveled with the baby to the Neverland Ranch. At the same time, he insisted that Debbie stay clear of the property. In fact, he demanded that she leave the LA area altogether. She protested, yet ended up going on vacation to Arizona. But she refused to follow Michael's instructions to dye her hair and cut it short in order to move about incognito.

In the weeks following the baby's birth, Debbie was deliberately frozen out from any communication with him. Michael simply gave her reports over the phone that the baby was healthy and doing well.

Eventually, with little to no mother duties to attend to, Debbie went back to her job working as a medical assistant for Dr. Klein.

There were repeated rumors that Michael treated Debbie as an employee and never as a wife. He avoided her in public. He went out by himself. He instructed his staff not to refer to her as "Mrs. Jackson," but only as "Miss Rowe."

When "Prince" Michael Jr. was two months old, Michael summoned Debbie to join him at a Beverly Hills hotel for a photo shoot. This session turned into a six-page exclusive spread, again in *The National Enquirer*, published April 28, 1997. But Michael didn't treat Debbie Rowe any better after the photo session than he did before it. Again, according to sources, he quickly banished her, virtually excluding her from contact with her son.

Michael had for years referred to women with contempt, according to those close to him.

One of his favorite words of contempt for women was "heifers." He was clearly treating Debbie as a heifer. As stated earlier, Debbie is either a clever business-woman or a foolish groupie of some kind. But the probability is that she is the former. Stories appeared during the time of her marriage that she was still dating old boyfriends and going out frequently herself. Michael liked and encouraged this, according to some reports. According to other sources, this type of behavior on Debbie's part was strictly forbidden by the "marriage" contract between Michael and her.

As far as Michael was concerned, more and more stories appeared about new special young male friends. Less than a year after the birth of Michael's son, it surfaced that Michael, now legally a father, was appearing in public with another young boy named Omar Bhatti. Michael met Omar while on tour in Tunisia. Three years earlier, Omar made quite a hit in Scandinavia by doing his very polished imitation of the pop star. Michael was described as lavishing gifts on the boy and on his family—much like he had others before him.

It was the old scheme again. Shower the kid with gifts. Bury his family in luxury compared to what they were used to. Dress the kid in designer outfits, with lots of them matching Michael's outfits. Make sure many of the clothes the kid wore made him look a smaller version of a toy soldier to Michael's larger version.

Whatever was going on here, with Michael's marriage to Debbie, it was entirely unorthodox, completely in keeping with Michael's sensationally odd life story. Because only fourteen months after Debbie gave birth to Prince Michael, she bore

Michael a daughter, Paris-Michael Katherine Jackson, on April 3, 1998. The new baby was born at the Spalding Pain Medical Clinic in Beverly Hills, and not, as their son was, at Cedars-Sinai. Reports circulated widely that Michael was hurting for money. Maybe the way daughter Paris came into the world lent some credence to these reports. Prince Michael Jr. was born on the VIP floor at Cedars-Sinai. His father rented the entire floor for the occasion. But now that daughter Paris came along, Michael only arranged a room in a modest clinic. And, whereas there was a whole host of security guards present when the boy was born fourteen months earlier, when his little sister was born, there was only one guard on duty.

But Michael repeated his earlier pattern and took the baby girl immediately from her mother. He again became the sole caregiver for the child, though he reportedly hired a raft of nurses and nannies to help him out. He also imported his mother Katherine to the Neverland Ranch to help raise his children. But, make no mistake, it appeared as if their birth mother had been banished—again.

"Michael did all the parenting," Debbie later said. "I didn't change diapers, I didn't get up in the middle of the night, even when I was there. Michael did it all."

There was one particularly crazy incident in 1999 where Prince Michael suffered a seizure that was competently handled by the boy's doctor, yet his father had it put out on the news wires that the boy had nearly died.

Mother Debbie in Los Angeles learned all of this from televised news reports and became hysterical. It soon appeared that Michael had exaggerated his son's illness in order to avoid traveling to Modena, Italy, to perform on stage at a concert to benefit charity with tenor Luciano Pavarotti. Pavarotti, compassionately, asked the audience at the concert to pray for Michael Jackson's supposedly dying son.

It was also reported that Michael himself was back on a deadly cocktail of painkillers.

He was regularly connected to an intravenous drip that fed him large doses of the powerful painkiller Demerol. Word also came out of Neverland that Michael might once again be addicted to drugs. To add to the general air of craziness that always seemed to surround him, more stories emerged about videos that had surfaced that showed the singer playing in the private garden at Neverland with two and three adolescent boys at a time, often with their shirts off.

Michael clowned with them on the merry-go-round or on the jungle gym. He often liked to videotape these youngsters at play, much like the video filmed in South Africa described at the beginning of this book. This private video collection of Michael's apparently drove his ex-wife Lisa Marie to intense anger when she discovered it at their home, sources said.

There were, at this point, two children Michael called his own, but his old patterns of inappropriate behavior went right on as they had before. Nothing seemed to really be changed, or probably ever would be.

Some sources claimed that Debbie's marriage was scheduled to last six years, but that she couldn't take it any longer. Her contract with Michael, according to sources, verified the reports that it had clauses in it that would not permit her to be seen in public with other men, and she could no longer hack this abstemious lifestyle. She moved out of her small apartment and into a nice house costing more than a million dollars on the periphery of Beverly Hills, which she purchased with money from Michael, according to sources. Then Rowe filed for divorce in October of 1999.

Amid speculation about Michael not being the biological father of Rowe's children—fueled by reports that Debbie claimed she had been artificially inseminated by a stranger, which would explain why the children did not look anything like their pre-surgeries father—she received a divorce settlement from Michael that paid her $36 million over six years, according to well-placed insiders who spoke to this author.

Of course, the payoff came replete with a gag order.

If Debbie discussed any aspect of her relationship with Michael or her marriage and child-bearing activities under his direction, she would forfeit the settlement.

But years later, Debbie eventually came clean about her generous gestation arrangement with the superstar.

"Michael was divorced, lonely, and wanted children," she stated in a 2009 interview. "I was the one who said to him, 'I will have your babies.' I offered him my womb. It was a gift. It was something I did to keep him happy."

Debbie also revealed that she had gone to a medical clinic—that she and Michael referred to as "the office"—and had been artificially inseminated by doctors.

"It was very technical," she confessed. "They impregnated me. Just like I stick the sperm up my horse, this is what they did to me. I was his thoroughbred."

On February 21, 2002, Michael added one more son to his brood, Prince Michael "Blanket" Jackson II.

This time, however, Michael opted to simplify the process.

"I used a surrogate mother with my own sperm cells," he admitted. "I had my own sperm cells with my other two children—they're all my children—but I used a surrogate mother. And, uh, she doesn't know me, I don't know her."

As Michael watched his family grow, he saw his music career tumbling in an irreversible freefall.

The singer had been banking on his tenth studio album—the 16-track *Invincible*—to put him back on top, but unfortunately, it only reinforced that the forty-four-year-old performer was remarkably vulnerable.

It would be his final record.

CHAPTER SEVENTEEN

BALANCING THE BOOKS

In July of 2002, when Michael attacked Sony for the failure of his latest album, *Invincible*, he joined a crosstown march led by the Reverend Al Sharpton in Manhattan to protest the racism in the music industry.

He even went so far as to ride around Midtown on the open upper deck of a double decker bus holding a placard depicting Sony boss Tommy Mottola, the one-time husband of Mariah Carey, as the devil. In the media, Michael also blasted Mottola as "racist."

These characterizations of Mottola took everyone in the music industry by surprise. They felt that Michael was reacting to the failure of his latest album and not to anything Sony or Mottola had failed to do for him or for that album. On the contrary, Sony and Mottola had backed the *Invincible* album to the tune of $60 million. But it flopped. That's the simple explanation.

It sold just two million copies or, to put it in perspective, a mere five percent of what *Thriller* had sold two decades earlier. A music insider was quoted regarding Michael's protest against Sony and Tommy Mottola to this effect: "Michael finally flipped and it's cost him what few friends he had left among music's power people. What he did was commit career suicide, plain and simple."

This insider added, "What Michael did was to make it seem as if he was dumping Tommy rather than the other way around. The failure of *Invincible* made Michael realize he was all washed up and he desperately wanted to save face."

Michael no doubt wanted to save face as well with all of the articles appearing in the media claiming that he was nearly broke. There were rumors that people were suing him for bills that had gone unpaid, even for his hospital bill for the delivery of his son Prince Michael Jr. A Beverly Hills jeweler sued Michael over an eighteenth-century watch he agreed to buy for just under a million-and-a-half dollars. But Michael used the watch for six months and then returned it, never having paid for it. It was scratched and obviously used, so the luxury jeweler sued.

Another news item reported that two former Jackson financial advisers sued him for non-payment of their monthly fees.

Stories in the press speculated that Michael needed $14 million a year just to run the Neverland Ranch.

His monthly personal expenses were also estimated at $8 million.

In light of such revelations, it was easy to see how the once flush Michael Jackson really could be going broke.

Then in August 2002, it was reported that Michael's family had attempted an intervention with him. They feared from reports given to them by members of Michael's staff that he had suffered a serious slide back into painkiller and booze addiction, mixing Demerol with wine.

Some alleged that this regime of wine and painkillers explained his outlandish behavior toward Sony and Mottola. Members of Michael's family feared that he would turn up dead—just the way Elvis had.

He was a man who was only a few days away from being embarrassed on national television at the MTV Awards when Britney Spears, in an offhand remark, referred to him as the "artist of the millennium." When he reacted to her words as though they conferred an official award, he was ridiculed and mocked in the press, as well as on numerous late-night television shows.

It seemed he was more an object of curiosity or contempt than anything else. Like Peter Pan looking for his shadow, Michael Jackson, like all abused children, was looking for something to make him feel whole and fulfilled.

What he did find in his futile search for that magic "something" that would make him happy was that it's very easy to go from the very top to the very bottom in one swift move. He had gone from being the King of Pop to the Sultan of Flop. In the new millennium, Michael was considered a music industry joke.

On August 28, 2002, Michael held court for visiting book publishers in the Westin Hotel in Stamford, Connecticut, a city some sixty miles northeast of New York City. In years past, Michael had taken over sumptuous suites at places like the

Waldorf-Astoria or Trump Tower, smack in the core of the Big Apple. But on this day, he was relegated to the suburbs.

Michael was "in town," though sixty miles out of it, for two reasons.

First, he had been lured to the MTV Music Awards ceremony to be held at Radio City Music Hall. Second, he was hawking a book on his life that he hoped would set the record straight once and for all.

On this hot summer day, Michael sat slumped on a sofa in the penthouse suite, lights dim, and dressed in black, slippers with rhinestone studs on his feet and sunglasses covering his eyes. His complexion, already pale, was smeared with white makeup. He had some peach fuzz on his face. It wasn't a beard exactly—not a five o'clock shadow—but more like some weird and unsuccessful hybrid of the scruffy look. It didn't come off right, one editor who saw him at the time described.

Michael appeared disoriented. He asked the publishers what company they were from. They answered him for a second or third time. Sometimes a fourth. This was doubly odd because the publishers had handed Michael sample promotional materials and their latest catalogs.

The names of the companies were clearly visible on all of this.

Michael pulled himself together enough to explain to the publishers that when he wrote his 1988 autobiography, *Moonwalk* with Jacqueline Kennedy Onassis, he really wasn't ready to talk. Jackie had twisted his arm. But now, he wanted to open up. He was misunderstood, and, Michael explained, had long been slandered and vilified in the press by writers who knew nothing about him.

He was, he assured his audience, a regular guy.

He wanted to counter the lies and distortions and clear his reputation once and for all.

Then, out of the blue, Michael suddenly burst into tears, crying quietly on the sofa while the publishers waited in silence for him to resume his pitch, but he withdrew into a ball, trying to make himself smaller.

On the Jacksons tour in 1981 for the *Triumph* album, Michael disappeared in a tremendous puff of smoke at the conclusion of singing his show stopping number "Don't Stop 'Til You Get Enough." Here in the penthouse suite, it was as if he wanted to disappear in a magical puff of smoke the way he had done in his glory days.

Michael managed to compose himself long enough to explain that when he had met Shirley Temple, she asked if he was disappointed in her. He elaborated on how this legendary child star, like himself, sacrificed her youth to entertain others. At this stage in her life, when fans met her, she told Michael, it was as though she had let them down somehow by growing up. They wanted her to remain a cute little kid forever. So, naturally, she had wondered aloud if Michael felt disappointed in meeting her, too. The truth was he harbored only compassion. He felt so isolated, he admitted, that sometimes he had gone up to complete strangers and asked them to be his friend.

As Michael's attention drifted away, one publisher tried to refocus him by asking if he exercised.

"I hate exercise," he replied. "I really don't do anything."

"How can you say that?" the publisher countered. "You have to be in fabulous shape to do your dance routines and to burn such energy during your performances."

Michael sighed and said, "When I have to perform, I get in shape. I work out fourteen hours a day."

With each publishing group, Michael spoke with sadness of his loneliness. He said that he barely kept in touch with his family and that they rarely got together. Jehovah's Witnesses do not believe in holidays, so there were rarely traditional family gatherings for the Jacksons.

There was mention, he said, of plans for a reunion in Hawaii. There was also talk of the entire family going on a camping expedition. At this prospect, Michael rolled his eyes.

Michael worked into the discussion that he had no friends among his contemporaries. He cited the older cadre of Liz Taylor, Liza Minnelli, and Marlon Brando. Ironically, he never mentioned his habit of keeping company with pre-adolescent boys and child stars like Emmanuel Lewis and Macaulay Culkin. He illustrated for the publishers how tough it was to be him. Michael Jackson could not go anywhere he pleased like a normal person.

During a trip to Las Vegas, Michael explained, he decided to leave his suite and go down on the gaming floor. That's when the awful thing happened, the awful thing that always happened.

"It was terrifying," Michael said in a soft, sad, and wistful voice.

"People had to touch me. They had to keep coming up to me and touching me. Other than the Pope, I'm the most recognizable man in the world."

Michael went on to tell the editors that he was extremely uncomfortable with the press. He didn't want publicity—he just wanted to write a real book to set the record straight and "clear up" misunderstandings. He tried doing it years earlier with the infamous Diane Sawyer interview, but he felt that Diane had let him down, even though the perception in the rest of the media was the exact opposite. Others accused the network of cutting a deal with the star to get an exclusive interview—a total rarity—simply to boost their ratings.

Even so, Michael explained that he still felt that Sawyer let him down by not annihilating any hint that he was ever guilty of pedophilia. "How could anyone even think such a thing?" he asked rhetorically of the gathered publishers.

He, Michael Jackson, loved children; everyone knew that. He couldn't do enough for them. His many gifts of money and time to charities and groups aiding children were a matter of public record.

Rambling with the wind, Michael started to explain how he loved his own children more than words could explain. But it was hard to raise them because they had everything, he declared. And on top of having everything, his friends in showbiz gave his children even more. What seemed illogical to others made perfect sense to Michael, and as he fought back tears, the stories continued.

Jackson insisted he was nothing but a regular guy. All else written about him to the contrary was false. All of it. Of course, he told his guests, he was edgy. He said he had always thought and acted outside the box. But first and foremost, he was a typical guy, not like one of the sideshow exhibits that he had been fascinated by all of his life.

Michael described an unusual habit he had of going up to kids and asking them who they would go to see if they had a choice between Prince and Lionel Richie. Whose music would you rather hear? Michael said that they always said they'd rather hear Richie. This, he stated, confirmed his theory that regular guys are preferred. Michael felt he was just a guy from Gary, Indiana, and so, by default, he too was preferred by kids.

When the spirit moved him, Michael let the publishers in on another plan. He wanted to write at least one book for children. He loved to read children's books and it was an obsession he carried into his adulthood. He was practically addicted to them. He had a whole library of children's literature in his bedroom and he read those books all the time. He didn't have to tell his visitors, for they all knew that he was crazy about children. But he told them anyway. If he wrote the first children's book and it was successful, he intended to write many more. He would become a children's book writer and parents would naturally flock to his books. They would buy them for their children with enthusiasm. After all, they would be written by one of the world's foremost entertainers and a man whose charity toward children was celebrated the world over.

The children's book he planned would be as well-meaning and as wholesome as his song "Heal the World." He intended to use the same sensibility in the children's book that he used to create this altruistic and award-winning song that had done so much to benefit the poor and starving children around the world, especially in Africa and Asia. His name on children's literature would be magical. It would be a kind of seal of approval.

At the end of each session with the visiting publishers, Michael handed out a DVD of his 30th Anniversary Madison Square Garden retrospective as a takeaway gift. In each of the interviews in Stamford, to illustrate the horrors of all-encompassing fame such as his, Michael stated that he was thoroughly bored with himself, with being The Michael Jackson.

Apparently, he was not alone in this emotion.

Not one of the half dozen or so elite Manhattan publishers who visited with him offered to option his new book proposal. For the first time in his life, Michael Jackson, recipient of the Grammy Living Legend Award in 1993, the very year his downfall began, found himself in a buyer's market.

And ultimately, there were no takers.

CHAPTER EIGHTEEN

HANG TIME

Even in defeat, even in declining popularity, Michael still couldn't escape the public spotlight.

In November 2002 he found himself in a Santa Barbara area courtroom in a role he wouldn't have chosen: defendant in a civil lawsuit. News reports of lawsuits brought against the entertainer barely registered a blip anymore, as it seemed that litigation involving Michael was churning out faster than he'd ever manufactured top ten hits.

But this time Michael was being sued for $21.2 million by European concert promoter Marcel Avram, who claimed Michael cancelled two concerts to celebrate the dawn of the new millennium, costing Avram millions of dollars. Michael lost the case and in March 2003 he was ordered to pay Avram $5.3 million.

More notable than the ultimate verdict, however, were pictures of Michael on the stand during this trial, photos published worldwide. What made these images so startling was not that he seemed dazed, confused, and even drugged—which he was—but the tip of his nose appeared to be missing.

Either Michael was in such a stupor that he no longer cared about his appearance, or the damage incurred to his nose after countless plastic surgery treatments was beyond repair.

A reporter at the trial was completely taken aback by Michael's appearance and her description of Michael was shocking: "He wears a black pageboy wig, his face is caked with white makeup, he uses red lipstick and perfume, pencils and dyes his eyebrows and has black eyeliner that looks as if it's tattooed on."

In Judge Zel Canter's courtroom, Michael took the stand like the masterful performer he is, never failing to entertain.

At times he appeared to fall asleep on the stand, at other points he made devil ears at the spectators, other times he simply waved. He hobbled into the courtroom on crutches, claiming his foot was swollen because of a spider bite. He was dressed in a satin tuxedo and surgical mask.

But Michael's appearance was soon to be the least of his worries. A new controversy was just around the corner.

Barely a week later, on Tuesday, November 19, Michael was back in the lap of luxury, halfway around the world in Berlin, Germany. A source said he was staying, along with his three children, in the Hotel Adlon's $7,500-a-night presidential suite; a bulletproof, soundproof, and fireproof fortress fit for a king. This level of protection, though, was not enough for Michael, the source said. "He insisted that it [the suite] be swept for recording devices prior to his arrival. And he secured confidentiality pledges from the chamber maids, busboys, and bellhops. He also feared germs in the air-conditioning system and demanded industrial-strength filters be installed."

If Michael Jackson went to such great lengths to protect his children's health and well-being, then how could he explain what would soon become one of the most infamous events in his strange life?

With fans swarming sixty five feet below the fourth floor, hoping for a glimpse of the pop icon, Michael did not want to disappoint. He swung open the doors on the short balcony and emerged with his then nine-month-old son, Blanket, who, only months earlier, had made his public debut at a Siegfried and Roy show in Las Vegas.

Within seconds, Michael dangled little Blanket over the balcony, covering his face with—what else?—a small blanket. As the baby squirmed—visibly agitated and scared—Michael appeared to cackle in delight despite the dangerous maneuver that was photographed and soon to be witnessed by the world.

He pulled the baby back over the balcony and retreated, like a modern-day ghoulish version of Norma Desmond, back inside.

Just moments after returning little Blanket to safety Michael reemerged, this time with his own face covered by the hotel's white lace curtain. He then paraded out his elder son, Prince Michael Jr., then five years old, his face shrouded in a towel.

Within a few short hours, images of Michael's reckless act were beamed around the globe. The initial public response was shock, followed quickly by anger. What kind of father would deliberately place his child in such danger?

Michael worked feverishly to quell the rising storm.

The next day he took Michael Jr. and four-year-old Paris to the Berlin Zoo, a visit that for any other child would be a delightful, normal excursion. But nothing was ever normal in Michael's outlandish life. Both youngsters' faces were shrouded in Taliban-like veils. As fans approached to get a closer glimpse, Michael's security team steered them away with opened umbrellas. Cameras, however, were encouraged to capture pictures of the seemingly devoted father escorting his children for a happy day as a family out and about. But no one could tell whether his children were happy because their faces were always covered.

The reality is, though, that no one could get a clear picture of Michael's kids. Why? Michael said he covered his children's faces for safety purposes, because he didn't want his children's photographs splashed across newspapers.

But others inside the Jackson camp disagreed. La Toya's outspoken ex-husband, Jack Gordon, insisted that Michael simply didn't want the world to see the obvious— that his three kids have no physical resemblance and biological connection to him.

In spite of the fact that Michael had insisted he and ex-wife Debbie Rowe enjoyed a robust sex life, Gordon said that Michael's "two children by Debbie Rowe were fathered by an anonymous sperm donor. Their real father is a Caucasian, whom Debbie picked from a list of donor profiles available at the sperm bank. When you see Michael's kids it's obvious he's not the father. That's why he makes them wear veils. They all have white skin, white features, and straight blonde hair. Paris even has blue eyes."

No one may ever know the truth about where Blanket, or for that matter, Michael Jr. and Paris, are from. While Michael dropped hints that he was, in fact, Blanket's father, it's impossible to know the truth.

In Beverly Hills, just two days after the already infamous baby-dangling incident, a prominent psychiatrist and child welfare advocate, Dr. Carole Lieberman, registered an oral complaint with the Santa Barbara County Child Protective Services and voiced her concern that Michael Jackson was "not emotionally stable enough" to take care of his own kids.

Dr. Lieberman said, "Michael's so out of touch that he wasn't even aware that the baby was frightened. He didn't blink an eye."

What was most scary, the doctor explained, was how "he treated the baby like a rag doll, a thing—not a human being. Child custody authorities should go in right now and take Michael's children away until he gets psychiatric help!"

But Michael had always enjoyed reverence and adulation in Europe, where his music continued to sell briskly, even while US audiences tended to brush off anything by Michael as irrelevant and uncool. Whether or not they didn't want to anger their much-beloved King of Pop, or because they chose to wash their hands in Pontius Pilate–style indifference, German authorities were quick to pronounce that Michael had been cleared of any criminal wrongdoing.

Yet no one was willing to let him off the hook for poor judgment.

So, there it was: The man who claimed no one loved children more than him was once again back in the spotlight with regards to his alleged mistreatment of children. But when Michael's behavior was examined and scrutinized, he always had an excuse at the ready.

One of his most reliable explanations for deviant behavior was that he was suffering with addiction issues. Insiders revealed that even before this most recent scandal, Michael's family, especially mom Katherine and sister Janet, were deeply worried that Michael was only steps away from a nervous breakdown. Just a few months prior to the Berlin incident the family had staged an intervention, hoping to get Michael professional help because he was once again addicted to Demerol and alcohol, seemingly unable to cope with the realities of everyday life.

Michael's life was in real jeopardy.

No one would have thought the sideshow that was Michael Jackson's life could get any stranger—but Berlin was only the beginning.

CHAPTER NINETEEN

FOOTING THE BILL

Just as the baby-dangling furor was dying down, ABC broadcast a two-hour *20/20* special on February 6, 2003, called "Living with Michael Jackson."

The television special was hosted by British journalist Martin Bashir, perhaps most famous for his 1995 interview with Princess Diana, in which she admitted both she and Prince Charles had been unfaithful throughout their marriage. Michael had welcomed Bashir into his inner sanctum, allowing the esteemed journalist nearly eight months with him. In return for his time and trouble Michael expected a glossy, positive production.

Nearly 30 million viewers—ABC's best Thursday night ratings in more than a decade—tuned into a spellbinding spectacle of riveting television which collectively left a nation speechless.

At the time, no one realized that this broadcast was the precursor to the greatest fight of Michael's life, the door that led to a world of trouble unlike anything he had ever dealt with, the lynchpin to a series of events that would have him fighting to stave off a prison sentence.

In the documentary, instead of sugar-coating Michael's peculiarities and troubles with the law, Bashir grilled Michael incessantly about his physical transformation and about his bizarre relationships with young children, especially boys.

These were not unfair questions. Any responsible journalist would be obligated to ask them. Nonetheless, Michael was not skilled at answering personal queries, and these went right to the heart of who—and what—he was. The interviewer knew it and Michael knew it. So did the home audience.

Bashir eased his way into the conversation by praising the wonders of Neverland and asking general questions about the star's youthful loves and sense of wonder.

Michael started out with relative confidence and poise, answering questions from Bashir about his lifestyle.

He said that the attacks began as soon as he started to break sales records.

"They called me weird, overnight. Strange. Wacko. You know, they said I'm a girl, homosexual. He wants to buy the Elephant Man bones, he sleeps in a hyperbaric chamber. None of that stuff is true. All completely made up. All a lie. I sleep in a bed."

That was true, as far as it went. There was a famous, indelible image of Michael lying prostrate in just such a device. It occurred after his scalp was seared filming the Pepsi commercial. Michael was told it would help him heal and that regular use might prolong life. The truth is, though, he did not take the plunge.

But then Bashir's probing went deeper.

Watching Michael squirm under such intense scrutiny was nearly unbearable. Yet at the same time, it was impossible to turn away. Almost like a car crash. Viewers became unwitting witnesses to what can only be described as a first-rate freak show.

Some of the shocking disclosures on the show were:

- Michael's admission that he had "slept in bed with many children," despite his multi-million-dollar child molestation settlement in 1993. When Bashir asked him if sleeping in bed with children was right, Michael responded incredulously, "It's very right. It's very loving. That's what the world needs now, more love."
- Michael claimed that Debbie Rowe bore his two oldest children "as a present."
- Despite mounting debts and lawsuits, Michael told Bashir that his worth was well over $1 billion dollars.
- Michael declared that he had only two cosmetic surgery procedures— both on his nose, in order to help him breathe better and enable him to sing higher notes. "I had no plastic surgery on my face," he said. "Just my nose . . . honestly."
- He announced that he hoped to adopt more children from each continent.

But the most important thing about the documentary was also one of its most striking images: a dark-haired boy, just sprouting facial hair, sitting meekly by Michael's side as the singer described how normal it was for him to share his bed with a young boy. This twelve-year-old boy at times rested his head on Michael's shoulder and at other moments held Michael's hand. Who exactly was this boy?

His name was Gavin Arvizo and he was just ten years of age in 2000, when he was given a few weeks to live. Doctors had found an eight-pound cancerous tumor on his left kidney, which subsequently was removed, along with the boy's spleen.

Sadly, by this point, the cancer had already spread to his lungs and liver, and despite the best efforts of his doctors, the prognosis was not good. "They told him he was going to die," Michael said of Gavin.

Making matters worse was the fact that his blood type was the very rare O-negative/CMV negative. Gavin Arvizo needed a miracle.

Jamie Masada, an Iranian immigrant and the owner of The Laugh Factory comedy club on the famed Sunset Strip section of Los Angeles, ran the Comedy Camp, a program for disadvantaged children. Masada had learned that a young boy was gravely ill with cancer and he desperately needed something, anything, to lift his spirits. Masada developed a very close relationship with Gavin, boosting his spirits throughout the cancer treatments, and Gavin, along with his younger brother and older sister, even participated in Masada's camp.

Well-connected in the entertainment business, Jamie hoped to boost the boy's mood by offering to introduce him to some of his favorite entertainers. Gavin, who lived a near-destitute existence in a ramshackle section of East Los Angeles, had a wish list of celebrities he wanted to meet, including Adam Sandler, Chris Tucker, and Michael Jackson. In that order. Apparently, when the youngster was asked to come up with names, he glanced up at the television and saw Michael on MTV.

Almost as an aside, he pointed out that, yes, he wanted to meet Michael Jackson, too. Masada was able to make good on these wishes.

In August 2000, Gavin, both of his parents, and his two siblings all made the two-hour drive to Neverland to meet Michael, whom they had heard was generous with his love and money when it came to children. Over the months the youngster would make repeated visits to Neverland, where he, along with his brother, would sleep with Michael, while his sister stayed in a guest room and his mother Janet stayed in a guesthouse, away from the main house.

Michael and Gavin seemed to hit it off almost immediately, much to the delight of the boy's family and Jamie Masada. Gavin regained a certain zest for life. Michael had a way of making him feel special, even if the older entertainer was different from all the other adults in his life. The boy had never heard any other grown up but Michael say, "If you love me, you'll sleep on the bed." But after all, that line had worked so well almost a decade earlier with the boy who eventually sued Michael.

Getting into Michael's bed was no easy feat without an express invitation.

One of his former business managers described Michael's bedroom in minute detail, pointing out that it was the most secure room at Neverland. When one entered the hall leading to the sleeping quarters, an alarm went off to alert Michael that someone was approaching. A camera mounted above a second door, about six feet down the hallway, displayed the image of the approaching visitor on a monitor in Michael's room. Upon passing through the second door, one would enter a sitting chamber that's roughly 500 square feet. Inside the actual bedroom there was a closet, in which there was another secret closet, made of cedar. There were five vertical stainless-steel panels between the two closets, that, when triggered by a secret five-digit code, lowered to another room, smaller, but with books, photos, and videos—yet not much bigger than Michael himself. This secret room was off-limits to everyone except those issued a special invitation by the singer.

Less ominous and certainly more inviting than the overblown security measures were the arcade games, the 80-inch plasma screen television, and the grand piano. This display of lavish living was something that Michael's new pal—who, when he was going through chemotherapy, had lost all of his hair, even his eyebrows—certainly had never seen before.

After the ABC special aired, it barely took twenty-four hours for the impact to fully sink in. The flurry of media interest and recriminations against Michael began almost immediately. On February 7, the singer issued a statement clearly angling for the public's sympathy, stating, "Today I feel more betrayed than perhaps ever before."

Meanwhile, Michael's ultra-protective brother, Jermaine, took a more pugnacious tone, telling the press: "I look at it as a modern-day lynching."

But Michael, never one to underestimate the power of publicity, whether good or bad, knew ahead of the February 6 airdate that the impending documentary would take a negative tone, as it had already aired in Great Britain. Just one day before it aired in the United States, Michael whisked Gavin, his siblings, and his mother away to Miami, Florida, for what was ostensibly a business trip, but was really an attempt to shield the family from the documentary and the press surrounding it.

Tucker, the actor who had befriended the boy after Masada introduced them, along with his wife, also accompanied the group on Michael's private jet. A source described how Michael attempted to keep the family and other guests from seeing the TV special, pointing out that, "The day before the show aired, Michael flew the family down to Miami in his private jet and put them up in a four-star hotel. I think Michael felt the family would be distressed to the point of seeking legal action, so he devised his own blackout."

Michael's idea to have Tucker accompany the family was nothing short of a stroke of genius. Having one of Gavin's favorite actors join the entourage in Miami all but guaranteed that everyone would be too distracted to tune in to the ABC special.

Michael may have also used another distraction on the boy, one that he reportedly called Jesus Juice, which was really white wine disguised in a Coke can.

Michael allegedly insisted to his young friend, "Jesus drank it, so it must be good."

Upon returning home, Gavin's mother, Janet, began to get a sense of the enormity of the situation. She was not equipped with the savvy and know-how to deflect media attention; after all, money was so tight in the family that the mother had once lived in a horse stable with her children.

Now, however, she was in a panic because schoolmates immediately began teasing her son about his "special" relationship with Michael, calling him derogatory names like "fag boy" and "gay boy." Much to Janet's surprise, a school official who saw the ABC special and who recognized the boy and his brother, had called the Los Angeles Department of Children and Family Services.

The official was concerned because the boy had not been back to school.

Scared and in way over her head, Janet turned to her new family friend for advice on how to deal with the brewing media storm. Michael soothed the mom's frayed nerves with the outer calm and ease with which he faced any hint of scandal. Michael even arranged for members of his entourage to drive her and the kids to the meeting with the child protective services officials. Michael's camp also asked to sit in on the interview. Feeling a little uneasy with the level of control Michael's inner circle was attempting to enforce, Janet balked at anyone joining her at the meeting.

Whether or not it was on Michael's orders—or if it was requested independently of him—his people asked the mom to record the session with the child welfare officials. She obliged.

The details of the ensuing meeting might have remained secret except for a memo that was leaked to the media some ten months later. Curiously, the memo detailing this February meeting was dictated on November 26, six days after Michael was arrested on another round of child molestation charges.

It would later prove a bombshell piece of evidence in Michael's favor.

Los Angeles authorities had launched an investigation on February 14, spurred by the previously mentioned phone call from a school official who had watched the Bashir special.

Janet was called to the child protective services meeting as a result of this call.

By February 27, the Los Angeles authorities decided that the charges of abuse were "unfounded."

But the timing of the leak—in the month between Michael's subsequent arrest and arraignment—was suspicious. Why was a memo from this February meeting released to the press immediately after Michael's arrest the following November? To Michael detractors, it smelled fishy. They assumed that someone in Jackson's camp had pulled some strings to get the memo released at just the right moment.

Shaken and flabbergasted at the suggestion that the man who had befriended and cared for her gravely ill son would ever harm him, Janet went into the meeting with Los Angeles authorities believing the whole mess was just a big misunderstanding, blown out of proportion by the vultures in the media who preyed incessantly on their close friend, Michael.

"The children's mother stated that she believed the media had taken everything out of context," the memo read (coincidentally or not, similar to Michael's own

One of 182 illustrations created by the King of Pop, which were valued at $902.52 million. This one is of the elaborate doors he dreamed of installing at the Neverland Ranch, with Disney's Peter Pan front and center.

Santa Barbara County Sheriff's Department's raid of Neverland Ranch: the evidence seized.

During the raid, investigators stumbled upon a hidden panel concealed with clothes in Jackson's wardrobe. (*Santa Barbara County Sheriff's Department*)

The room contained items Jackson had collected and wanted kept secret. (*Santa Barbara County Sheriff's Department*)

One memento was a headshot of former child actor Macauley Culkin, now thirty-five. (*Santa Barbara County Sheriff's Department*)

A messy closet of various collectibles, which "paint a dark and frightening picture of Jackson," an investigator on the case told this author. (*Santa Barbara County Sheriff's Department*)

Mixed in with some of the more sinister evidence were children's toys, like a Mickey Mouse stuffed animal and various Disney memorabilia. *(Santa Barbara County Sheriff's Department)*

The singer had a penchant for the creepy, including dolls that lined this staircase. *(Santa Barbara County Sheriff's Department)*

Some have suggested that Jackson's love of toys hid his dark side. *(Santa Barbara County Sheriff's Department)*

The master bedroom in Jackson's mansion where he died on June 25, 2009. *(MEGA)*

Jackson's bedroom in disarray after his death, with medical equipment strewn on the bed and the floor. *(MEGA)*

Jackson's bedroom with a hanging bag for medication. *(MEGA)*

Oxygen tanks in Jackson's bedroom. *(MEGA)*

Closet in Jackson's Bel Air mansion. *(MEGA)*

Jackson's infamous embroidered costume jackets hanging in the closet. *(MEGA)*

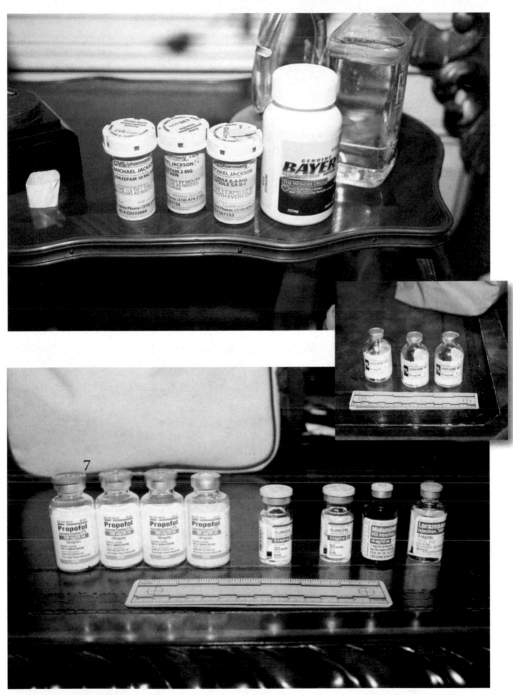

Top: Prescription medication bottles in Jackson's name on the bedside table, including Diazepam. *(MEGA)* Inset: Bottles of Lidocaine prescriptions found in Jackson's bedroom. *(MEGA)* Bottom: Four bottles of Propofol, and four other bottles of prescription medications found in Jackson's bedroom. *(MEGA)*

Dr. Conrad Murray's medical bag with medication hiding in the closet of Jackson's Bel Air mansion. *(MEGA)*

Sadly, Jackson's three young children were permitted to go inside the drug-strewn room, the authors claimed. *(MEGA)*

Outside Jackson's rented mansion, the day of his death. *(MEGA)*

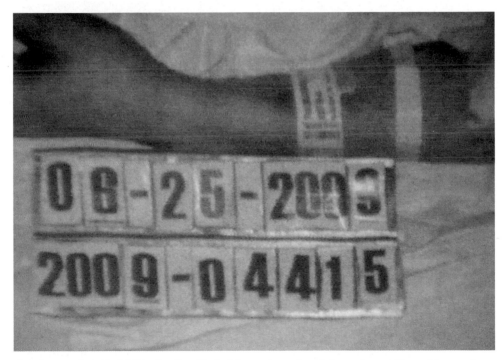

On September 3, 2009, the family held a private burial service at Forest Lawn in Glendale, California. The entertainment icon's empty casket was entombed in a structure known as the Great Mausoleum. Jackson family matriarch, Katherine, decided to cremate his remains, according to a source. *(MEGA)*

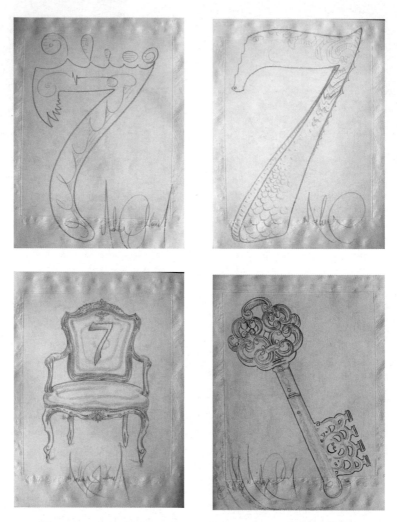

In addition to his fascination with Peter Pan and oddities, such as the Elephant Man, Jackson was obsessed with the number seven. It played a large part in his life, such as him signing his will on 7/7/02; his two biggest hits—"Black or White" and "Billie Jean"—were No. 1 for seven weeks each; his top three albums—*Thriller, Bad,* and *Dangerous*—each producing seven Top 40 hits.

Jackson learned his illustration skills
from Australian artist Brett-Livingstone
Strong, who was also a close friend. The
image at the bottom is of a rocking chair
once owned by John F. Kennedy.

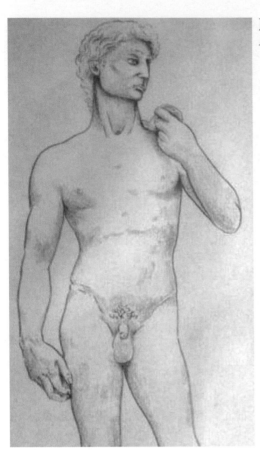

Jackson's drawing of Michelangelo's *David*.

MJ's sketch of his own feet doing
the famous "Moonwalk."

The most priceless of Michael's art pieces—his very first work—entitled *We the People*. It was said to be valued at a startling $3 million.

After seeing the Wright brothers' plane in the Smithsonian National Air and Space Museum, he sketched several versions of the historic aircraft.

Jackson drew a self-portrait he intended to use on the Neverland entrance gate.

explanation). "Mother stated the twelve-year-old was in stage four cancer and had received a year of chemotherapy in addition to having his spleen and one kidney removed. Mother stated that the entertainer was like a father to the children and part of the family."

The report went on: "The child was interviewed . . . as to the allegations and he denied any form of sexual abuse. He denied that he ever slept in the same bed as the entertainer. Both children expressed a fondness for the entertainer and stated they enjoyed visiting his home, where they would often ride in the park, play video games, and watch movies."

In addition, the Los Angeles authorities interviewed the boy's older sister, sixteen-year-old Davellin, who said that "she had accompanied her brothers on sleepovers at the entertainer's home and had never seen anything sexually inappropriate between her brothers and the entertainer."

With that, Los Angeles officials closed their investigation.

Unbeknownst to almost everyone associated with the case, the Santa Barbara authorities had also opened their own investigation on February 18—but closed it for lack of evidence on April 16.

At this point, the pressure must have been nearly unbearable for the boy's family; therefore, it's not surprising that the cash-strapped family willingly accepted any and all of Michael's help.

The family had gone into hiding at Neverland.

Michael had managed to ease Janet's worried mind to a degree by promising to put her three children through private school so they wouldn't have to endure any more taunts from the mean-spirited children who had targeted her son after the airing of the ABC special.

The superstar also promised to support the family for the rest of their lives.

In addition, about a month after the ABC special aired, Michael's newly hired criminal attorney, famed defense attorney Mark Geragos, whom Jackson retained before there was even a notion of criminal charges, got the mother to state on audio and videotape that Michael was a wonderful man.

Again, Janet was only too happy to oblige, at the very least as a token of thanks for the man who had given so much of himself to her son. Besides, Michael had convinced her that the extra measures were taken to ensure her safety and well-being as much as his own.

Meanwhile, Michael was preparing to launch his own counteroffensive into action.

CHAPTER TWENTY

TAKE TWO

After the ABC special aired, Michael lodged formal complaints with both the British Broadcasting Standards Commission and the Independent Television Commission, and he immediately began planning his own two-hour special for Fox. Hosted by Maury Povich on February 23, 2003, *The Michael Jackson Interview: The Footage You Were Never Meant to See* major television event was bought by the network for a staggering $5 million and utilized hours of Michael's own footage with Bashir and the boy—compiled by videographer Moslehi—none of which was included in the ABC special.

According to reports, the deal for the special was negotiated by Michael's friend and sometime business partner, F. Marc Schaffel, a gay pornographic producer whom Michael had met about four years prior at a charity event.

Michael's inner circle had long tried to convince him to sever contact with Schaffel, and Michael may well have wished he had listened to his advisors.

It is nearly impossible to believe that Michael, having somehow survived the 1993 accusations, would still risk his reputation—and possibly so much more—to do business with this man.

Yet, Michael had a way of constantly defying reality and common sense.

In addition, Michael's camp encouraged the sick boy's mother to blast the ABC special for showing her son's face. The idea was to give the impression that Michael and Gavin's family both felt betrayed by the documentary. In fact, in Michael's complaints to the two British media watchdog groups, he claimed that Bashir breached a basic journalistic code by showing footage of his three children and by interviewing Gavin without his parents' express permission.

Janet also released a statement through Michael's spokesperson, declaring, "At no time has [my son] ever been treated with anything other than love, respect, and the deepest kindness by Michael. His constant support, both practical and emotional, helped give my beautiful little boy the strength to fight his cancer."

But should the family turn on Michael, he and his camp knew they had one major trump card in their favor—the boy's estranged parents were locked in a bitter feud and neither had a clean record.

Janet immediately came under fire for even allowing Michael unsupervised visits with her sick son. Her ex-husband, David, even lashed out at her publicly, in his own attempt to regain custody of the kids, for allowing their children to have unsupervised sleepovers with Michael. He implied that his ex-wife was selfish and told a newspaper that "she just sees prestige for herself from the connection. [She] always dreamed of being a celebrity. That's what she thinks she's become."

David's attorney at the time, H. Russell Halpern, claimed Janet had committed "reckless abandonment of your parental duties." As for Janet, the mom had once complained in a request for a restraining order against David that "instances of violence in our marriage were a daily occurrence."

David, meanwhile, pleaded no contest in 2001 to a charge of beating his wife, and the following year, he pleaded guilty to a misdemeanor charge of willful cruelty to his daughter. Further tarnishing the family's reputation was a lawsuit from 1998. The family had carried clothes out of J. C. Penney which they had not paid for, and although there was no explanation for this action, the family sued J. C. Penney for rough treatment. In the end, they received a settlement of $137,500.

But despite the damaging evidence against the Arvizo family, the tidal wave against Michael was building. Gloria Allred returned to the Jackson spotlight and demanded that child welfare officials take custody of Michael's children from him, and she implored authorities to reopen a criminal investigation into Michael's contact with minors, as did A. Sidney Johnson III, president of Prevent Child Abuse America.

In a letter to the DA, Johnson wrote, "Michael Jackson has raised enough red flags for us to be concerned about protecting the welfare of children he comes in contact with, including his own."

Even another one-time ally of Michael's was also voicing doubts about his psychological well-being. Michael's ex-wife, Lisa Marie, told a Boston radio station that Michael "needs help." In another radio interview, Lisa Marie said that Michael's behavior was "erratic."

"He's not the person he likes to present himself to be in public. There's a very different person behind the scenes," she said.

Of course, at this time the sick boy's mother had no idea that any improprieties had ever occurred between her son and Michael. Although she did find it odd when, according to a source, Michael's entourage, with the help of Beverly Hills private investigator Bradley Miller, obtained passports for her family and encouraged them to take a one-way trip to South America, with Brazil and Argentina mentioned as possible specific destinations. To sweeten the deal, Michael offered, without reserve, to pay for the family's airfare, accommodations, and all of their medical bills.

"You'll love it down there," Michael cheerily explained.

The mother may not have yet realized it, but the picture was coming into focus for others.

"They were trying to shut them up," said a family friend, about the offer to send the family to South America.

Michael's explanation for sending them abroad was far simpler and innocent: he wanted to ensure their privacy.

Because the commotion over the ABC special was leading to the revelation of all kinds of facts and secrets, it was only a matter of time before Janet learned that sources claimed Michael was not only serving wine to her cancer-stricken son but encouraging him to drink it because Jesus had done so.

Had the mom known about the wine allegations when she went into the meeting with the Los Angeles child protective agency, she may have painted a different picture rather than singing Michael's praises as an erstwhile father figure. After all, most people would string up anyone who served a cancer-stricken twelve-year-old alcohol. Even if she didn't have all the facts yet, it was too late to go back on any statements she had made to the Los Angeles authorities. But that didn't mean she wasn't going to give Michael a piece of her mind.

Privately, she blew her stack at Michael, sources told me.

"How could you do that? Why would you do such a thing?" she hollered at Michael. "He's a little boy! And he's on chemotherapy for his cancer. It's dangerous and irresponsible to have someone drinking when they're on cancer treatments. There can be very bad, even fatal, side effects."

Michael did his best to calm her down.

By all accounts, Michael is a very shrewd man, and even he must have sensed that she was turning against him at this point. So, Michael swung into action. He must have known that as soon as outside influences started bearing down on Janet, she'd hire an attorney to look out for her best interests.

Michael hoped to keep her where he could watch her, preferably within the gates of Neverland.

But she was furious about stories that Michael was serving her child wine and she wanted out of Neverland right away, which would later, supposedly, turn into a house of horrors for her and her family.

But breaking free from Michael wouldn't be so easy.

CHAPTER TWENTY-ONE

A HOUSE DIVIDED

A source close to the Gavin Arvizo investigation revealed that "when the mother grew suspicious of Michael's clandestine activities with her older son, tensions came to a flashpoint. Michael kept track of Janet's every move, not allowing them to leave the property without an escort and having them followed by Neverland employees wherever they went on the ranch."

After Janet confronted Michael about serving her child wine, she decided she needed to get her kids and get out of there. But Michael reportedly told her flat out, "You cannot leave here."

Michael allegedly went so far as to have exits sealed off and doors locked. The source said, "Finally, after 11 o'clock one night, the panicked mother approached the Neverland house manager and said, 'We need to get out of here.'"

The sympathetic house manager agreed to help the mother and her children get off of the ranch. The manager loaded the family into a vehicle and drove them 100 miles to their home in Los Angeles.

Not surprisingly, Michael had the house manager fired.

Around April, even though Janet and Michael were on the outs, they still shared one thing in common—they both knew they needed professional help. One of Michael's first calls in the wake of the ABC special was to high-powered legal eagle Mark Geragos (who had defended Academy Award–nominated actress Winona Ryder on charges of stealing more than $5,500 worth of merchandise from a Beverly Hills, California store in 2001) and private investigator Bradley Miller.

In May, Janet was referred to an attorney who knew quite a lot about Michael Jackson—Larry Feldman, the same lawyer who had represented the accuser's family in 1993 and helped them negotiate the multi-million-dollar settlement.

Feldman's first order of business was to see to it that Janet got her son into psycho-therapy right away.

There was a therapist Feldman knew and trusted, Stan Katz, the exact same therapist who, along with Dr. Mathis Abrams, saw the 1993 accuser a decade ago. Over the course of three therapy sessions, away from the influence of Michael's money and power, Gavin dropped the bombshell everyone suspected: he admitted that Michael had sexually abused him.

A source revealed that Katz "asked the boy over and over again if it was true. He insisted it was. It was a shocking realization."

Gavin also told Katz that Michael gave him copious amounts of liquor, includ-ing wine, vodka, and tequila, and that Michael eagerly showed him pictures of naked women he'd downloaded on his computer. Bound by law to report the boy's charges to law enforcement authorities, Katz set in motion the investigation that would ultimately lead to Michael's arrest.

Upon hearing about the boy's allegations to the therapist, Santa Barbara offi-cials reopened their investigation on June 13. The child, who was struggling for his life at the time of the alleged abuse, could scarcely imagine taking a witness stand against his former father figure. What's more, the ill child didn't even know if he'd survive to witness the outcome.

One man who had long been intrigued with what went on behind the scenes with Michael was Thomas Sneddon, the Santa Barbara district attorney who called the entertainer out after the *Primetime Live* interview with Diane Sawyer.

The sixty-three-year-old prosecutor, a Vietnam veteran and staunch Republican, was known to colleagues and friends as "Mad Dog"—a nickname the chief prose-cutor earned early in his career because of his dogged determination and commit-ment to his criminal cases.

Sneddon couldn't be more different from Michael. He was intense, combative, aggressive, abrasive, and highly competitive; more of a modern-day John Wayne, as opposed to Michael's Peter Pan.

Interestingly, both Michael and Sneddon had a pull-yourself-up-by-the-bootstraps ethos, rising from working class beginnings to reach the pinnacle of their respective careers. Sneddon was born in the dreary confines of Lynwood, a suburb of Los Angeles very near the mean streets of Compton. The Sneddon family business was a bakery, and with his father's prodding, Sneddon—raised Catholic—aimed to get himself out of the dead-end future that awaited him. The first of his family to graduate college, Sneddon attended Notre Dame University, where he excelled at boxing and found his calling in law. Sneddon earned his law degree at UCLA, the well-manicured campus of the state-run University of California system that is nestled at the South end of one of Los Angeles' richest and most exclusive neighborhoods, Bel Air. Sneddon met his future wife, who is a book author as well as a writer for *Christian Parenting Today*, on a blind date while he was a law student.

Sneddon worked from the ground up in Santa Barbara, beginning in the DA's office in 1969, and by 1983, he was elected to the highest county legal office.

Michael first came into the prosecutor's sights in 1993, when he was accused of molestation by three boys, including the one who eventually filed a civil suit against him. After a year of building what he thought was a rock-solid sexual molestation case against Jackson, based primarily on the allegations from the boy who sued, the attorney was forced to drop the criminal case because of the settlement, and because the alleged victim then refused to testify against Michael.

Michael apparently viewed Sneddon as Javert to his Jean Valjean in their own very personal production of *Les Miserables*. Michael immortalized Sneddon on his 1995 *HIStory* album, on a song called " D.S.," about a "TA" named "Dom Sheldon." Even though Michael made a meager attempt to conceal the identity of his target with a fictitious name, the aim of his vitriol was obvious.

Michael sings, "You know he really tried to take me/Down by surprise, I bet he missioned with the CIA/He don't do half what he say/Dom Sheldon is a cold man."

Michael went on, "You think he brother with the KKK?/I know his mother never taught him right anyway/He want your vote just to remain TA/He'll stop at nothing just to get his political say/I bet he never had a social life anyway."

Sneddon was unmoved by the audacious showmanship.

When asked about the song once, Sneddon replied, "I have not, shall we say, done him the honor of listening to it, but I've been told that it ends with the sound of a gunshot."

As cavalier an attitude as Sneddon attempted to cultivate, the truth is that he had never gotten over narrowly missing his chance to prosecute Michael, on what Sneddon believed wholeheartedly were truthful allegations. In the wake of the collapse of the 1993 molestation case, Sneddon was instrumental in changing California law, so that civil lawsuits must be put on hold during a criminal case.

Now facing his second chance to nail Michael, Sneddon believed he had the force of the law behind him.

After the ABC special aired, reporters dogged Sneddon for his thoughts and asked him whether he was still after Michael. Sneddon begrudgingly dubbed the 1993 case "open but inactive." But, in light of Michael's admissions on the program, Sneddon came out swinging again, encouraging anyone who felt victimized by the superstar to come forward. The two long-time enemies were about to come face to face again.

Early in the morning hours of November 18, 2003, ten months after the Martin Bashir special had aired, the calm over the Eden-like playground of Neverland was disrupted by the whirling of helicopters overhead, and the appearance of a procession of police cars, a forensic van, a locksmith truck, a paddy wagon, and an ambulance. After filing an eighty-page affidavit seeking permission to raid Michael's home, some seventy members of Santa Barbara County Sheriff's Department and staffers from the DA's office methodically, with laser-like focus, swooped in on Michael's compound, armed with a search warrant and an arrest warrant for the King of Pop.

At first the Santa Barbara District Attorney's office obliquely called their surprise visit part of an "ongoing criminal investigation," but by 5:30 p.m., when workers installed a generator and floodlights, it was clear that the worst days of Michael's life were ahead of him.

After fourteen hours of intense digging, police were reported to have confiscated computers, photographs, and videotapes, some material related to S&M, and medications. An employee of Neverland said, "During the search, the police cleaned out the medicine cabinet. All of Michael's prescriptions were gone. They took home videos that were in his master bedroom. They also took cameras."

One report claimed that police also found personal letters and poems that Michael wrote to the alleged victim. With much less fanfare, police also raided the West Hills, California, home of Hamid Moslehi, Michael's videographer, and seized videotapes showing Michael with various children.

The offices of Michael's private investigator, Bradley Miller, were also raided.

A source close to the investigation said, "Police seized several secret videos during their multiple raids. Now the cops are going to try to match these secret videos with descriptions that the alleged victim gave them. He was able to give very specific details about what happened, where it happened, and how it happened."

Where the alleged victim couldn't fill in the blanks, Gavin's younger brother Star could. Prosecutors looked upon Star as their secret witness who could provide further details about Michael's not-so-innocent slumber parties.

In particular, the child told authorities about a specific sleepover in which Michael and Gavin stayed on the bed while he stayed on the floor. As key as the little brother was to bolster the DA's case, their witness could hardly be thought of as impartial. Still, some reports said he was an eyewitness to the alleged abuse.

One piece of information from the alleged victim seemed to be proven true by the search and was very damaging to Jackson. According to a source, the Sheriff's Department alleged that "the victim told officials of a location at Neverland where Michael kept his porn magazines hidden in a briefcase. When the Santa Barbara Sheriff's Department conducted their search at Neverland, they allegedly found several pornographic magazines in the briefcase—exactly where the youngster told police they would be. One of the magazines police confiscated was *Barely Legal*, which features adult women dressed in sexy young outfits to make them look like teenagers. Police believed Michael showed *Barely Legal* to the victim to excite him."

The informant claimed that during their raid, the sheriffs even cut the top off of Michael's mattress pad and had a lab test it for the victim's semen.

Further tightening the web around Michael were charges that over the previous two years Michael used another unnamed teen to access pornography on the internet.

Michael was formally charged on December 18 in an explosive nine-count felony complaint, including seven counts of lewd and lascivious acts upon a child under fourteen and two counts of administering an intoxicating agent.

The complaint stated that the "lewd and lascivious acts" were committed "with the intent of arousing, appealing to, and gratifying the lust, passions, and sexual desires" of both Michael and the alleged victim.

Sneddon and his fellow lawmen alleged that Michael began abusing the boy just one day after the ABC special aired.

Almost as soon as the charges were filed, rumors spread that Sneddon's case was weak; that's why he waited so long after the alleged crime and the raid on Neverland to file charges. Michael's defenders also pointed out that Sneddon implored other victims to come forward, suggesting that Sneddon might lack the goods to send Michael up the river.

What's more, the secret memo from the Los Angeles Department of Child and Family Services, which was leaked after Jackson was arrested, cast further doubt on Sneddon's charges.

But Sneddon was quick to acknowledge that his office was aware of the Los Angeles authorities' findings prior to issuing search warrants and the arrest warrant for Michael. Sneddon brushed off the meeting as an interview, not an investigation.

"Los Angeles is a big place," he snuffed. "They have a lot of problems down there and that office has a lot of problems."

But who leaked the memo and why? Was it possible that Michael's shrewd attorney, Mark Geragos—who vowed to use the Los Angeles document as proof of his client's innocence—manipulated his multitude of law enforcement connections to get the memo released at a critical time in Michael's saga? No one may ever know the answer to this critical question.

It is important to point out that someone in Michael's camp learned of the boy's interview with Los Angeles authorities in February, and that Michael had a chance to speak with the family before they sat down with the Los Angeles Department of Children and Family Services. Although Sneddon remained unmoved by the suggestion that his case was flawed, Mark Geragos made his point clear, saying that Michael would fight the charges "with every fiber of his soul."

He charged like a bull: "These charges are driven by two things: money and revenge. And we will prove that."

As part of their investigation, authorities also looked into the possibility that Michael, who was no stranger to the effects of wanton pill popping, used "knockout drops" on the unsuspecting boy. The authorities, according to the *Enquirer's* reporting at the time, "had questioned the mother of the boy extensively about drugs that Jackson may have used on her son. They also spoke confidentially with other parents of kids who were at Neverland around the same time as the boy."

While Neverland was swarming with cops and the most serious trouble of Michael's life was unfolding, the singer was in Las Vegas, behaving as if blithely unaffected. If this was indeed his last hurrah, Michael had decided to go out with a bang.

CHAPTER TWENTY-TWO

FACING THE MUSIC

From November 3 to November 19, 2003, Michael was ensconced in a lavish, private two-bedroom villa at The Mirage Hotel in Las Vegas. He checked in under the pseudonym "Parker," along with his three children and a gang of underage kids.

Michael's staff and entourage spread out among a three-bedroom villa at $5,000 a night, an additional suite at $1,500 a night, and a regular hotel room at $500 a night. The singer was in town to shoot a video for the first single, "One More Chance," from his greatest hits collection called *Number Ones*, which was released the day of the raid. The only adult supervision for the pack of kids, mostly boys, was Michael, who often calls his young male charges names like "doodoo head," "apple head" and "smellies." An insider said he even made it clear to hotel staff that no one but he and his young charges were allowed inside the villa.

The bacchanalian vacation was a complete free-for-all. Sources said hotel staff delivered cigarettes, along with Absolut vodka, Crown Royal whiskey, and Baileys liqueur to the private villa. Eyewitnesses to the shocking comings and goings reported that an African American boy seemed to be drunk most of the time, slurring his words.

One of Michael's first stops after he checked into The Mirage was at the Art de Vignettes art gallery.

"He had one girl and three boys—in the twelve- to thirteen-year-old range—with him when he arrived at my store," remembered gallery owner Barbara Lee Woollen.

"Michael wanted a $6,000 bronze statue of a bare-chested boy."

Another eyewitness described the image of Michael up close: "Michael was decked out in full makeup. It wasn't just a little bit of foundation, but heavy showgirl makeup. He was wearing very thick pancake on his face along with black eyeliner. He wore the same purple, gray, and black silk pajamas with two sets of buttons at the top. He looked like a geisha."

A longtime friend of Michael's put an even finer point on it.

"Michael Jackson has become a traffic accident, a spectacle," said Blood, Sweat & Tears drummer Bobby Colomby, who knew Michael since he was a child, at the time. "I'm not an apologist for the guy, but this is all so unbelievably sad."

Because no one, not even maids, were allowed in Michael's villa, the room was a mess by the end of the group's stay. A source inside the hotel reported:

> When Michael and his party checked out of the Mirage, it looked like a bomb had hit it. The carpets and upholstery on the chairs and couches and the bedspreads were all ruined with stains and had to be replaced. And a number of prescription pill bottles—some unopened—were left behind in the trash heap. The destruction in the Villa was so bad that the hotel actually videotaped the room as Michael and his guests had left it. The hotel made arrangements to send a bill for $25,000 in damages to Michael's managers.

The staff also found blankets and pillows stuffed in the bathtubs, which explained where some of the boys may have slept.

While Michael partied, prosecutor Sneddon had his own business to attend to, namely, organizing a splashy news conference on November 19. Announcing the arrest warrant for Michael, Sneddon brushed aside the suggestion that he was so consumed with exacting revenge on Michael that he had spent the past ten years doing anything and everything to collar the King of Pop.

"I can tell you it's BS, but it isn't going to change people's observations," Sneddon claimed.

During the meet and greet with reporters, many of whom had traveled from all corners of the globe to cover what surely promised to be the trial of the century, Sneddon cracked jokes and, unwittingly, set himself up for a serious bashing for the inappropriate tone that he set for such a serious matter.

At one point, Sneddon joked to the gathered media, "I hope that you all stay long and spend lots of money, because we need your sales tax to support our offices."

While no one could doubt that Michael always took every opportunity to exploit center stage, Sneddon seemed equally intent on squeezing every last ounce of attention from the firestorm. With his arrogant behavior, Sneddon had given the defense an advantage. Now Michael's attorneys would pound the theme of the DA's overzealous pursuit of their client, and how he had turned a routine investigation into a full-scale witch hunt.

The stage had been set for a monumental clash of egos, wits, resolve, and power. Sneddon did eventually appear on CNN, apologizing for his behavior at the news conference. But with the stakes so high, the bell could not be un-rung.

Sufficiently relaxed from his adventure in Las Vegas, and apparently ready to tackle his legal crisis, Michael boarded a private Gulfstream jet on November 20 for the roughly hour-long plane ride back home. Reports suggested he was calm and even snacked on an apple. Michael arrived, with lead attorney Mark Geragos in tow, and surrendered to Santa Barbara authorities at 12:05 p.m., after Sneddon, in his press conference, had earlier admonished Michael, to "get over here and get checked in."

Michael was driven to the Santa Barbara County Sheriff's department and led inside, hands cuffed behind his back. Michael was booked and his mug shot was taken. The picture reveals a crestfallen man: sad eyes accentuated by heavy eyeliner, a wisp of black hair hanging over his right eye, lips pursed, as if caught like a deer in headlights. Michael's vital statistics were listed as 5 feet 11 inches, and 120 pounds. He surrendered his passport, as is customary when one is arrested on felony charges, though Sneddon would eventually return it to Michael so that the performer could fulfill "contractual obligations" in Britain.

Michael's camera-ready attorney spoke briefly to the 100-plus reporters waiting outside the sheriff's department. A defiant Geragos told them: "Michael is here. He has come back specifically to combat these charges head on. He is greatly outraged by these charges and has authorized me to say the charges are categorically untrue. He looks forward to fighting this in court."

The authorities and Michael Jackson told two immeasurably different versions of what went on during the booking process, an event that took exactly sixty-three minutes. On Christmas Day 2003, Michael taped an interview with correspondent

Ed Bradley for *60 Minutes*, which aired three days later, in which he laid bare his account of the gruesome and humiliating details of being booked in Santa Barbara. Michael showed Bradley a picture of himself with a huge, bulging, discolored bruise on the underside of his arm, the result, Michael claimed, of manhandling by the officers from the Santa Barbara County Police Department.

Furthermore, Michael alleged, his "shoulder is dislocated, literally," the result of the sheriff's roughly handcuffing his arms behind his back. Michael went even further, saying that he was locked for forty-five minutes in a jailhouse bathroom and that "there was doo-doo, feces, thrown all over the walls, the floor, the ceiling."

Upon hearing Michael's allegations, Santa Barbara Sheriff Jim Anderson called for a state investigation into Michael's complaints. If the entertainer's outrageous claims were determined to be unfounded, then the sheriff threatened to seek criminal charges against Michael. Sheriff Anderson added that he was "shocked and troubled" by Michael's tales of mistreatment.

More questions were raised than answered by Michael's bizarre confessions to Ed Bradley. If, as Michael claimed, he was locked in a bathroom for forty-five minutes, then how could it be that he was only held at the Santa Barbara County Jail during the booking process for a total of sixty-three minutes? Once again, Michael was stretching the confines of believability.

Still, though, many longtime fans stood by their fallen hero, lapping up his every outlandish word. In good times and in bad, Michael has never failed at delivering top-notch entertainment, and his sit-down interview with Bradley in prime-time Sunday night was no exception.

In Sheriff Anderson's version of events, Michael was "escorted to a holding cell designed to hold up to seven individuals and had a toilet in one area. He [Michael] was alone in the holding cell for approximately fifteen minutes." The cell had been cleaned by a work crew prior to Michael's arrival. Common sense begged the question: Why would Santa Barbara authorities, who must have known that the world was watching, risk their credibility by flouting basic procedure?

Sheriff Anderson also provided video and audio tapes, one of which documented Michael's drive from the airport hangar to the jail. Michael can be heard whistling and humming, and when a deputy asked the singer how he was faring, Michael responded, "Wonderful."

At least one bystander saw part of the spectacle unfold inside the police station. Steve Balash, who was representing another prisoner at the jail, told the media that his client saw Michael "with his legs spread and his two hands up against the wall, and they were patting him down."

Balash went on to explain that as Michael was being led along to be finger-printed, he waved to a group of prisoners. If, as Michael said, authorities dislocated his shoulder, then how was he able to wave to prisoners inside the jail, and how could he have raised his arm and waved when he exited the jail?

Finally, if Michael had been treated so poorly, with such gross indifference to the law, then why hadn't his lawyer filed a formal complaint? The usually talkative and visible Geragos did not respond to media requests for a comment, only issuing a statement that Michael stood by the allegations he made.

The wording of Geragos' response left one to wonder if Geragos actually stood by Michael's allegations too.

Nevertheless, as Michael was formally charged, the very few who always stood steadfast by his side were quick to jump to his defense. Elizabeth Taylor issued a statement, saying simply, "I believe Michael is absolutely innocent and that he will be vindicated." She also included a message to the media, saying that she looked forward to when he was vindicated because they would all eat crow for dragging her close friend through the mud.

Michael's older brother, Jermaine, was in the forefront of his brother's defense. He speculated that race was the primary motive behind the whole mess when he went on CNN the same day Michael was booked.

Jermaine denounced the charges and stated: "The whole family supports Michael 100 percent . . . 1,000 percent. Michael is in very strong spirits because he is inno-cent. My brother is not eccentric. We had an incredible, wonderful childhood."

Despite the rosy picture Jermaine attempted to paint, the outlook wasn't good for Michael.

It seemed that with each move he made, the superstar dug himself deeper into a hellish pit. Michael was clearly trying to shelter himself from the gravity of the situation.

For example, soon after he was released on $3 million bail, he and members of his entourage immediately boarded a plane and headed right back to Sin City, where they set up camp in the penthouse suite of the Regency Tower at the Las Vegas Country Club.

On the outside, at least, it appeared Camp Michael was operating business as usual, but the truth is that problems continued to mount, one on top of another.

Like a sideshow to a circus extravaganza, a scandal-within-a-scandal was brewing about the day Michael flew back to Santa Barbara to turn himself in to authorities. For his journey home, Michael had chartered a Gulfstream IV through a Santa Monica–based aviation company he often used, named XtraJet.

What both Michael and his attorney did now know, however, was that someone had surreptitiously installed two hidden cameras in the plane's main cabin, thus recording intimate details of conversations aboard the flight.

Geragos wasted no time in swiftly filing a lawsuit against XtraJet, promising to "land like a ton of bricks" on anyone who deigned to besmirch Michael's reputation or character, and the lawyer also obtained a temporary restraining order barring any release of the tape, citing attorney-client privilege.

Yet, before he had a chance to halt the spread of details from the tapes—which someone was secretly shopping around to the highest bidder—some details managed to slip out. While aboard the flight, Michael spent a good deal of time slamming DA Sneddon, and much to the surprise of those who had heard or seen the tape, there was no evidence of Michael's meek, little boy voice.

Instead, Michael spoke with an authoritative tone in a deep voice.

While no particular legally damning information had leaked, the few morsels of information that managed to seep through cast more shadows upon Michael's image. To some who have long maintained that Michael is nothing like the scatterbrained innocent rube he cultivates through his image, the suggestion that Michael comes off as cutthroat and downright macho was something of a vindication.

Throughout the years, Michael has managed to engender a great deal of sympathy, continually painting himself in the role of victim. On the tape, however, according to those who heard snatches of it, Michael sounded nothing like an overmatched victim, rather a man hellbent on fighting until his last dying breath.

One cannot help wondering if Sneddon was aware of this secret side of Michael, the fighter and, indeed, the survivor.

CHAPTER TWENTY-THREE

FALSE PROFIT

Throughout his career, and more importantly, in the midst of his sundry legal quagmires, Michael had always relied on an inner circle of consiglieres, personal advisors, family members, business managers, accountants, lawyers, publicists, and others to handle his affairs, both personal and professional.

Once again finding himself under such a sharply focused microscope, Michael turned to his most trusted confidante: his brother Jermaine.

Fearing for Michael's safety—presumably self-inflicted as well as threats coming from Jackson haters—Jermaine, who had converted to Islam in years prior, advised his brother to seek the security services of the controversial Muslim splinter group, the Nation of Islam.

This move, Jermaine reasoned, would also help Michael curry favor with the African American community, who had long ago turned on Michael because of his apparent self-loathing, which manifested itself in his attempts to whiten his skin and reshape his nose and other African features, to more resemble a white man.

Desperate to clear his name and feeling like a man trapped inside a prison of his own making, Michael reached out to Leonard Muhammad, son-in-law of the organization's militant leader, Louis Farrakhan.

The fifty-eight-year-old Muhammad had a spotty record, at best, for his business acumen.

Once known as Leonard Searcy, Muhammad—a former tavern owner—was largely responsible for the economic development of the Nation of Islam, and remains its chief of staff today. Before that, he was involved in a company that sold a questionable AIDS treatment to the poor in Chicago. Several of his companies were reportedly closed by the state of Illinois due to documentary improprieties or failure to pay taxes. These included Nationway Ventures International Ltd., DiNar Products, and Economic Solutions Inc. One company, POWER Inc., reportedly owed the government and creditors hundreds of thousands of dollars. It culminated in a 1995 *Chicago Tribune* report that read, "ALLEGATIONS OF FRAUD TRAIL FARRAKHAN AIDE."

Whatever expertise Muhammad had in managing the affairs of a worldwide entertainer was a mystery to all, including Michael's trusted and credentialed business managers.

A chasm immediately formed within Michael's inner circle over his decision to bring the controversial group into his fold. Michael's business managers, Ronald Konitzer and Dieter Wiesner, and his spokesperson, Stuart Backerman, argued with Muhammad over how large of a role the Nation of Islam would play in his private and public life.

Likewise, Michael's longtime advisors, many Jewish, did not appreciate the Nation of Islam's anti-Semitic stance and openly voiced their distaste for the group's beliefs. (The Nation of Islam had once referred to Judaism as a "gutter religion.")

On December 20, Michael fired Backerman, who had dutifully served as a buffer between the ferocious press and his client, reportedly because Backerman spoke out the loudest and most fervently against the splinter group.

Publicly, though, the Nation of Islam staunchly denied anything but a passing acquaintance with Michael. They issued a statement saying they had "no official business or professional relationship" with Michael, despite claims from those inside Michael's camp that the group had all but taken over his affairs.

One can only wonder how Michael reconciled his marriage to Debbie Rowe with the Nation of Islam, which opposes interracial marriage. Perhaps the $5.5 million "donation" that Michael allegedly made to the militant group was enough to make members bend their rules and beliefs?

The truth appeared to be that Michael, always reliant upon his contingent of yes-men, was fragile and easily influenced. Facing a doomsday public relations disaster, let alone criminal charges that could see him locked up for decades, Michael scrambled for a new spin.

His first order of business was to rally the support of African Americans. But by aligning himself with the sometimes racist, hate-spewing Nation of Islam, Michael's people feared he would only compound the mess he was in. Certainly, Michael's affiliation with the Nation of Islam did not make him an attractive commodity, to say nothing of the molestation charges.

Geragos was quick to dismiss the claims that Michael was being controlled by Muhammad and his cronies. Another close associate of Michael's had a different view, stating that the singer was "a little paranoid and has a tendency to turn all the members of his team against each other, to cause chaos. He thinks this way he'll have more control and he'll have a better team. Usually it's a fallacy."

Michael also had to contend with another nasty rumor—that he was yet again quickly going broke.

Michael owed a $70 million loan to the Bank of America and a $200 million loan guaranteed by Michael's greatest asset, the music catalogue he owned, which included the highly valuable Beatles songs. If Michael was forced to sell the catalogue to pay the Bank of America debt, he would have been left penniless. But this concern seemed to have done nothing to stop Michael from his wild spending sprees, which included renting a lavish Beverly Hills home for $70,000 a month.

While facing a trial that could drag on for an extended period of time, Michael's ability to partake in money-generating ventures was certainly hampered. Facing the trial of his life, the trial for his freedom, Michael also faced the prospect that he could be bankrupt within two years.

The self-styled King of Pop no longer possessed the magic to create monstrous record sales, as each of his successive records cost more to produce but sold less than the one before. Furthermore, three of Michael's past four albums had been nothing more than repackaging of old music. Never one to stop trying, however, in late June 2004, Michael announced that he was releasing a four-disc *The Ultimate Collection* box set of his music that would include remixes, rare and hard-to-find songs, and a *Live in Bucharest: The Dangerous Tour* DVD of his 1992 concert. Ultimately, sales of the set were lackluster. It peaked at 154 on the Billboard 200.

Michael's spending was clearly in inverse proportion to his ability to generate sales. And even though Michael continued to shoulder the enormous financial burden of maintaining Neverland, there were liens against the property (Sony

Music was one of the holders), and Michael still owed an enormous sum of back taxes on the sprawling estate.

Michael's attempts to put a glossy sheen on his financial situation were often pathetic. In the Martin Bashir special, Michael, in an attempt to demonstrate how wealthy he was, went on a lavish spending spree, dropping nearly $6 million on home furnishings and decorations. He may have duped viewers, but Michael returned all of the pricey merchandise just days after the purchase.

And the wanton spending showed no signs of abating before Michael went to trial. The very same December day that Michael fired spokesperson Backerman, he hosted a gathering at Neverland, attended by some six hundred Jackson supporters, friends, and family.

The event was billed as a "homecoming." It had been planned five days earlier and dubbed "You Are Not Alone."

Comedian Tommy Davidson emceed the evening's festivities and Michael, his sister La Toya, and his parents sat in the audience basking in the attention and adoration from commoners and celebrities alike, including comic Eddie Griffin, MC Hammer, and Backstreet Boy Nick Carter. Michael even opened the event up to some of his fans who had been staked outside of the Neverland gates.

Michael was feverishly trying to hold fast to the image of himself as a benefactor to hordes of disadvantaged youth.

The lavish party was another of Michael's well-crafted public relations events which the media was sure to report. No amount of money was too much to spend in an attempt to redirect the public's attention to Michael's self-created reputation as a philanthropist and protector of children.

But in a few short weeks, Michael would once again be facing his toughest critic, the man whom Jackson attorney Howard Weitzman described as "an overly-zealous, ethically-challenged, and ultimately disgraced prosecutor . . . who looked anywhere and everywhere for supposed 'victims' of Jackson's": District Attorney Tom Sneddon.

CHAPTER TWENTY-FOUR

ALL-TIME LOW

On January 16, 2004, Michael was arraigned on seven counts of child molestation and two counts of administering an "intoxicating agent with intent to commit a felony" at Neverland between February 7 and March 10, 2003.

He was squarely in the public spotlight again, the place where he had spent almost his entire life, and despite the dire circumstances he was determined to milk every moment to his benefit.

Michael arrived twenty minutes late to the courtroom, exasperating prosecutors and even the judge. Geragos came armed with extra artillery; he'd recently added another high-flying legal eagle to Michael's team. Benjamin Brafman, who had previously defended high-profile cases involving everyone from Sean "P. Diddy" Combs to high-ranking Mafia figures and would go on to represent disgraced movie mogul Harvey Weinstein against a magnitude of sex abuse charges, now joined Michael's defense. (In the fairness of full disclosure, Weinstein and this author, through a past employer, American Media Inc., had a television production company prior to his much well-reported fall from disgrace in 2017.)

Besides the not guilty plea, which everyone had anticipated Michael would enter, the judge issued a protective order—not quite as restrictive as a gag order that Sneddon was hoping for—but meant, nonetheless, to put a lid on the rampant run of rumors and prevent both sides from using the media to try their case in the court of public opinion.

Outside, about 2,500 fans gathered who had traveled to catch a glimpse of their hero. Some dedicated fans had even lined up outside the courthouse the night before. Anyone could be forgiven if they mistook this legal event for a free concert;

some eyewitnesses, including one CNN legal analyst, likened the proceedings to the hysteria that surrounded Beatles' concerts in the 1960s.

Before Michael sped away in the backseat of an SUV, sitting directly behind his mother, the King of Pop treated his fans outside the courthouse to an impromptu performance atop an SUV, stomping his feet and clapping, while alternately blowing kisses to the rapturous crowd. No one seemed to care much that recent reports suggested that the alleged victim's health was in major decline.

In spite of the seriousness of the charges against him, Michael still saw fit to reward those fanatical fans who showed up with invitations to a party he was hosting back at Neverland. The invite read:

> In the spirit of love and togetherness, Michael Jackson would like to invite his friends and supporters to his Neverland Ranch. Please join us Friday, January 16, from 11 a.m. to 2. Refreshments will be served. We'll see you there.

Anyone wishing to attend was instructed to bring along either a driver's license or passport to serve as identification.

The most notable addition to Michael's support system on this day was his sister Janet, who had kept a healthy distance from the circus surrounding Michael's arrest. But Janet did show up at Michael's arraignment to offer her support, and in several weeks, Michael had ample reason to thank his sister for deflecting some media attention away from him, when she exposed her breast on live television during a halftime show for the Super Bowl with Justin Timberlake.

When the child molestation charges of 1993 first surfaced, Michael hightailed it into London's Charter Nightingale Hospital for a month of drying out and rehab. Addiction is largely thought to be a disease out of the sufferer's control, a wrenching vice that discriminates against no one. Michael has claimed that his post-1993 struggles with addiction were the direct result of the stress he suffered while being probed on child molestation charges back in 1993.

So, there was an element of déjà vu when in February 2004 Michael flew to Aspen, Colorado, to begin treatment for alcohol and painkiller addiction—twin demons that had haunted him for years.

This time, according to one report, Michael was under the care of Honduran-born herbologist, Dr. Alfredo Bowman.

Michael was holed up at a $125,000-a-month, nine-bedroom villa where Dr. Bowman (who was also known as Dr. Sebi) treated the superstar with herb-based pills that work to break down toxins, thus freeing the body of addiction. Jackson emerged from his luxury villa only two weeks into his treatment on February 24, and then it was only a trip to the local Wal-Mart, where police stopped him because he was wearing a ski mask in the store.

While Michael submitted himself to a new age treatment for his addictions, back on the East Coast, yet another bizarre sideshow was playing out, once again with Michael in the starring role.

A New Jersey contractor, Henry Vaccaro, had bought hundreds of boxes of memorabilia belonging to the Jackson family at an auction after the family neglected to pay overdue bills on storage.

No doubt capitalizing on the flurry of Jackson interest since his arrest, Vaccaro had sold the items—which included stage costumes, items from Neverland, MTV music awards, and even note pads with sketches of a face with variously shaped noses.

There was also a list of rules for a private club Michael created, called the Rubberhead Club. Requirements for participation in the club included a mandate that "members of the Rubberhead Club must be idiots and act crazy at all times, members must read and know the story of Peter Pan fluently, all members must be vegetarians and fast on every Sunday for good health, all members must have the brain power of a two-year-old child, all members must watch at least two episodes of *The Three Stooges* every day"—and finally—"every member of the Rubberhead Club must take flying lessons at the Peter Pan School of Flying."

Vaccaro's stash, especially the Rubberhead Club rules, offered a rare glimpse into the twisted, adolescent world of Michael Jackson, demonstrating how, by appealing to juvenile impulses, Michael is able to gain the trust and love of whatever boy he chooses.

The private cache also included pornographic videos and sex toys, which was of major interest to prosecutors. Another precious piece of property which Michael must have wished remained in his possession was a letter he allegedly wrote to his now-deceased sister-in-law, Dee Dee. In the note, Michael wrote:

> Please read this article about child molestation. It brings out how even your own relatives can be molesters of children, or even uncles or aunts molesting nephews and nieces. Please read. Love, MJ.

Prosecutors in Santa Barbara were swift to act, requesting that New Jersey authorities seize specific items in Vaccaro's collection, namely two pairs of white Calvin Klein briefs, purportedly worn by Michael, and photos of him posing with young boys. Vaccaro was told that Santa Barbara authorities, who took possession of the items on March 17, planned to use the underwear for DNA comparison.

While Michael attempted to get his alcohol and pill addiction under control, DA Sneddon continued to work to bolster his case. On March 29, he took the unusual step of convening a grand jury of nineteen citizens (with six alternates) who would decide if the prosecution had enough evidence to try Michael on the molestation charges, thus forgoing a public preliminary hearing. After thirteen days of testimony from nearly a dozen witnesses, including the alleged victim, his younger brother, and their mother, the grand jury voted in the prosecution's favor, thus freeing the prosecution from the requirement of laying out their evidence in front of the defense. Sneddon's decision to secure a grand jury indictment may have been motivated by the fact that defense lawyers are not allowed to take part in the proceedings.

This way, Sneddon was able to keep the media locked out, and he was also able to prevent his witnesses from being cross-examined.

On April 21, the grand jury formally indicted Michael Jackson, and just four days later, on April 25, Michael abruptly fired his legal team of Mark Geragos and Benjamin Brafman, and replaced them with fifty-three-year-old Thomas Mesereau, notoriously part of actor Robert Blake's defense team. Blake was on trial for solicitation of murder, conspiracy, and special circumstance of lying in wait regarding the May 2001 death of his wife Bonnie Lee Bakley. In March 2005, a jury found Blake not guilty. The attorney also represented boxing legend Mike Tyson in an investigation conducted by the San Bernardino County, California DA in 2001 for alleged rape. Those charges were dropped.

Seeing that a trial, and not a plea deal, was inevitable, Michael lashed out the only way he'd ever known how—by blaming others. He only meant to spread love. He was all about love. It was others who willfully misinterpreted his message, who exploited it to hurt him and shake him down. He was frustrated and scared and he was ill-equipped to deal with either emotion. He had not been this frightened since he was a boy. The only people who seemed to understand were his siblings.

Mesereau was a shrewd choice for Michael because of his close ties to the African American community. In addition to the Tyson connection, the lawyer was known to volunteer two Sundays a month at the First African Methodist Episcopal Church's legal clinic in Los Angeles. Though he was white, with flowing white hair, Mesereau was unabashedly liberal (in stark contrast to his nemesis, Tom Sneddon), his girlfriend was an actress, and like Sneddon, he was an amateur boxer in his college days. Reportedly, Michael had originally implored Mesereau to take on his case a year prior, but he was too tied up with Robert Blake to devote himself to Michael.

That had to have felt like more rejection, the kind that Michael was facing everywhere he turned. What he needed was to feel protected.

Mesereau was surely behind many changes in the Jackson camp. Gone was the Nation of Islam, whom Michael had come to agree was more of a liability to his image. Also stepping into the background was Jermaine, having been replaced by younger brother Randy, whom Michael had turned to in the prior weeks.

The shuffling of Michael's inner deck was nothing new, as noted before. No one knew for sure whether Michael hoped to inject new vigor into his defense team or whether he was merely flailing about in a desperate bid to beat the charges. What was immediately clear was that Michael's newly hired lawyer was ready to put a lid on the high-flying spectacles of past court appearances. Michael would put forth the image of a contrite man, ready and willing to cooperate fully with authorities, though still vigorously denying any wrongdoing.

But the long, sad decline of Michael Jackson—once a chart-topping, record-breaking pop superstar, international celebrity, and self-proclaimed world-wide emissary of peace and love—seemed to have nearly reached its nadir. Since Michael's musical career had stalled years ago, most industry veterans predicted that—even with a successful legal ruling—it was a near impossibility that Michael would ever be able to reclaim a viable singing career. Even though diehard fans still professed undying love for their idol, the ranks were indeed shrinking.

The biggest question still remained: was Michael's time as a free man also running out?

CHAPTER TWENTY-FIVE

THE WESTERN FRONT

On Friday, April 30, 2004, Michael appeared in court to be indicted on the original child molestation charges, as well as new charges of conspiracy involving child abduction, false imprisonment, administering an intoxicating agent to commit molestation, and extortion. A newly transformed Michael Jackson arrived forty minutes early with lawyer Mesereau to a jam-packed Santa Maria, California courthouse, not far from his sprawling Neverland estate.

Michael walked to a microphone and addressed his fans, saying: "I would like to thank the fans around the world for your love, your support from every corner of the globe."

The sartorial flair and outlandish getups Michael had become so famous for were now only hinted at in the form of a red armband he wore around his black velvet jacket. Rather than his ever-present germ-resistant face mask and aviator sunglasses, the fallen superstar wore understated rimless eyeglasses. In place of the various military medallions that usually adorned his clothes, Michael wore a very businesslike red tie.

As one reporter pointed out, "He looked like he was going to do a science project."

Several hundred spectators watched and waited outside the courthouse for a Michael Jackson–style extravaganza, but the consummate showman persona was not to be found that spring day. This scene was in marked contrast to the circus-like atmosphere on January 16, 2004, when Michael arrived twenty minutes late to Superior Court Judge Rodney Melville's courtroom because he was outside the courthouse greeting the nearly 2,500 fans and spectators who showed up to support him.

But Judge Melville's patience was again sorely tested. Whenever one of Michael's relatives entered the courtroom the fans cheered, an obvious breach of courtroom protocol. Although the judge warned Michael at the time—"you have started out on the wrong foot with me"—Michael seemed unfazed, even flippant. That was fear and anxiety talking, not confidence.

When his attorney offered a limp excuse, Judge Melville cut him off.

"I don't want to hear it."

The Jackson clan sat stoically in the courtroom behind the crestfallen forty-five-year-old entertainer, holding each other's hands, no doubt imagining the worst-case scenario for Michael—a conviction of committing lewd acts on a child.

All told, if Michael was found guilty of all charges, he would go to jail for roughly twenty-nine years.

On the other side of the courtroom sat prosecutor Sneddon. Although it isn't customary for district attorneys to try cases, this lawman clearly relished the opportunity to confront Michael directly.

Michael listened intently and quietly as Judge Melville read aloud each charge from a grand jury indictment of the felony charges. With a slight nod and in a soft voice, Michael pleaded not guilty to all counts, just as he had at his January arraignment.

The latest charges against Michael involved two of his former employees and the role they both allegedly played in allegedly threatening Gavin's mother and the rest of her family, as well as preventing them from leaving the Neverland estate.

The conspiracy charge appeared to be a major problem for Michael.

While Sneddon and his team faced an uphill, but not impossible, battle in proving the child molestation charges, proving a crime of conspiracy—which basically amounted to a defendant trying to cover up certain actions—was relatively easier.

Laurie Levenson, a former federal prosecutor and teacher at the Loyola Law School, explained it succinctly: "I would call this the Martha Stewart phenomenon. If you don't get the defendant on the critical act, then you try to get him on the cover-up. Prosecutors love conspiracy charges. They're not hard to prove. You just have to prove two or more people agreed to commit an illegal act."

Sneddon obviously wanted Michael to feel cornered by the charges.

Though Michael's new defense team was taking a less bombastic tone, they still planned to depict the accuser's mother as a money hungry opportunist. A source close to the case told *The National Enquirer*, "A major part of the defense will be that the woman and her son sought revenge on Michael, their benefactor, when he no longer wanted to support them in luxury. They'll show how Michael's help and kindness enabled the boy to get his cancer into remission."

Defenders of Michael claimed that the case lacked the classic courtroom "smoking gun"—some definitive piece of evidence that could guarantee Michael's conviction. Despite the mountains of so-called evidence authorities took during their raid, early indications suggested they were unable to come up with that one key piece of evidence.

So, Michael's attorneys worked overtime to paint the accuser's family as greedy opportunists with a shady background who hoped to get rich quick off the good will of Michael Jackson, the undisputed King of Pop.

Sneddon, in turn, painted a vivid picture of a strangely eccentric man trapped in a Peter Pan fantasy life; a grown individual who never matured past his adolescent years, who preys with precision on disadvantaged children.

It was a somewhat misleading tactic. All but the last part was demonstrably true. Whether that would sway a jury into accepting the predatory allegations was the big question.

Outside the courtroom, Michael's fanbase was losing some of its luster. Michael's supporters had dwindled from the thousands who had shown up at his January arraignment.

Nonetheless, Michael pledged on his website that free chartered buses, dubbed the "Caravan of Love," would be provided for fans to ferry them to and from the court proceedings. He needed his supporters more than ever, no matter what actions he had to take to secure their devotion.

Michael's presumption of innocence was fading faster than his once red-hot musical career. Those qualities that Sneddon had cited, Michael's eccentricities, were creating a perception of culpability: if he's this weird, who knows what he's capable of? Hoping to keep public opinion in check, Mesereau also issued a statement.

"I want to make clear what this case is about," the attorney stated.

"This case is not about lawyers and anyone else becoming celebrities. This defense is going to be conducted with dignity at all times."

Dignity was something Michael desperately needed to reclaim.

Years of one album selling worse than the last, of a grotesque physical transformation, and increasingly bizarre behavior robbed Michael of any sense of dignity in the eyes of the public.

On May 28, a two-hour hearing was held in Santa Barbara Superior Court, which Michael did not attend. Michael's father Joe sat in the courtroom's first row, just behind Michael's lawyers. In addition to the very few Jackson supporters outside the courthouse, this time there was also an equal number of child abuse activists in attendance, as a show of solidarity for the alleged abuse victim. The judge heard arguments from Michael's lawyers that the $3 million bail was set excessively high, though he eventually ruled in early June 2004 that bail was to remain at $3 million.

The judge set a tentative trial date of Friday, September 13, 2004—not a date even slightly superstitious people would want to be bound by, and a date far earlier than most experts predicted.

Although Judge Melville conceded that the trial date could change, he wanted to set "a bullseye that we're shooting at here."

The judge continued, "It is critical I set a trial date. I understand the problem. It may be necessary to change the date later. But someone has to set the goal, to get things going."

Prosecutors had already turned over a mountain of evidence which they believed would put Michael behind bars for many years—2,202 pages of reports, nine audiotapes, two videotapes, and a CD-ROM's worth of photographs.

As for the issue of Michael's bail, prosecutors posited that the more Michael began contemplating life behind bars—which surely wouldn't have offered any of the comfort he had so long been afforded at his Neverland Ranch or at the slew of five-star hotels he had frequented throughout the world—that the superstar might give serious consideration to fleeing the country. Indeed, when Michael was first accused of child molestation, he had taken his time returning to the United States.

Before the trial even started, one outcome seemed certain: the accuser and his family were permanently scarred. In February 2004, the Santa Barbara district attorney's office offered the family twenty-four-hour police protection after they started receiving death threats. The death threats began almost immediately after the Bashir special aired on ABC and continued long after.

Again, this presented a sense of déjà vu.

In 1993, Jackson's accuser and his family also faced death threats. The accuser's father even had a safe room built in his house, had recording devices attached to phones and kept a bulletproof vest and a loaded shotgun by his side. Intimidation of potential witnesses was something that concerned Sneddon, and as he prepared for trial, he intended to show how Michael might have tried to prevent the new accuser from going to the authorities. A source close to the case disclosed that Sneddon was "looking to show that Jackson not only molested the child, but also created a sense of fear for the victim and his family."

By late May 2004, ABC News revealed new details that continued to chip away at Michael's credibility. Two flight attendants who worked on a private plane chartered by Michael, with the accuser and his brother onboard, came forward to say that Michael had asked them to serve him wine in Coke cans.

This would seem to support Gavin's assertion that Michael served him alcoholic beverages disguised as soda pop.

And another witness, a security guard at Neverland, claims he saw the boy so drunk and out of his mind that he was stumbling around the complex.

Another alleged incident, harkening back to when the accuser's family was still on good terms with Michael, occurred when Gavin needed to provide a urine sample to his cancer doctor. Jackson insiders said Michael begged the mother to cancel the appointment because he feared traces of alcohol would show up in the urine. When Janet insisted on going to the appointment, sources said one of Michael's assistants drove them to another doctor's office with the urine sample, where the urine mysteriously disappeared. The assistant's reported excuse to the mother was that the sample had accidentally spilled.

At that point in his life, Michael's future, his fate, and even his legacy hung delicately in the balance.

Sneddon left nothing to chance in his second go-round with Michael. Stung by his experience in 1993, when Jackson's accuser accepted a civil suit settlement and then refused to cooperate with criminal prosecution, Sneddon reportedly had the new accuser's family attorney "solemnly swear" not to pursue a civil lawsuit against Michael until the criminal prosecution was complete.

As Michael's day of reckoning in a Santa Barbara courtroom approached, the world watched as he feverishly tried to prove that he was not a horrible pied piper leading children down a path of depravity.

CHAPTER TWENTY-SIX

THE PEOPLE V. MICHAEL JACKSON

Before he could convince the world that he was not guilty of the charges brought against him, Michael first needed to persuade twelve members of the jury.

Jury selection began approximately one month before the trial, on January 31, 2005.

"I wanted women," Michael's attorney Mesereau said of the potential jurors. "We thought they would be more open-minded about an eccentric artist like Michael Jackson, less prone to judge."

Given Mesereau's preference, the final jury lineup seemed stacked in Michael's favor.

The final roster included eight women and four men. Of those, eight were Caucasian, three were Hispanic, and one was Asian. Although the members of the jury came from all walks of life, several of them had had negative experiences with the law. One juror griped that her grandson should not actually be a registered a sex offender, and another juror's ex-husband was on the Santa Maria police force. Mesereau felt they would sympathize with his client, whose rights and liberties he claimed had also been unjustly violated.

On Monday, February 28, 2005, Michael arrived at the Santa Maria courthouse for the first day of his trial. The performer appeared cool and collected and, most importantly, healthy and sober. He seemed prepared to face his accuser and whatever DA Sneddon would throw at him.

The small courtroom was packed and atypically cramped. The legal battle was scheduled to begin each day at 8:30 a.m. and remain in session for six hours, with only a few brief bathroom breaks.

"It felt like an eight-hour economy-class flight," one reporter noted.

"You were all squeezed into this courtroom with the first-class passengers—Michael Jackson and his family. And the cattle car—the rest of us—we were all squeezed together."

No live media was allowed inside the courthouse.

On that first day, Sneddon led by reading the charges against Michael. They were extensive—though not all of the most egregious claims actually involved Michael. And those that did are not always presented in an explanatory context. That would be Mesereau's job.

Sneddon went through the allegations slowly and carefully. Listening to the lengthy recitation, Michael had to feel shell-shocked and hopeless.

The prosecutor began with "overt acts" which, in law, are acts from which criminal behavior may be implied; that is, an act committed in the pursuance of an intent or design toward criminality before moving on to the counts themselves. There is a twofold reason for overkill in these presentations: first, to meticulously detail what is being alleged and why; but also, to suggest by the sheer mass of information that a defendant must be guilty of something. (Full the full indictment, see Appendix I.)

Because he was a minor, young Gavin had been cited anonymously in the charges. At trial, he was given the option of using an alias with his true name concealed, but the fifteen-year-old bravely opted to use his real name. Before the trial officially started, Sneddon revealed this decision to the judge.

"I discussed it with the family and explained to them the technical problems of trying to go through all the redaction process with every tape and video and everything else," Sneddon told Judge Melville.

"They understood—and they said that they were comfortable with it."

Sneddon then proceeded with his opening statement to the jurors. The DA first explained how Michael's "world was rocked" by the Martin Bashir interview from February 3, 2003, during which the singer's close relationship to Gavin was exposed.

Sneddon maintained:

This case is about the defendant. It's about his manipulation of the young boy's adolescence through exposing him to strange sexual behavior and introducing him to sexually graphic adult magazines. It's about how he traded on the boy's obvious and often expressed admiration for the defendant. And it's about how he exploited the knowledge of the fact that the child had no father in his life . . . He exploited this paternal relationship and created another relationship with the child as a surrogate father, encouraging the child, Gavin Arvizo, the mother, and other members of the family to refer to him as "Daddy" or "Michael Daddy."

Instead of bedtime discussions and children's books, this forty-four-year-old man is sharing with thirteen-year-old Gavin . . . his collection of sexually explicit magazines . . . he's talking to Gavin about masturbation, and he's telling him that it is normal, and that it is okay, and that everybody does it.

The private world of Michael Jackson reveals that instead of cookies and instead of milk, you can substitute wine, vodka, and bourbon.

In defense, Michael's attorney Mesereau presented a scenario that Michael was conned into paying for Gavin's cancer treatment by Gavin's shifty mother Janet.

"The Arvizo family is from Los Angeles," Mesereau began. "We are going to bring in witnesses to tell you about their behavior. For example, Janet and Gavin called comedian Jay Leno and tried to get money from Mr. Leno. Mr. Leno has told the Santa Barbara police, 'Something was wrong. They were looking for a mark. It sounded scripted. The mother was in the background, and I terminated the conversation.'"

Michael's attorney claimed that the Arvizo family had attempted to hit up a slew of celebrities for money.

Mesereau stated:

Comedian George Lopez was approached by Gavin and Janet. He was asked for money. He didn't want to give money, and then they accused him of stealing $300 from Gavin's wallet. An actress named Vernee Watson, who has appeared on *Fresh Prince of Bel Air* and the movie *Antwone Fisher*, met this family at a dance school. As soon as she met

Janet and Gavin, they wanted to move into her house and wanted money. She refused. A comedian named Louise Palanker was approached by Janet, told they needed money for medical bills and living expenses. She was not told that insurance was covering all the medical bills. . . . Efforts were made to reach Adam Sandler, Jim Carrey . . . a number of celebrities. And we will prove to you that the best-known celebrity and the most vulnerable celebrity became the mark: Michael Jackson.

Mesereau portrayed Michael as someone who spared no expense to keep Gavin's spirits up.

Mesereau claimed without equivocation:

Michael Jackson wanted to help Gavin Arvizo. He let them come to Neverland. He sang songs to Gavin. His parents were around, his brothers and sisters were around. And he tried to help Gavin in ways he thought might work. The child was described to him as having very serious cancer, as having had three rounds of chemotherapy, various organs removed . . . that this child was on his last legs. He took him around Neverland. He showed him the animals. He showed him the kind of Disney-like atmosphere that he thought and believes and knows children like. He did things that were unusual. Michael is a voracious reader. He loves to read books on all subject matters. He has close to a million books at Neverland. And he tried to use techniques that he had read about to help cancer patients. For example, he asked Gavin to envision he's playing Pac-Man, and the cancer cells are being gobbled up. . . . He taught him to climb trees when he was well. He did the kinds of things his mother and father had asked Michael Jackson to do. He took a lot of time away from his career to help this child and help his family, never knowing that the trap was being set.

Mesereau's lengthy opening statement continued into the second day of the trial, when he turned one of the most damaging allegations against Michael into an asset.

"Michael Jackson will freely admit that he does read girlie magazines from time to time," Mesereau stated in an attempt to thwart claims that Michael used adult viewing materials strictly to arouse boys like Gavin. "A member of staff will go to the local mart and pick up *Playboy* or *Hustler* from time to time. He absolutely denies showing them to children."

The attorney argued that Michael caught Gavin looking at one of his pornographic magazines and seized it from the boy, thus explaining why both Gavin's and Michael's fingerprints were discovered on the same issue.

Over the next several days, many major players in the case were called as witnesses and each testified against Michael.

First to the stand was television journalist Bashir, whose documentary arguably caused the courtroom clash to ensue. Jurors watched his nearly two-hour documentary *Living with Michael Jackson* before Bashir was grilled by attorney Mesereau.

"Do you consider yourself to be a professional journalist?" the defense attorney prodded.

"My academic studies were not in journalism," Bashir admitted. "They were in the arts and humanities. So, I don't have a formal qualification, if that's what you're asking."

Mesereau hammered away at Bashir, asking dozens of questions about footage that didn't make the final cut of the TV special. Bashir—invoking the California Constitution's shield law that protects the independence of journalists from being called to testify—declined to answer most of them. Mesereau hoped to cast serious doubt on Bashir's journalistic integrity.

Santa Barbara County sheriff's deputy Albert Lafferty, who shot footage of Neverland during the November 18, 2003, police raid, was called to the stand on days three and four of the trial.

The officer recounted the all-day "search warrant" experience and provided commentary for a video of the search that was shown to jurors.

"When the warrant was executed, there were different teams that were assigned to search various locations," deputy Lafferty told Sneddon. "When those people would conduct a search and find an item that they would like to have documented, they would contact us, and we would go and take still photographs of that item before it was collected."

Michael sat in the tense, silent courtroom and watched in horror as his private life and prized possessions were systematically exposed to the world. Only tear-smudged eyeliner revealed the intensity of his distress.

Gavin's older sister, eighteen-year-old Davellin, and his younger brother, fourteen-year-old Star, subsequently testified against the singer.

Davellin claimed: "Mr. Jackson was laying on the bed, and then Gavin was next to him, and then Star. . . . I saw empty bottles or half full bottles of alcohol. . . . Some were on the nightstand."

She shared with the jurors how inappropriate Michael's relationship with Gavin seemed to her.

"Michael Jackson was constantly hugging him and kissing him on the cheek or on the head," Davellin stated under oath. "He didn't want to be hugged; he didn't want to be kissed."

When fourteen-year-old Star was questioned, he stated, "Me and my brother were watching a movie, and Michael walked up naked. And he walked to the corner of the room, picked up something. Me and my brother were grossed out. And he sat on the bed and he told us it was natural, and then he walked back downstairs."

The teenager recounted several occasions at Neverland that put Michael's innocence directly in the crosshairs.

"He asked me if I masturbated," Star testified. "I said, 'No.' He said to me that, 'Everyone does it. You should try it. It's okay.'"

Star said that Michael's "left hand was in my brother's pants and right hand was in his pants."

"When you saw that, did you see what, if anything, he was doing?" Sneddon asked the boy.

"He was masturbating," Star answered, noting that Gavin was asleep during the alleged assault.

"How could you tell that?" Sneddon pressed.

"Because he had his hand in his pants and he was stroking up and down," the boy responded.

Sneddon asked Star if he saw Michael's "private parts."

"Yes," the boy stated. "He had a hard-on."

Star also revealed that, while on a private jet, the King of Pop served him and his brother cans of soda filled with alcohol.

"He leaned over and he handed it to me," the boy told Sneddon. "I thought it was Diet Coke. I didn't want to be rude, so I took a drink, and it tasted like the smell of, like, rubbing alcohol . . . so I handed it back to him. I asked him what it was, and then he said it was wine."

"Did Mr. Jackson have a term that he referred to in connection with the wine?" Sneddon asked.

"He called it 'Jesus Juice.'"

If Michael used that expression at all, it was a reference, no doubt, not to the properties of the wine but the fact that Jesus miraculously made it from water. There was no indication before this that Michael had ever been irreverent in that way. Not with his strict religious upbringing and life as a Jehovah's Witness. In fact—and this pertains to any and all allegations of criminality and immorality—that would have been a big barrier for Michael to overcome.

Years later, after Michael's death, he was briefly eulogized by Michael Bearden, who was to be the music supervisor and keyboardist on Michael's "This Is It" tour—which Michael himself had prophetically described as "the final curtain call."

Bearden says that he and Michael were talking about their musical talents and Michael said, "We gotta be humble. I don't want God to take our gift away. We have to use our gifts together to help others figure out what their gifts are."

The keyboardist was genuinely moved by that, remarking, "He had the humanity. He actually cared about people."

Was it possible, then, that this same man could be guilty of the crime of inebriating a young boy?

Star explained that Michael gave Gavin the same alcohol and that it made his brother act "really weird."

"After a while he didn't feel too good. So, my brother leaned over on Michael's chest and I saw Michael's head licking my brother's—the top of his head."

"What do you mean?" Sneddon inquired.

"He was just licking his head," Star clarified.

"How long did that last?"

"I don't know. Six seconds probably," the boy answered.

To defend Michael's character, attorney Mesereau showed the jury footage of Gavin's mother Janet giving her highest approval of the singer.

"It disturbed me greatly when I saw the innuendos that there was something dirty about it," Janet said on the video, recorded shortly after the Bashir interview aired.

"I am the most vigilant, the most sensitive to making sure my children and I are not subjected to any harm. . . . He took us on as a family unit and I appreciate it with all my heart. We met Michael Jackson when something traumatic and tragic happened to us. Something traumatic was turned into something beautiful."

Mesereau also entered into exhibit a Father's Day card the Arvizo family gave to Michael.

"You always heal us in a very special way," Mesereau read it to the court.

"Michael, you are special to us . . . We loyally and faithfully love you more . . . We love you unconditionally, to infinity and beyond forever . . . Thank you, Michael, for being our family."

"That was before all that happened," Star argued, referring to Michael's alleged sexual abuse.

The notion that Michael had suddenly gone from saint to devil was a difficult point to sell to the jury.

For the duration of the trial, Michael had been sitting silently as he watched each witness attempt to take him down. He felt, at that point, that he and his legal team had been adequately weathering the storm. But as Star was wrapping up his third and final day of testimony, Michael knew that the next witness could decide his fate.

"Nothing further, Your Honor," Sneddon and Mesereau both concurred after questioning Star.

"You may step down," Judge Melville instructed the boy.

The judge then asked Sneddon to call his next witness.

"Gavin Arvizo, Your Honor," Sneddon announced.

Moments later, Michael and his accuser were within a few paces of each other. Neither made eye contact as Gavin took his seat near the judge.

The next four days would be among the most painful Michael Jackson would ever endure.

CHAPTER TWENTY-SEVEN
THE ACCUSER

The punishment began when Gavin took the stand on March 9.

He was cancer-free, healthy-looking, and a robust teenager who had grown considerably since appearing in the videos that were shown to the jury.

The hulking teenager's five o'clock shadow made him seem more like an intimidating young man than a child who was abused by the increasingly withering defendant.

The startling contrast between the younger, sickly version of Gavin was marginalized by the courtroom confessions about his rocky childhood.

"My stomach was hurting a lot," he recalled of the day he discovered he had cancer. "I couldn't sleep at night. I would put my pillow on my stomach because it really hurt. And then I looked at myself in the mirror and lifted up my shirt, and I saw there was a big bump."

Gavin confirmed that doctors removed his infected kidney and spleen. He also confirmed that he had several visitors while recovering at the hospital.

"My old coach, George Lopez, came," Gavin said, referring to his one-time mentor at The Laugh Factory comedy club in Los Angeles. "Then Louise Palanker would visit me. My grandparents would visit me a lot. George Lopez would always bring me shirts and stuff because a lot of my clothes didn't fit me anymore."

The boy also testified that his doctor didn't think he was going to pull through.

"They thought I was sleeping in my bed and they were talking to my mother and my biological father," Gavin told DA Sneddon. "My doctor told them to prepare for my funeral—and that if the cancer didn't kill me, the chemotherapy would. Because the chemotherapy is toxic and they were giving me adult dosages."

After presenting Gavin's emotional journey to the jury, Sneddon steered his questions to how the boy and Michael Jackson became fast friends.

"Gavin, at some point in time, did you have some contact with the defendant in this case, Mr. Jackson?" Sneddon asked.

Gavin admitted that, while still in the hospital, he received an unexpected call from the legendary entertainer.

"I was like, 'Who is this?'" Gavin recalled, confessing that at first, he didn't believe it was really Michael on the phone.

"And how long did the conversation last?" Sneddon inquired.

"That was a pretty short conversation. It was only about, like, five minutes long."

"Now, did you have other conversations with Mr. Jackson?

Gavin told the jury he had.

"Between the time you received the first telephone call from the person identifying themselves as Michael Jackson until you went to the [Neverland] ranch, how many calls did you think you had between you and Mr. Jackson?"

"I don't know, like twenty, maybe," Gavin told Sneddon.

"Were some of them quite lengthy?"

Gavin said they were, and that Michael continued calling him long after the hospital stay.

"So how did you get up to the ranch?" Sneddon asked.

"There was a limousine that came to my grandma's house and then we went up in a limousine."

After firing off several questions regarding Gavin's adventures in Neverland, Sneddon turned the jury's attention back to the true purpose of the case: to decide whether or not Michael Jackson was a pedophile.

"Would you tell the ladies and gentlemen of the jury how it came about that you ended up sleeping with Mr. Jackson in his bedroom?" the prosecutor asked.

"Me, my brother, and Michael . . . we were all in his office, and we were talking," Gavin began. "Then Michael said we should sleep in his room. . . . I was like 'Okay, yeah,' because we, like, wanted to sleep in his room, too. Then he told us to ask in front of our parents if we could sleep in his room. So, I think it was, like, at dinner, we had asked our parents if we could sleep in Michael's room . . . my parents said yeah, it was okay."

Of that first night in Michael's bedroom, Gavin recalled, "We were going to watch some Disney cartoons, and a bunch of these videotapes of *The Simpsons*. And then [Michael's personal assistant] Frank Tyson had a computer . . . and then Frank started doing stuff on the Internet. And then they started looking up, like, adult material sites."

"Was Mr. Jackson there?" Sneddon inquired. "Was Mr. Jackson involved in that?"

"He was, like, pointing out girls. Like, "Oh, I like her." But, he wasn't typing. Frank was typing."

"How many different sites do you think you went to?" asked Sneddon.

"Maybe, like, seven sites," the teenager said, estimating they spent approximately half an hour online. "One time we were looking at the site and there was this girl with her shirt up . . . it was all quiet and stuff, and Michael was like, 'Got milk?' We started laughing because he said that."

Gavin then revealed that Michael's children Prince and Paris were asleep in the same bed. He alleged that, "Michael leaned over to Prince in his ear and he said, 'Prince, you're missing all the pussy.'"

Another round of questions revealed that Gavin had made multiple trips to Neverland and that the youngster was rarely joined by his mother, and then Sneddon switched the topic to the Bashir interview.

"Michael introduced me to Martin Bashir," Gavin stated. "[Michael] was telling me, 'Hey, you want to be an actor, right?' And I was like, 'Yeah. I want to be comedian though.' And then he was like, 'But you can act too, right? Well, I'm going to put you in the movies. And this is your audition, okay?' And he told me, 'Okay. I want you to go in and then tell them about how I helped you.' And he told me to make sure to tell them 'that you call me dad' . . . and that he pretty much cured me of cancer."

"Was it true?" Sneddon questioned.

"Not really," Gavin confessed. "During my cancer, he wasn't really even there."

***

On the second day of Gavin's direct examination—the day he was supposed to provide his "tell-all" testimony to the jury—Michael was still a no-show in the courtroom by 8:30 a.m. Mesereau informed Judge Melville that Michael was suffering from debilitating back pain and would not be in attendance that day.

Judge Melville was unpersuaded by Mesereau's excuse for his client.

"I'm issuing a warrant for his arrest," the judge announced with impatience.

"I'm forfeiting his bail. I will hold the order for one hour."

Meaning, if Michael did not appear in the courtroom by 9:30, he would spend the rest of his trial behind bars and lose the $3 million he put up to remain free during the proceedings.

A short time later, Mesereau gave Judge Melville an update on the defendant.

"Mr. Jackson is at Cottage Hospital in Santa Ynez with a serious back problem," Mesereau informed the court. "He does plan to come in."

According to Michael, he was hospitalized due to a fall at his home.

"I was coming out of the shower," he later claimed.

"All my body weight—I'm pretty fragile—fell against my rib cage . . . I bruised my lung very badly."

Ultimately, Michael finally arrived at the courthouse, though he was a few minutes over the one-hour deadline. He was also a vision of unintentional disrespect for the venue and the proceedings. His hair was untidy. He was wearing Gucci slippers and was dressed in bright blue pajama pants with a black sports coat buttoned up over his casual white shirt.

"I had told Michael he couldn't go home and change," Mesereau recalled. "He had to get to court as quickly as he could. . . . The jurors told me later that they didn't even notice. Michael was sitting down at the defense table when they came in."

Entering the courtroom, Michael was supported on both sides by two men holding his arms as he slowly walked to his place at the table. Even if his malady had been a made-up excuse to avoid an exceedingly tough day in court, at best, Michael seemed emotionally wrecked.

Judge Melville did not fail to notice and went easy on him. Before resuming Gavin's controversial testimony, the judge wanted to make Michael's situation clear to the jury.

"I'm sorry for the delay," Judge Melville announced.

"Mr. Jackson had a medical problem this morning, and it was necessary for me to order his appearance. I'm telling you that because I don't want you to draw any adverse inference about his guilt or inference from the fact that I had to order him here. If one of you had called in and had not appeared, or one of the attorneys, I would have had to do the same thing. The trial is going to go forward."

With Michael firmly planted in his seat, the attention of the courtroom shifted back to his accuser. Sneddon continued his mission to expose Michael's dark side.

"That portion of the video that shows you sitting on the couch with Mr. Jackson, there's a point in time where you place your head on his shoulder and hold hands with Mr. Jackson," the attorney said, resuming his examination of the Bashir interview. "How did that come about?"

"Well, the holding hands part—that was one of the things that Michael told me to do. But I put my head on his shoulder. . . . I was really close to Michael, and he was like my best friend."

Gavin stated that he was disappointed that he didn't hear from Michael again until a few days before the Bashir interview aired on television, and he recounted how their subsequent trip together got out of hand.

"Michael gave me a Diet Coke can," Gavin explained, corroborating his brother's story about Michael serving them "Jesus Juice."

"He told me, 'You know how, like, Jesus drank wine.' I drank a little bit of it and I told him that it tasted ugly."

"And what did he say?"

"He said that, 'It's okay, because it will relax you' and he told me that he knows that I'm all stressed out because of all the media stuff that's going on . . . I probably drank like three-fourths of it."

Gavin confirmed the alleged misdeeds happened on several occasions and with various alcoholic beverages.

"I drank Bacardi, vodka, and Jim Bean [sic]," the minor confessed.

"Did you ever tell Mr. Jackson that you only had one kidney?" Sneddon asked.

"I told him that it was bad for me to drink alcohol. And he said, 'it's okay,' that 'it's fine,' that 'nothing's going to happen.'"

It was after one such instance that Gavin said Michael first sexually assaulted him.

"We just came back from drinking in the arcade, and then we went up to his room. And then we were sitting there for a while, and Michael started talking to me about masturbation. . . . He said that if men don't masturbate, they can get to a level where they might rape a girl or they might be, like, kind of unstable . . . and then he said if I didn't know how that he would do it for me."

"What did you say," Sneddon pressed.

"I said I didn't really want to," Gavin stated. "Then he said it was okay, that it was 'natural,' and that it's natural for boys to do it. And then, so he—we were under the covers, and I had his pajamas on, because he had this big thing of pajamas and he gave me his pajamas. And so I was under his covers and then that's when he put his hand in my pants and then he started masturbating me."

"Did you have an ejaculation?"

Gavin admitted that he had climaxed.

"I kind of felt weird," the boy said of the alleged encounter. "I was embarrassed about it."

Gavin said the "same thing happened again" the following day.

"He said that he wanted to teach me. And then we were laying there and then he started doing it to me. And then he kind of grabbed my hand in a way to try to do it to him. And I kind of—I pulled my hand away, because I didn't want to do it. . . . He would always say that it was 'natural' and 'don't be scared' and it 'was okay.'"

On Gavin's third day in court, during his cross examination, Mesereau accused the teenager of changing his story.

He asked Gavin if he'd confessed to a schoolteacher that Michael was innocent.

"Dean Alpert looked you in the eye and said, 'Are these allegations that Mr. Jackson sexually abused you true,' right? You said they were not true, right?"

"Yeah," Gavin told Mesereau. "I told him that Michael didn't do anything to me."

Looking to further discredit the witness, Mesereau also challenged Gavin's recollection of who told him that men who don't masturbate "might rape a girl."

"You told the police your grandmother made that quote to you," Mesereau stated. "You came into court under oath and told the jury Mr. Jackson made that quote to you."

"That didn't change, because Michael tried to explain to me first," Gavin argued.

"He was more pushing on me that men have to masturbate. Now, later when I came back from Neverland, I guess my grandmother saw that I was very confused about sexuality and things like that. My grandmother explained to me a lot of things."

"What you're telling the jury is it was sort of a coincidence that both your grand-mother and Michael used almost the identical phrase about raping a woman."

"Both my grandmother and Michael were trying to talk to me about the—pretty much the birds and the bees story."

"Okay, and they pretty much said the identical thing," Mesereau said, feeling as though he'd made his point.

During his final day on the witness stand, Gavin clarified why he told his teacher that Michael Jackson hadn't molested him.

The boy told Sneddon, "All the kids would laugh at me and try to push me around and stuff, and say, 'That's the kid that got raped by Michael Jackson,' and stuff like that. . . . I would sometimes not say anything and just walk away. If they got close enough, sometimes I would fight them."

"You were asked yesterday whether you had a conversation with Dean Alpert where he asked you whether or not Mr. Jackson had touched you," Sneddon said.

"You recall that you told him it didn't happen. . . . Why did you tell him that?"

"Because all the kids were already making fun of me in school," Gavin main-tained. "I didn't want anybody to think that it really happened."

For his final question to Gavin, Sneddon asked the boy to give his opinion of Michael "in light of what he did to you."

"I don't really like him anymore," Gavin responded. "I don't really think he's deserving of the respect I was giving him as the coolest guy in the world."

When Gavin's testimony ended on the eleventh day of the trial, both lawyers felt they were ahead in the high-profile case.

"I could see that Sneddon believed he was winning the case because the media said he was winning the case," Mesereau later admitted. "I could see that at least a couple of the jurors were getting more and more disgusted with the prosecution witnesses . . . at least a couple didn't believe a word Gavin Arvizo said."

Mesereau sensed that Sneddon's case was "falling apart." Unfortunately, so were Michael's nerves.

"Even though we were doing well, and he knew it, the trial turned into an immensely exhausting and painful experience for Michael," Mesereau later recalled. "We all believed the most dangerous prosecution witnesses were yet to come."

Indeed, Michael would have to remain in the hot seat for a nearly unbearable period of another fifty-four days.

CHAPTER TWENTY-EIGHT

BREAKING NEWS

Throughout the remainder of the trial, more than Jackson's reputation took a beating.

"It was clear to everyone his health was suffering," one reporter noted. "He became frailer, a lot thinner. . . . It was tragic to watch."

Day after day, Michael sat in the courtroom, seemingly unblinking and devoid of emotion.

"I gain strength from the fact that I know that I am innocent," he said at the time.

"None of these stories are true. They are totally fabricated. . . . It's very painful and, at the end of the day, I'm still a human being, so it does hurt very, very, very much."

Michael listened as his legal team challenged the claims of each of the prosecution's witnesses. After Gavin testified, lead investigator Sheriff's Sergeant Steve Robel took the stand to recap the accuser's allegations of sexual misconduct.

"During my initial interview with [Gavin], he had told me that he was specific about two events that he recalled occurring. And he also told me that he believes that it happened between five and seven times. And he could not articulate exactly what occurred, but he believes that it happened more than twice."

Additional testimony revealed that Gavin may have been unknowingly molested several times by Michael while sleeping. Michael's co-counsel, Robert Sanger, accused the officer of being biased against the defendant. The attorney cited a portion of Davellin's 2003 statement to police, after which Robel attempted to reassure the Arvizo family:

"One thing I wanted to say and emphasize to you is that you guys are doing the right thing here," Robel reportedly said. "You know what, I know it's scary, and I realize that you guys are going through a lot and you've been through a lot as a family. They're the ones that have done wrong, not you. And trust me in this, and trust Detective Zelis, we're law enforcement. We're going to try our best to make this case work. I can't guarantee it, where it's going to go from here, but that's why we're interviewing everybody involved. I don't care how much money they have. . . . You guys are the victims. Your family is. He is wrong in what he's done. We're going to try our best. Can't guarantee it. We're going to try our best to bring him to justice." Did you say that?

"I definitely said that," Robel responded.

"That's not the statement of somebody who has an open mind who's looking to see whether or not these people are telling the truth, is it?" questioned Sanger.

"Through my courses that I've had—you have victims that are terrified in coming forward to law enforcement," Robel said. "That is to reassure them that they are not the suspects or they are the victims in the case. I was reassuring them through that and letting them know that they are doing the right thing, because they were terrified when they came forward. It took us about two weeks to get them to come forward and up here to be interviewed."

After Robel stepped down, the prosecution began one of the most contentious portions of the trial. For several hours, the covers and interior pages from adult magazines—all seized from Neverland—were displayed on the big screen in the courtroom. Michael and his family, spectators, and members of the press, watched as the slideshow of nude women was presented to the jury. None of the pictures showcased child pornography. The prosecution was presenting pages and pages of evidence that Michael used these easily accessible magazines to arouse boys.

"We're all sitting in back of poor Mrs. Jackson," one reporter recalled. "At one point, she started nodding off . . . and Mrs. Jackson wakes up and says, 'What's going on? Oh, more porn.'"

Investigators noted that all of the exhibited adult materials were recovered from Michael's bedroom during the raid in November 2003. However, some of the dates on the evidence presented an issue for the prosecution. One magazine—"confirmed" to have been shown to Star Arvizo by the defendant—was from "August 2003," but the Arvizo family hadn't set foot on Neverland after March 12.

The embarrassing pornography presentation seemed to only reinforce that Michael Jackson was very much into women, not boys.

On March 30, 2005, a major development in the trial put Michael's quest for vindication in jeopardy. Judge Melville decided to allow testimony from several other children—Wade Robson, Brett Barnes, Macaulay Culkin, and Jason Francia—the latter of whom had claimed that the defendant sexually abused him on three occasions. And, once again, Michael was forced to square off against his former accuser Jordan Chandler.

"I knew that three of those boys—Robson, Barnes, and Culkin—were not going to testify for the prosecution," Mesereau later claimed. "I wasn't that afraid of Jason Francia. The Jordan Chandler allegations, though, those were a major concern. I knew we might win or lose this case on whether or not the jurors believed Michael had molested Jordie."

Rather surprisingly, Jordan "had no interest" in testifying against Michael.

The twenty-five-year-old had been living under the radar since his 1993 lawsuit and he informed the FBI that he would "legally fight any attempt" to force him to appear in court.

Instead, Sneddon put Jordan's mother, June, on the stand.

On April 11, after rehashing how Jordan befriended Michael, and how Michael begged June to let them share a bed, the mother recalled a strained conversation she had with Michael regarding her son.

"'Why are you objecting to Jordie staying with me?'" June claimed Michael asked her. "'Why can't we be a family? Why don't you trust me?' He was upset that I wanted my son back. I didn't like the situation. It was getting out of hand."

Although June demonstrated that Michael was guilty of throwing tantrums, she did little to persuade the jury that Michael was guilty of molesting her child.

During Francia's testimony, the twenty-four-year-old told the jury how, when he was around seven, Michael used to constantly tickle him.

"I was sitting on his lap," Francia stated.

"I was young, and I was small . . . my back was to his chest . . . and I was just sitting there watching TV and so was he. I think we were watching cartoons. He just started tickling me . . . and then I'm tickling and he's tickling, and it eventually moved down to my little private region . . . around my crotch area."

"Did he actually make contact with your genital area?" Sneddon asked.

"Not skin to skin, but, yeah. Yeah, he was on my clothes."

Later in his testimony, Francia admitted, "Every time I was being tickled, there was always some sort of money exchanged. Not exchanged. There was money given . . . and it was kind of a 'Don't tell your mom about the money.'"

"What would he give you?"

"A hundred-dollar bill."

"Did he do this on more than one occasion?" Sneddon pressed.

"Yeah," the witness said, "because I had a lot of money."

But Michael's defense team rattled Francia by revealing that the witness's mother had sold his story to *The National Enquirer* and a primetime television news program. Unaware that she had done that, Francia's testimony became inconsistent and he started contradicting his own statements.

Prosecutors also called several members of Michael's Neverland staff to testify against their employer. Ralph Chacon, a former security guard at the ranch, stated that he saw Michael kiss Jordan and that "Mr. Jackson's hands went down to his crotch."

"The boy's?" Sneddon clarified.

"Yes, sir," Chacon said.

Former maid Adrian McManus recalled seeing "Mr. Jackson and Macaulay in the library, and Mr. Jackson was kissing him on his cheek, and he had his hand kind of by his leg, kind of on his rear end."

"What was the next thing that you saw that caused you concern?" Sneddon asked Adrian.

"Brett Barnes," she said.

"I was up in the video room, and Mr. Jackson had me taking videos out of the wall . . . and there was like—I don't know what you call them—like wood things that would hold the videos, and they had, like, screws in the wall. So, I was pulling those all out because he had heard that you could see down into his bedroom."

"So, did you, in fact, remove videotapes?"

"Yes."

"Could you see down into the bedroom?"

"Yes," she admitted.

Subsequent questioning by Michael's defense team illustrated that the two ex-employees were bitter about a "wrongful termination" lawsuit and sought to "get even" with Michael, who had sued them for a million dollars.

Flight attendant Cynthia Bell testified that Michael did, in fact, drink wine from soda cans. However, she claimed he did to keep the adult beverage "private from his children." She did not recall seeing any inappropriate contact between Michael and Gavin.

On April 27, Michael's scorned ex-wife Debbie Rowe was called to testify, seemingly a solid witness for the prosecution. However, the mother of two of Michael's children—who had not seen her ex-husband since their divorce in 1999—had a change of heart when she took the stand.

"As soon as she took one look at Michael, everything changed," Mesereau recalled. "The reality of it all hit her. . . . He was vulnerable, and she didn't want to hurt him."

During her testimony, Debbie made her attitude towards the entertainer very clear.

"I promised him that I would always be there for him and the children," she stated, admitting that she was hoping to "renew a relationship with Mr. Jackson."

The prosecution rested on May 4, having presented over five hundred pieces of evidence and eighty-five witnesses. The defense took control of the trial the following day.

Heading into the third month of the trial, Mesereau called several key witnesses in Michael's defense. On May 5, Robson took the stand and contradicted claims that Michael touched him "in a sexual way."

"Never, no," the twenty-two-year-old said.

On May 11, Culkin admitted that he often slept in Michael's bed, but the *Home Alone* star "never saw it as an issue."

"What do you think of these allegations?" Mesereau probed.

"I think they're absolutely ridiculous," Culkin insisted. "It was amazing to me that they—that nobody approached me and even asked me whether or not the allegations were true. . . . They didn't even double-check it."

Towards the end of the trial, multiple celebrities weighed in on Michael's innocence and the dubious experiences they had with the Arvizo family. Jay Leno testified that he felt his interactions with Gavin were "suspicious."

"It was unusual to have a twelve-year-old child leave you a long voice message," the former *The Tonight Show* host stated, but acknowledged that "no one asked me for money."

Actor Chris Tucker admitted to the jury that he had a similar experience with Gavin at a fundraiser held to help pay for the boy's cancer treatment.

"He was just real sad-looking and said they didn't raise any money, and they needed some money," the *Money Talks* star said.

"Now, you saw people at that fundraiser, right?" Mesereau inquired.

Tucker said he had.

"Were you a little suspicious when Gavin made that statement to you?"

"Yes," Tucker acknowledged, "but I was always thinking I was helping him, so I just did it."

By May 27, the defense had called nearly fifty witnesses. But as both attorneys wrapped up their cross-examinations, several unsettling details from the trial remained uncontested.

It was confirmed that, over a two-year period, Michael shared his bed with a young Brett Barnes on more than 450 occasions.

Michael had visible, readily available porn stashes scattered throughout the main residence at Neverland. He frequently telephoned compliant parents late at night and requested the company of their boys in his bedroom. On one occasion, he spent nearly a half an hour arguing with June about letting Jordan sleep in his bed. Although these startling facts were irrefutable, they weren't crimes.

In the closing arguments for the prosecution, Senior Deputy District Attorney Ronald Zonen hoped to show the jury how susceptible the boys who visited Neverland were to Michael's unchecked corruption:

> They did whatever they wanted to do during the course of the day and at night, they entered into the world of the forbidden. At night they went

into Michael Jackson's room, which is a veritable fortress. It is a room that nobody else has access to. It is a room that has codes and locks and multiple doors and alarm systems, and they knew all of those alarm systems and all of those codes, and they stayed there, and they knew all of that information because Michael Jackson wanted them to know all of that information. And inside that room, in the evening time, they entered the world of the forbidden and they learned about human sexuality from somebody who is only too willing to be their teacher. And that discussion began with looking at magazines, looking at pornography, looking at a collection of sexually explicit material. It began with very frank discussions about sexuality designed to reduce their inhibitions. It began with discussions about masturbation. It began with discussions about nudity. It included a presentation by himself, nude, to them, to these children. It included an act of simulating a sex act on a mannequin that was up in the room. . . . The grooming process takes a while. Not a terribly long while, but a while. And it begins with the selection of a vulnerable child. Gavin Arvizo, demonstrating remarkable courage in coming into this courtroom, gave testimony to you about a series of events that took place in Michael Jackson's bedroom when Michael Jackson, not for the first time, took sexual liberties with a thirteen-year-old boy. That information and testimony is entirely credible, entirely accurate, and entirely truthful. It should be believed, and Michael Jackson should be held responsible for what he did.

The closing arguments made in Michael's defense were given by Mesereau. In his lengthy final plea to the jury, the attorney stated:

The issue in this case is the life, the future, the freedom, and the reputation of Michael Jackson. That's what's about to be placed in your hands. And the question you have before you is very simple. Do you believe the Arvizos beyond a reasonable doubt, or not? If you don't, Mr. Jackson must go free. . . . If you have any reasonable doubt about this case, about the testimony, about the double-talk, the lies, about their past, about their motives, it's over. You must acquit Michael Jackson to follow the law.

Michael's trial had lasted an anguishing and somewhat agonizing sixty-six days, and the degree of his innocence was now entirely up to the jury. "There really wasn't anything to do but wait," Mesereau later recalled.

During the next ten days, the jury spent over thirty hours debating the outcome. After their first vote, the tally was split nine-to-three in favor acquitting the singer. But their verdict had to be unanimous.

By June 13, the jury was ready to make their announcement.

That day, Michael shuffled slowly into the courtroom, visibly crushed under the weight of the pending charges, the bare-all trial, and his crumbled charisma. He seemed perilously drugged and overtly convinced that he was "guilty."

"He was strained beyond description," Mesereau explained. "He looked more emaciated, frailer, more out of it than I had ever seen him."

Shortly after 2 p.m., with tension so thick it was like a spectator, the jury read through each charge. Michael Jackson was found "not guilty" on all counts.

The superstar appeared to be the last person in the courtroom to react to the breaking news.

"His first reaction was gratitude," Mesereau recalled.

"Gratitude to God, gratitude to his defense team, gratitude to his family and friends . . . he said the words, 'Thank you, thank you, thank you.'"

Judge Melville made the official announcement to the defendant, "Mr. Jackson, your bail is exonerated, and you are released."

Outside the courtroom, armed guards surrounded Michael, who was whisked away amidst a media firestorm. Mesereau did not hurry off. He used the opportunity to address the press and did so as he had defended Michael: with dignity, sincerity, and directness.

"This prosecution was a travesty of justice and one of the most mean-spirited attacks on an innocent person in legal history," Mesereau stated.

"Justice was done. The man is innocent. He always was."

In response to a question about Michael's habit of allowing boys to sleep in his bed, Mesereau answered flatly, "He's not going to do that anymore."

The sad coda for Michael, apart from the shredding of his privacy, is that after the trial, he never returned to his beloved Neverland and the ranch was officially closed. Although he was fully exonerated of any legal wrongdoing, the compound and everything on it, every memory, every corner, was tainted. His quality of life seemed permanently ruined.

Those close to him ached for him. In particular, his goddaughter Lucy, the daughter of Michael's friend, child star Mark Lester. She was so close to Michael's children that they considered themselves cousins.

During the trial, Lucy was in anguish for her beloved godfather. She remembers waiting for her parents to pick her up one day when she heard two girls talking trash about Michael.

"They weren't to know he was a friend of the family," she said recently, "but it was all I could do not to say something to them."

The truth about the Michael she knew is that when he would see her and her siblings, he would hug them, "and just start talking about normal stuff like how we were getting along in school? He was very down to earth, and he'd just talk about the family and everyday things.

"It's weird because the media make him out to be wacky and eccentric, but for me he was just a family friend."

Now, the personal, private part of that friend was irreparably damaged. The question was: did anything survive?

Not surprisingly, showing the same grit and courage he had mustered to stand up to his father, Michael was determined to defy the odds—and climb the charts—one more time.

CHAPTER TWENTY-NINE
HELL TO PAY

Even though Michael had persevered against his accuser, it was hardly a celebratory moment. To those closest to the singer, he appeared defeated. The media had sold the public on Michael's guilt. His songs no longer played on the radio and he was over $400 million in debt. Michael had about $600,000 in cash—a relatively modest sum when compared to the $2 million a month it took to run his personal empire.

Michael, almost involuntarily, went into seclusion.

"He was depressed, anxious, and unable to eat or sleep," an insider said. "You don't just bounce back after something like that."

Even weeks after the trial ended, Michael admitted, "I wake up feeling upset and scared to death, and it takes me a half hour to remember that it's over."

Michael distanced himself from anything—and everyone—that reminded him of his courtroom nightmare. He didn't want to see his parents or siblings. He couldn't face the press. And maybe most sadly, he wanted nothing more to do with Neverland.

During the trial Michael had remained at his ranch, but he hadn't slept in the main residence. He felt—and rightly so—that his Shangri-La estate had been desecrated by the police during their raid. Instead, Michael stayed in the nearby guest quarters. But following the trial, Michael wanted out of Neverland—for good.

On June 17, the Jackson family held a party for Michael at a casino in Santa Ynez. Tito performed, Janet mingled with fans, and "Beat It" was blasted over the sound system. But Michael was not in attendance.

"I think that by the time the trial was over, Michael wasn't sure he wanted to live anymore," Mesereau confessed.

The attorney advised his client to leave town, recharge, and prepare to reboot.

"Michael had been drained of his strength, of his happiness, of his hope," Mesereau said. "I just had this gut feeling that the authorities in Santa Barbara weren't going to let it go, that they were going to find a way to make a new case against Michael."

On June 19, 2005, Michael went into exile. The singer, his three children, and their nanny, Grace, quietly flew to Paris. Within the week they'd relocated to Bahrain, a small bustling urban state in the Persian Gulf. The Jacksons stayed with Michael's friend, Sheikh Abdullah bin Hamad bin Isa Al Khalifa, who had loaned the singer over $2 million to pay off some of the $30 million he racked up during the trial.

A year earlier, Jermaine had introduced Michael to Sheikh Abdullah.

The men had discussed possibly teaming up for a music-related fundraiser to aid victims of natural disasters. Abdullah, an aspiring songwriter, decided to build a recording studio so he and Michael could one day collaborate. He was hoping that day had finally come.

Abdullah afforded Michael and his family a luxurious refuge and provided them with the extravagances to which they were accustomed: a posh residence, high-end cars, expensive trips, and handpicked attendants. Abdullah even paid some of Michael's past-due Neverland bills. But Michael had a different, less career-minded plan.

Instead being married to his music, Michael spent his days being a father to his children. At that time, his kids were all he was truly passionate about. He was no longer concerned about maintaining his worldwide fame or his foothold in the music industry. The nearly fifty-year-old man just wanted to be left alone.

He took his children to the movies and spent the summer trying to relax. To conceal his identity while moving throughout Bahrain, the singer would dress in an *abaya*—a customary head-to-toe dress worn by Arabic women. He realized he just wanted to disappear, to live off the grid—perhaps to finally grow up.

Rather coincidentally, around the same time, Sheik Abdullah was beginning to think that Michael was simply sponging off him—and quite understandably. To raise some quick cash, Michael had made a lucrative music deal with the sheik. Abdullah had given the singer a $7 million advance to write and record new songs that the sheik would release on his label, Two Seas Records. After accepting the money, Michael backed out on the deal. He claimed the cash had been given to him as a gift. Abdullah did not, and he sued Michael for the full amount.

In mid-2006, Michael left Bahrain on a "vacation," never to return.

After a brief stay at the Cliveden House mansion in rural Southeast England, Michael and his family settled at the remote Grouse Lodge in County Westmeath, Ireland, where they remained throughout the summer. Grace had staked out the farmyard lodging—a nearly 300-year-old stone-structured estate known for its state-of-the-art recording studios—which reportedly cost the singer $150,000 a month. Michael and his clan stayed in a three-bedroom cowshed-turned-cottage.

Although he was in the middle of nowhere, Michael seemed to have everything he truly needed. His family was chauffeured around by a local taxi driver who blacked out the car windows to keep the Jackson's European occupation top secret. And the staff at Grouse Lodge cooked fresh, healthy meals for Michael, who preferred fish and poultry with a side of veggies.

"The guy was fit," Grouse Lodge owner Paddy Dunning recalled. "He was getting stronger."

In Westmeath, Michael began to experience something he hadn't felt in a long time: inner peace. When he decided to stick around, Paddy moved Michael to their more spacious neighboring estate, Coolatore. The rustic six-bedroom, five-bathroom Victorian manor boasted high vaulted ceilings and long hallways, decadent living and dining rooms, and a library with a secret staircase that descended to a bar in the basement. The refreshing locale got Michael's creative juices flowing.

Michael rented out one of the music studios at Grouse Lodge. To help him lay down some new tracks, the singer flew out several musical collaborators, including The Black Eyed Peas star will.i.am.

"When he called me to ask him to work with him, I didn't believe it was him," the rapper said, admitting that the music they recorded will never get released. "Those songs weren't perfected in the way someone like him wanted them to be perfected."

Paddy recalled one special evening where he, Michael, and music producer Nephew all jammed together.

"Michael was on the drums, I was playing guitar, and Nephew was on the keyboards and we just started getting a rhythm together," Paddy said. "Slowly but surely, Nephew just creeped the song into 'Billie Jean.' It was just mad playing 'Billie Jean' with Michael Jackson."

But the extended stay in Ireland might have relaxed Michael just a smidge too much. During a dinner with his newfound friends, the singer bragged that he had a secret vault buried at Neverland that the police missed during their 2003 raid.

"I've tricked them all," Michael reportedly admitted.

"They think they found strange things in my house. But really, they will never see the real stuff."

Those present at the dinner party believed he was referring to a stash of child porn as well as photos and videos he made showing him abusing a string of children.

A source revealed:

In the aftermath of his trial, Michael was angry and very anti-authority and one night over dinner it just all came pouring out. He specifically boasted that anything that he really cared about wasn't in the house at Neverland, so the FBI had been looking in all the wrong places when they staged their huge swoop operations on the property. He said he was always ready for the raid because he felt people were trying to set him up and get him jailed.

So, he built a hidden vault in the woodland area of the property where he spent so much of his time. He claimed under one of his favorite trees there was a "dummy tree stump" and that's where the "really personal stuff" was hidden. He said they'd never get it.

But the insider said Michael might not have been as clever as he thought, as it is believed the vault may be buried under the singer's favorite tree at Neverland, which he loved to climb while acting out fantasies he was Peter Pan.

One source added:

A lot of pedophiles like to record their acts so they can watch them back, and Michael had the means to set up secret cameras all over

Neverland. He even had a secret bedroom in the home that has long been suspected he used to molest children. If the vault he spoke of can be found, the FBI may finally have the smoking gun that proves Jackson was abusing kids. There could be pictures and videos in there that would shock the world and his millions of fans.

Michael's Irish acquaintances claimed they withheld reporting the information to the FBI out of respect for his musical legacy; however, they now admit being "haunted by guilt as new allegations seem to keep emerging about Jackson."

The source added, "If a report is made that Jackson has a stash of potentially incriminating child pornography and videos on the grounds of Neverland, the FBI cannot be seen to do nothing, especially as the allegations against Michael seem to keep coming each year."

Although Michael had gone house hunting in Ireland, the singer and his family covertly returned to the US at the end of 2006, only a few days before the new year. The singer holed up in Las Vegas, where he rented a seven-bedroom, $150,000-a-month mansion near the legendary downtown Strip.

Of course, his arrival didn't remain secret for long.

Paparazzi swarmed the palatial residence and rumors began to circulate that the King of Pop was staging a comeback, perhaps even considering a "residency" concert series in Sin City.

But the rumors remained purely speculative.

Fatefully, the only person seen regularly coming or going from Michael's rental home was the family's new physician, who was recommended by a member of Michael's security team when Paris was reportedly battling the flu.

The doctor's name was Conrad Murray. And soon, Michael would become his patient, too.

CHAPTER THIRTY

DOMESTIC HARMONY

In the spring of 2007, Michael was faced with the very serious threat of losing everything. The pop star hadn't toured in a decade. His tarnished "image" was only generating approximately $100,000 a year—or about two percent of what his brand used to command. Michael had used his Beatles song catalogue as collateral to secure loans, but even those had been refinanced several times. His expenses exceeded his income by millions, and yet, Michael's spending showed no signs of slowing down.

Unfortunately, the same was not true for the singer himself.

Michael knew he needed to make a change, but he seemed physically and psychologically incapable of it. He was rarely seen in public, and when he did surface, he wore a surgical mask while being carted around in a wheelchair, flanked by his security team and his increasingly rambunctious children. While publicly it appeared that Michael was in no rush to save his career, privately he was battling something more serious than public humiliation.

Michael was reportedly suffering from an inherited genetic condition called Alpha-1, a disease that destroys the body's ability to defend the lungs from inflammation. The liver makes Alpha-1 antitrypsin (AAT), a protective protein that is sent to the lungs.

In Michael's case, these AAT protein cells would get stuck in his liver. It gave him chronically inflamed lungs and made him especially susceptible to adverse health effects. More obvious symptoms of Alpha-1 include shortness of breath, reduced mobility, weight loss, respiratory infections, and a rapid heartbeat, all of which Michael seemed to be plagued with.

While there is still some debate about whether he truly had the disease, it's clear that Michael liked the theatrical effect of fighting for his life.

A source who was close to the star at the time called him "a publicity hound who thinks that news of illness will make him more sympathetic to the public. He learned this from Elizabeth Taylor . . . the kooky former King of Pop is just fine, playing with his kids, and living large in a house he can't afford."

If Michael didn't actually have an ongoing medical emergency, perhaps he needed the appearance of one to hide that he was getting daily doses of Propofol—a doctor-administered anesthesia only used on patients in hospitals—in the privacy of his home. Michael relied heavily on the intravenously injected drug to help him sleep, which meant he also needed a full-time doctor to give it to him.

More than likely, both dreadful medical scenarios kept Michael perpetually backed into a corner.

For the next year, Michael traveled back and forth between Las Vegas and New York City, but committed himself to neither city—likely because he couldn't lay down the cash on a King of Pop–worthy home.

Although he was keen on buying a $50 million estate in Las Vegas once owned by the Sultan of Brunei, Michael couldn't even pay the security team that helped him tour the property. While in Las Vegas, Michael was subsisting off the hospitality of others, like casino mogul George Maloof. The tycoon invited Michael and his children to live in the five-figure sum per night penthouse suite at The Palms, free of charge.

"He touched base about every other day just to say 'Hi,'" Maloof said. "He was always a gentleman, never asked for anything outrageous."

During his two-month stay, Michael worked in the resort's lavish recording studio, Studio at The Palms. The singer was revamping *Thriller* for a special 25th anniversary release called *Thriller 25*. The album included new versions of his classic songs, like "Beat It" featuring will.i.am and Fergie, and "Billie Jean" featuring Kanye West.

Thriller 25 debuted in February 2008 and, much to Michael's surprise, it was a hit.

"I can't believe people actually bought it," the demoralized singer admitted. "I'm really shocked."

The re-issued record sold over 150,000 copies in its first week and reached number two on the US charts, number three in the UK, and went all the way to the top in nearly a dozen countries.

On August 22, just over of a week before Michael's fiftieth birthday, the compilation album *King of Pop* was released. The record featured a collection of Michael's songs as voted on by his fans. It launched in over twenty-five countries—the US not included—and the track list varied from region to region. "Billie Jean" was the only song featured on all twenty-eight different versions.

Despite impressive sales of both albums, Michael didn't see a dime from either. All of his royalties were withheld to repay his debts to the record label.

Although Michael was flooded with lucrative job opportunities in Las Vegas, he turned them all down. He didn't believe he could go full throttle for five nights a week and 250 shows a year.

Michael stated, "I can't just be like the Osmonds. I can't just sit on a stool and sing . . . People want me to dance from beginning to end . . . that's a lot of work. I don't know how much longer I can do it. I don't know when it'll just not be possible."

Sadly, Michael wasn't using hyperbole; the fifty-year-old had severe arthritis. Even those closest to him were kept in the dark about how bad his debilitating joint disease had become. His spine, knees, ankles, and even his fingers were painfully inflamed and stiff from a lifetime of performing.

A close friend said at the time, "This is why he uses the wheelchair. He's breaking down in so many ways. It's hard to imagine him on stage. In fact, it's hard for him to imagine it."

As if things couldn't get any worse, Michael was staring down the barrel of dozens of lawsuits brought against him, many for delinquent bills. Even *Thriller* director Landis was suing the superstar for $1 million for his unpaid share of the film profits.

Fearing economic ruin, Michael called upon top tier financial advisor Tohme Tohme to help bail him out.

After analyzing his assets, the money whiz agreed that Michael's situation was grave. He gave the frazzled singer two options: one, file for bankruptcy; or two, go on tour.

Tohme agreed to spare Michael more big-league embarrassment by personally investing over $20 million to save Neverland from foreclosure. But his motives weren't entirely selfless. Tohme knew that if he could protect Michael from financially imploding, and help the star shoot back to the top, that his newest real estate investment would go way up.

Out of options, Michael followed Tohme's lead and took a meeting with concert producer Randy Phillips. Back in 2007, Phillips had propositioned him to headline the then-brand new O2 Arena in London, England. But, fearing poor ticket sales and lacking the confidence to perform, Michael had passed. But by mid-2008, Michael's tune had changed. He was determined to do a string of shows in 2009.

Eager to give Michael what he needed to succeed, Phillips spotted the singer nearly $20 million, a portion of which Michael used to pay off Sheik Abdullah. His front-end deal also included a luxurious rental property in Los Angeles, where rehearsals for the comeback concerts would take place. Technically, Michael was merely amassing more debt. But even after the advanced funds were repaid with his future concert revenue, Michael stood to clear $1 million per show. The big question was: how many performances did Michael think he could pull off?

"I would trade my body for his tomorrow," Phillips promoted at the time. "He's in fantastic shape."

On January 26, 2009, Michael agreed to do ten blockbuster shows, all to be held at the O2 Arena starting in July. He was finally ready to return to California, confident that the golden gate would once again welcome him home.

Unfortunately, he got way more than he bargained for.

CHAPTER THIRTY-ONE

TIME & PRESSURE

Michael Jackson's decision to perform again was being touted as his "comeback," but the thirteen-time Grammy winner had not "failed" at anything from which he needed to come back. He was really coming out of retirement.

Michael hadn't released a studio album since 2001. His last music tour, the *HIStory* World Tour, ended in 1997 and subjected the then-thirty-eight-year-old entertainer to eighty-two shows in over fifty cities. Michael hadn't planned on appearing on the global stage again. He did not yearn for it. The fifty-year-old veteran had to be coerced into it for financial reasons.

"The vultures who were pulling the strings somehow managed to put this concert extravaganza together behind his back," an insider told me. "They told him that this would be the greatest comeback the world had ever known. They were armed with all these studies conducted by a London agency showing that Michael could still sell out a stadium for weeks . . . that's what convinced him."

Tohme negotiated a deal that gave Michael an irresistible ninety percent of the net ticket sales. With nearly twenty thousand seats at the London arena, and an average ticket price of $100, the dollars added up quickly for the cash-strapped superstar. All he had to do was show up and perform ten times. At least, that's what he thought he agreed to do. He felt that he could manage that.

From an early age, Michael had learned to manage his own business affairs and to intelligently assess complicated contracts. Although everyone wanted to work with Michael, no one liked negotiating with him. He was sharp and made very few business-related errors in his forty-year career. But in January 2009, Michael signed his O2 concert contract without fully analyzing the documents—another red flag of his unrelenting decline.

And the oversight cost him dearly.

Initially, Michael only had a verbal contract for his ten-date set, to which he reluctantly agreed. But without warning, that number more than tripled and no one highlighted the change before the star signed the paperwork.

On page three of his formal contract, clause three explicitly stated: "Artistco (Michael Jackson) hereby pre-approves up to thirty-one shows, or such other greater number as agreed by Artistco and Promoter, at the O2 Arena in London, England between July 26 and September 30, 2009."

But the unexpected change-up did not end there.

The entire nineteen-page contract—not a very long contract, as these things go—is filled with caveats and very loose definitions, all of which had the potential to saddle the star with additional burdens, both physical and financial.

Michael didn't realize it at the time, but he was on the hook for every penny spent to produce the epic event.

On page fifteen of the contract, the producers decreed that the "Artist's Net Tour Income means the Contingent Compensation minus the sum of Production Costs." In other words, Michael would get paid once all tour-related overhead was paid off. And on page seventeen, the contract defined "production costs" as: "(a) all Artist-related production and related costs including, but not limited to sound and lights, rigging motors, staging elements, video, pyro, photos and bios of Artist, televised broadcasts; (b) the cost of all musical instruments as well as the cost of transporting, storing and insuring all such musical instruments; (c) personnel costs for the Tour Party (including transportation, feed and accommodations); (d) salaries, wages, per diems, payroll taxes and expenses, union dues and other labor costs and benefits of musicians and dancers and other non-management members of the Tour Party; (e) travel and transportation costs (including trucking, bussing and freight, and local ground and show transportation for the tour party; (f) tour design fees and tour creative art; (g) visa & immigration costs; (h) all such other costs for which an artist is customarily responsible, including, without limitation, worker's compensation and liability; (i) cancellation insurance to cover the risk of loss of Artistco's profits and Production Costs in an amount which, at a minimum, is equivalent to or exceeds any unrecouped portion of the Advances and costs related to naming Promoter as a loss payee on such insurance."

Essentially, he was financially liable for anything and everything that anyone might require to put on the Michael Jackson show every night. The contract also stipulated that should Michael have to cancel the show he would still be responsible for costs, even if the producers were reimbursed by the insurance policy, which Michael was also slated to pay for.

What's more, page fourteen of the contract stipulated that "facsimile copies of photocopies of signatures" were considered "as valid as originals." Meaning that if anyone representing Michael wished to change the scope or parameters of the contract, they did not need that star's actual signature or approval to do so.

Quite tragically, Michael's short-term residency at the O2 Arena had been turned into a life sentence.

Meanwhile, Michael was also battling to save his wealth of belongings from the auction block. He knew he had spent wildly and irresponsibly, but he thought the income stream would never stop. While Neverland faced foreclosure, elite Beverly Hills auction house Julien's Auction had combed the estate gathering the star's possessions, including memorabilia, antiques, cars, the ornate front gates of the ranch, and even his trash cans. Michael sued Julien's, arguing that he had never authorized the sale of his possessions.

In that instance, with millions of dollars and valuable reputations at stake, and with Michael seeking to save both his belongings and his dignity, both sides compromised. The two factions released a joint statement: "There was so much interest from so many of Jackson's fans that instead of putting the items in the hands of private collectors, Tohme and Julien's Auction House have made arrangements that will allow the collection to be shared with and enjoyed by Jackson's fans for many years to come."

Julien's put together a Michael Jackson exhibition in Beverly Hills. They charged a $20 entrance fee and sold high-end hardcover catalogues advertising the items that were previously headed for auction. A single volume went for $50 and the full five-volume set was available for $200.

"It was in our best interest to resolve it," auction house owner Darren Julien said.

"We continue to have great respect for Michael Jackson. I guess you could call it the greatest auction that never happened."

With his personal affairs seemingly under control, Michael gave his full attention to public obligations. The aging entertainer underwent a rigorous four-hour physical exam and multiple doctors deemed him fit to perform.

Likely still fresh in Michael's mind, however, was his last public performance three years earlier. The star delivered a messy rendition of "We Are the World" at the 2006 World Music Awards. Halfway through the number Michael had joined a chorus of teenagers. Although he looked virile dressed in a black suit and black cowboy boots, much like a rhinestone version of Johnny Cash, his vocals were scant and strained. His unexceptional appearance was over in minutes. Michael had seemed overwhelmed, as if he felt undeserving of the enormous outpouring of love from his fans at the event. And as he prepared for his 2009 show dates, Michael seriously doubted that the same diehard fandom would still be there to welcome him; to breathe life into him.

He got his answer on March 5, 2009.

Michael was in London to officially announce his highly anticipated "This Is It" concert series to the world. While staying in the Royal Suite at The Lanesborough hotel, the reclusive star grappled with the pressure of his looming press conference. His handlers were struggling to pull the star together. On the day of the press junket, Phillips contended that Michael wouldn't change out of his bathrobe and was "locked in his room, drunk and despondent."

In an email sent to boss Tim Leiweke, the producer wrote:

> Tohme and I are trying to sober him up and get him to the press conference with his hairdressing/makeup artist . . . I screamed at him so loud the walls were shaking. Tohme and I have dressed him, and they are finishing his hair and then we are rushing to the O2. This is the scariest thing I have seen. He is an emotionally paralyzed mess riddled with self-loathing and doubt now that it is show time. He is scared to death. Right now, I just want to get through the press conference.

A short time later, Phillips gave Leiweke another update: "I haven't pulled it off yet. We still have to get his nose on properly. You have no idea what this is like. . . . I just slapped him."

Thousands of fans and hundreds of journalists, all of whom had been standing for several hours for the brief occasion, were left waiting for two additional hours.

When Michael finally arrived at the press conference, the promoters blamed "traffic" for making him tardy.

Emerging through a red curtain backdrop, Michael finally appeared on the press stage.

"When he went through that curtain, there was Michael Jackson," Phillips admitted.

Michael was wearing a vibrant black suit adorned with his customary military-meets-floral sequins insignias. His raven black hair was shoulder length, much like rocker Joan Jett's shag style in 1970s, and he hid his eyes behind opaque aviator sunglasses, which only accentuated the latest prosthetic on the end of his nose. His pale face appeared gaunt, but intentionally so, as if he had jaw or chin implants to create a sunken-in cheek look.

The grinning singer approached the "This Is It"–branded podium.

Each fractional movement made by Michael triggered an impressively disproportionate response from the audience.

When he held up his hand to silence the hyper crowd, it only stirred them further.

"This is it," Michael chirped to the swarm of fans screaming, "We love you, Michael!"

Although his words were largely drowned out by the excitement, the singer went on with his public address with an eerie, prophetic choice of words.

"These will be my final show performances in London," he announced. "This will be it. This is it. When I say 'this is it' it really means this is it. Because, um . . ."

Michael spontaneously paused to collect himself, and then decided to soak up the unexpectedly emotional moment. Like an Olympic sprinter at the starting line—or a repentant man humbling himself before his creator—he placed both hands on either side of the podium and bowed his head. It was clear that the weight of the moment had caught him off guard.

After looking up and firing off a genuine smile, the star looked backwards, as if the crowd was cheering for someone more formidable standing behind him. But, of course, Michael—on that stage or any—was enough to make everyone feel loved, and he finally felt it too.

Michael stepped out from behind the podium, placed his left hand on his chest, and stood before his disciples. He extended his angelic arms and thanked them all before continuing his speech.

"I'll be performing the songs my fans want to hear. This is it; I mean, this is really it. This is the final . . . this is the final curtain call, okay?"

Michael raised his arms in triumph. He did an about-face, marched towards the back of the stage, turned around after several paces, and extended his right arm and clenched fist in a firm salute to the right side of the audience.

He dropped his arm, puffed out his chest, then saluted the remainder of those in attendance. Michael blew a single kiss to everyone, waved, then exited out through the red curtains.

That was Michael Jackson's final public appearance; and the last time his fans would see him alive on any form of stage.

Despite his rabid fan base at the press conference, the promoters still needed convincing that Michael was a reliable box office draw. But on March 11, when nearly one million "This Is It" pre-sale tickets were booked in twenty-four hours, the show's producers scrambled to meet the historic demand. When the general public tickets went on sale two days later, Michael's business partners bumped the number of shows from ten to twenty. Those additional ten performances sold out in hours also.

At first, Michael threatened to quit when he learned of the scheduling change, but Tohme reminded the singer that performing only ten shows barely made a dent in his unmanageable debt. Soon, the number of O2 shows ballooned to thirty-one, and then to fifty dates. Each performance sold out, one after the other.

The mind-blowing public response kicked Michael's mind and spirit into high gear. Instead of running from the onerous obligation, he did an about-face and embraced the beast.

Back in Hollywood, the newly inspired star took a more active role during the pre-production phase of "This Is It."

"Bigger," he instructed his creative staffers. "When I'm on that stage, this is the best place in the world to be."

Michael helped select his backup dancers and started rehearsing with the team in mid-April. But those closest to the entertainer wondered whether his "This Is It" concert series would become the greatest comeback that never happened.

"Literally nobody believed he would end up performing," an insider told me, pointing out that Michael "needed medical attention and couldn't go on" after only two rehearsals.

As Michael labored to get himself back into marquee-worthy shape, a camera crew captured the whole creative process on film. Their footage provided an incomparable glimpse into the final weeks of the King of Pop.

CHAPTER THIRTY-TWO

ODDS & ENDINGS

In early June 2009, Michael and the "This Is It" team started rehearsing together full-time at The Forum, an arena situated a few miles south of Los Angeles. Most nights, Michael arrived around 6 p.m., warmed up his voice for an hour or two, then practiced on stage with the band until around midnight.

His only audience was the "This Is It" performers and production staff.

Everyone on the project had the highest regard for Michael and his historic career, but there didn't appear to be a clear consensus on his abilities at age fifty.

"He can't do this," Michael's makeup artist Karen Faye said at the time, believing that her longtime friend "might last a week" performing at full blast in London.

Naturally, Michael was shedding pounds while rehearsing for "This Is It," however, the weight loss concerned his physicians.

A source behind the scenes revealed:

> He goes days at a time hardly eating a thing and at one point his doctor was asking people around him if he had been throwing up after meals. He suspected bulimia, but when we said he hardly eats any meals, the doc thought it's probably anorexia nervosa. He seemed alarmed and at one point said, "People die from that all the time. You've got to get him to eat."

Those suffering from an eating disorder increase their chances of going into cardiac arrest.

When Michael's former manager, Ron Weisner, dropped in on a rehearsal, he felt Michael "looked horrific."

"He had all of these people around him," Weisner stated, "but nobody was looking out for him."

A member of Michael's staff believed "there was just too much money at stake" for people to care about Michael.

"The people who had his ear told him he would be a laughingstock if he canceled," the employee stated. "They had to have known he was in no shape to go on. . . . I know his family was concerned, especially Jermaine. But Michael was kept very isolated during those last weeks."

To make his job a little more manageable, Michael limited his time on stage to thirteen consecutive minutes or less. Gimmicks like film clips, set changes, and dance breaks bought him valuable recovery time backstage.

To restrict the number of times he'd have to sing and dance at the same time, Michael also wove many pre-recorded vocal tracks into his songs. He also trimmed off entire sections of his music, like simplifying the vocally challenging Jackson 5 numbers into one verse-one chorus samples.

Those on stage with Michael had an entirely different perspective on the star's power.

"Whenever I gave him a hug, I was hugging a solid mass of muscle," percussionist Bashiri Johnson recalled, noting he "never heard him complaining about being tired or anything."

Guitarist Tommy Organ stated, "He would just fill the room up with joy."

Even Michael was captured on film during a table meeting telling his production crew: "I want to push it to the limit, all the way."

Michael had hired a film crew to document the "This Is It" rehearsal process for his personal library, although he intended to show portions of the material during the concert.

Ultimately, hundreds of hours of footage were edited into a two-hour film showcasing Michael's creative process as he sings and stages many of his popular songs.

To accurately highlight what the superstar was planning for each number, the film combines recordings of the same song from different practices, each splice clearly denoted by his ever-revolving wardrobe. Although Michael rarely goes full tilt in the practices, there's little else to suggest that he has any rust to shake off; his moves seem effortless.

The cinematic event became Michael's sad but oddly uplifting swan song.

The movie kicks off with Michael's backup dancers explaining how he inspired each of them to become professional performers. Many of his youthful team had flown halfway around the world simply to audition for the project. Hundreds were excused during the rigorous tryout process. Only a handful became Michael's principal dancers.

As "This Is It" director Kenny Ortega—who choreographed films including *Ferris Bueller's Day Off* (1986) and *Dirty Dancing* (1987)—explained, "The dancers in a Michael Jackson show are an extension of Michael Jackson."

Michael had conveyed to his production team that nothing was more important than providing the audience with a thrilling experience. With that note in mind, he requested that his team devise a way to maximize the crowd's anticipation of his arrival on stage. Production designer Michael Cotten recalls Ortega asking for "a pre-show that would create an air of mystery in the arena so as people were coming in to the arena they would see something about to happen on the stage."

"So, we designed a kind of cacophony of lighting equipment and chrome spheres on the stage that were sparking with energy and about to come to life as the show began," Cotton said.

Ortega also wanted to herald Michael's entrance with fireworks, pillars of flames, and a giant lit-up "Light Man" robot.

"Michael came up with Light Man," Ortega said.

The plan was to slowly open the robot's digitally illuminated "suit of armor" panels and to have Michael leap out on stage. Much like he had done at the Super Bowl, Michael intended to stand motionless for several minutes.

As exemplified by the use of combined rehearsal footage, Michael is clearly improvising his funky dance routine during the opening number, "Wanna Be Startin' Somethin'." At the end of the song, Michael takes a moment to give his bass player some instruction.

"It's funkier," Michael says. "I'm not feeling that part enough."

But Michael doesn't verbally explain what he prefers to hear, he vocally imitates the bass line he's looking for.

"It's not there," Michael critiques, then warmly encourages, "We'll get it there."

Michael and his dance team subsequently crush their way through "Jam" and "They Don't Care About Us," then simultaneously freeze in their final poses.

"Hold for applause, hold for applause," calls Ortega. "Fade out."

Next, Michael drills his backup singer on the tricky timing of a "why, why" vocal echo in the effusive song "Human Nature." Heavily saturated by pink stage lights, Michael employs his graceful hands to capture the rhythmic nuances of the melody.

As a lead in to the incredibly catchy "Smooth Criminal," Michael gets inserted into a series of black and white gangster films. First, he appears like he's sitting in the crowd of Rita Hayworth's showstopper "Put the Blame on Mame" from the movie *Gilda* (1946). When Rita tosses her glove into the audience, Michael seemingly catches it. The intimate event sets off a scene between Michael and the late Humphrey Bogart. They seamlessly move through the 1941 movies *The Maltese Falcon* (1941) and *The Big Sleep* (1946).

Back on the rehearsal stage, Michael explains to Ortega that he wants to "sizzle" after the film reel.

"I wanna turn first and face the audience and then just nothing," the star is seen telling his director, fully aware that, as gratifying as his dance moves are to an audience, doing "nothing" can sometimes be a more effective crowd pleaser. "Then when he gets my cue we go."

"The only thing is," Ortega inquires, "how will you see the video change from the marquee to the city?"

"I gotta feel that," Michael says very persuasively. "I'll feel it."

Michael gives a sharp hand signal and the group shoots into the chart-topping song.

"I need the artist to be hands-on," says "This Is It" musical director Michael Bearden. "MJ is always hands-on with everything that he does. He knows all of his records. He knows all of his tempos. He knows all of his keys of songs."

During the intro for "The Way You Make Me Feel," Michael directs the musicians to pull way back. He wants the live version to drag more than on the album track.

"You've gotta let it simmer!" the frustrated star says. "You're not letting it simmer. Just bathe in the moonlight."

They run through the lick again and incorporate the sluggish tempo Michael had asked for. After a few lines of the verse, Michael gives the cue to launch into the standard upbeat version. He spends the duration of the song playfully pursuing a leggy female model around the stage.

Following a major set change that invokes a 1970s TV variety show, the band bursts into a medley of The Jackson 5 hits. They start with "I Want You Back."

For the first time in the film, Michael gets flustered during a rehearsal. He pushes through to the end of the song before dishing out a complaint about his sound monitor earpiece.

"You guys, I gotta tell you this," Michael vents. "When I'm trying to hear and it feels like somebody's fist is pushed into my ear, it's really very difficult. I know you mean well, but. . . . I'm trying to hear and I can't. If we could just bring it down a little bit, please."

With everyone a bit on edge because Michael's on edge, the group revs into "The Love You Save." Michael again struggles, this time with hitting the high notes in the verse of the song. But he nails the next number, "I'll Be There."

All of his backup dancers are in the audience, swaying side-to-side with their arms raised.

After concluding the song, Michael thoughtfully remarks, "I'll say, 'Jackie, Jermaine, Marlon, Tito, Randy. . . . I love you. Joseph and Katherine, God bless you. I love you.'"

To liven up the somber mood, Michael snaps into "Shake Your Body Down To the Ground" and then oozes his way through an "I Just Can't Stop Loving You" duet with Judith Hill.

The *This Is It* movie leaves the rehearsal venue and takes viewers behind the scenes to the "Thriller" 3-D film set, where Michael and the dancers are shooting an all-new graveyard sequence for the concert. Each performer is getting the full "undead" makeup treatment. Ortega shows off the ghostly "dead brides" and the "dead grooms" props that will parade through the aisles during each live performance of "Thriller."

Back on the rehearsal stage, Michael unexpectedly emerges from a man-sized spider puppet at center stage. The remaining dancers flank him and they all perform the iconic "Thriller" dance. During a techno musical interlude, Michael steps onto an elevating platform that takes him to the back of the stage, where he exits.

As the production inches closer to the July show date, the special effects crew demonstrates their awesome pyrotechnic capabilities. "Who Is It" plays over the tech-savvy montage.

"We are including lighted elements into his 'Billie Jean' costume," reports wardrobe designer Michael Bush. "The cut of the stones, the refraction of the light . . . as we're applying them you almost need sunglasses for the reflection."

Before running through the pulse-pounding song "Beat It," Michael takes a quick test ride on his state-of-the-art hydraulic crane called a "cherry picker." The railed platform will carry him over the crowd during each sold out concert. Michael also takes a few minutes with musical director Bearden to create an epic new song ending, one that brings the singer to his knees a la Jimi Hendrix torching his guitar at the Monterey Pop Festival in 1967.

"Let it burn the lights out!" Michael cheers to his crew.

For "Black or White," Michael rises from beneath the stage to join lead guitarist Orianthi Panagaris. At this point in the rehearsal schedule, Michael's completely dialed in. He comes across as being in shape, in tune, and in control. But most noticeably, he's having a good time on stage. His energy is instantly infectious.

Before singing the show-closing "Earth Song," Michael provides some narration concerning his passion for all living things.

"I respect the secrets and magic of nature. I love the planet. I love trees. I have this thing for trees and the colors and changing of leaves. I love it. And I respect those kinds of things . . . I really feel that nature is trying so hard to compensate for man's mismanagement of the planet, because the planet is sick. Like a fever . . . this is our last chance to fix this problem that we have. It's like a runaway train and the time has come. This is it."

Michael utilizes the cherry picker to practice delivering his "save the world" lyrics to fans.

As an encore, Michael returns to the stage to sing the song that made him legendary, "Billie Jean." He performs the same exact opening routine that dazzled audiences in 1983.

Unlike Michael's other performances in the film, a single rehearsal is shown throughout the entire number. Although he brings several exciting twenty-first centuries moves into the mix, none measure up to the moonwalk. Michael ends the song performing a lengthy one-man dance-off set against the single beat of a snare drum. The backup dancers impulsively catcall to him from the audience.

"God bless you," Michael tells them after completing the routine.

Ortega gently reminds the hardworking performer to "get some water."

At the end of the film, the entire cast and crew gather in a circle on stage and hold hands. Michael gives them one final motivational speech.

"Everybody's doing a great job. Let's continue and believe and have faith. Give me your all, your endurance, your patience, and your understanding. But it's an adventure. It's a great adventure. It's nothing to be nervous about. They just want wonderful experiences. They want escapism. We wanna take them places that they've never been before. We wanna show them talent like they've never seen before. So, give your all. And I love you all, and we're family. Just know that. We're a family. . . . We're putting love back into the world, to remind the world that love is important, to love each other. We're all one. That's the message."

The close, temporary family huddles together, each member extending their hand into the middle and "on three" they all scream "Michael!"

Running one final sound check, Michael performs "Man in the Mirror." He stands alone on stage, awash in a sea of blue light. He concludes with his arms outstretched to the side, his face turned up to the heavens, and his belief in himself restored.

As producer Phillips would later note, "It's just amazing how close we came to having what would have been the greatest show ever."

CHAPTER THIRTY-THREE

GOING SEPARATE WAYS

On June 24, 2009, Michael had a magnificent rehearsal. Feeding off the energy of his fully costumed dancers, the newly installed set pieces, dynamic special effects, and a 130-foot long LED screen behind him, Michael belted out the entire "This Is It" set list and moved to his music as if he knew it was the last chance he'd get to do it.

"You could see it in him . . . that he was seeing the show finally come together for the first time," said Dorian Holley, Michael's vocal director dating back to the 1980s. "I think he was in top form."

After that first official run-through, everyone involved was finally on the same page: Michael was still the King of Pop.

"He was bioluminescent," director Ortega claimed. "He was so brilliant on stage I had goose bumps."

Musical director Bearden agreed, "You could see his confidence growing and you could see physically he was able to do the things that he wanted to do . . . Michael had a serious glow about him."

The three-hour dress rehearsal ended around 11 p.m., but everyone lingered till midnight, still transfixed by the electrifying performer. On his way to the car, Michael relayed his love to several people in passing. He also took a moment to reassure his producers.

"I know I can do this," he told them. "Thank you for getting me this far. I can take it from here."

Michael was driven home to his rented $40 million mansion in nearby Holmby Hills.

At the gated estate, he was greeted by the usual encampment of fans. Still buzzing from the occasion, he rolled his backseat window down and gave a few well-wishes before heading inside. With only a few rehearsals remaining before the production moved to London, Michael wanted to ensure that he squeezed in as much rest and recovery time as possible. But for the star, getting to sleep was always an uphill battle.

Michael believed his musical inspiration was channeled through him by a higher power, and those creative juices flowed most heavily at night.

"When it's coming you gotta work," Michael explained, joking that if he ignored the late-night messages from his supreme creator "then he might give them to Prince."

To call these gifts "demons" would be unfair to Michael's incredible abilities, but the star treated them as such. He often wanted these transmissions eradicated—and it was Dr. Conrad Murray who supplied the secret weapon.

A few months earlier, the singer had confidentially recruited the physician to live with him full-time.

Dr. Murray was earning $100,000 a month to obtain, administer, and monitor Michael's drug use.

At first, the doctor secured "downers" for Michael, including Xanax (alprazolam), Restoril (temazepam), Ativan (lorazepam), and Versed (midazolam). They made Michael seem so "out of it" that his handlers would cover for him by saying "he's tired" or "it's not a good day for him."

But Michael's dependency on painkillers became so severe, he racked up a $100,000 bill at a Beverly Hills pharmacy. And to prepare for his extended stay in London, Michael had Dr. Murray get him over 5000 ml of Propofol (or Diprivan, which is the brand name). That's the equivalent of what a busy hospital uses to anesthetize all pre-operative patients in one week.

Unfortunately, Dr. Murray wasn't an anesthetist—a medical specialist trained to administer drugs that render a person unconscious or unresponsive. He was a heart doctor and was operating dangerously outside his field of expertise.

When called out about his obvious bad habits, Michael irritably responded, "My body is the mechanism that fuels this entire business. I need my own personal physician attending to me 24/7."

At 1:30 a.m. on that fateful Wednesday night, Dr. Murray gave the persistent star ten milligrams of Valium to help him sleep. The doctor denied repeated demands for Propofol, which Michael referred to as "milk." Although Dr. Murray would later contend he was looking out for Michael's best interests, the doctor was probably more worried about his own.

Propofol kicks in fast, but wears off within minutes, so it must be given intravenously to keep a person under. Because Propofol lowers blood pressure and suppresses breathing, a patient's heart and lungs must constantly be monitored. A doctor's undivided attention is required when injecting the drug through an IV.

When Michael had arrived home from rehearsal in the middle of the night, Dr. Murray had likely been asleep, or at least close to it, and was probably not up to the monumental lifeguarding task.

But that night, a Valium didn't do the trick. Michael was still awake half an hour after taking the pill. So, Dr. Murray gave him a dose of Ativan, a federally regulated substance that relieves anxiety. When that also failed to facilitate slumber, the superstar was given Versed, a powerful sedative usually given to patients before getting surgery. A short time later, Dr. Murray gave Michael additional doses of both drugs. Neither medication subdued the ailing singer.

Michael was still awake at 10:30 a.m. He needed sleep. He demanded his "milk."

Dr. Murray—presumably having slept for a few hours—finally acquiesced. With Michael laid out on the right side of the bed, the doctor gave him 25 mg of Propofol through an IV.

To reduce the pain caused by the drug as it enters the blood stream, Dr. Murray diluted the IV drip bag with another anesthetic, lidocaine.

Around 11 a.m., Michael finally went under and fell asleep. The doctor left him alone.

According to Dr. Murray, he took the opportunity to use the bathroom, but promptly returned to the master bedroom only minutes later.

However, Dr. Murray's phone records reveal a completely different story.

At 11:18 a.m., the doctor called his Las Vegas clinic. The chat lasted over 30 minutes. Next, Dr. Murray called a patient, presumably to handle a matter discussed during the previous call. He left a voicemail.

"Just wanted to talk to you about your results," Dr. Murray stated in the message. "You did quite well on the study. We would love to continue to see you as a patient, even though I may have to be absent from my practice for, uh—because of an overseas sabbatical."

Finally, Dr. Murray spent several more minutes checking in with a cocktail waitress from Houston. They never finished their conversation. The doctor dropped his phone when he returned to the master bedroom.

Michael had stopped breathing.

In a hospital, heart monitors would have instantly alerted doctors of the life-threatening change to a patient's vitals. A heart-restarting defibrillator would also have been on hand to electrically stimulate a stopped heart.

But Dr. Murray had not provided Michael with what may have proven to be lifesaving advantages.

First, he gave Michael an injection of Anexate (flumazenil), a medicine used to bring people out of sedation or to reverse an overdose. When that failed to revive the lifeless star, Dr. Murray began mouth-to-mouth resuscitation and chest compressions. They also didn't work.

CPR (Cardiopulmonary Resuscitation) is most successful when the receiving subject is on a solid surface. A mattress has too much give for the downward thrusting technique to be effective. To compensate, Dr. Murray shoved one arm behind Michael's back and used only one arm to press on Michael's chest. The maneuver was completely useless.

In a panic, the doctor called out for Michael Jr., who was in the kitchen eating lunch. Dr. Murray ran downstairs and told the twelve-year-old and his younger sister, "Something may be wrong with your dad." Both terrified kids began sobbing.

Then Dr. Murray phoned Michael's personal assistant Michael Amir Williams and informed him that Michael had "a bad reaction." Williams immediately summoned internal backup while Dr. Murray cleaned up incriminating evidence scattered around the bedroom. He removed the IV tubing that was inserted into Michael's stiffening left leg, collected the glass Propofol vials, shoved them into a bag, and put everything in the closet.

At 12:21 p.m., someone finally called 911.

A member of Michael's security team, Alberto Alvarez, calmly informed the 911 operator of the crisis:

911 Operator: What is the address of the emergency?

Alvarez: Yes sir, I need an ambulance as soon as possible, sir.

Operator: Okay, sir. What is your address?

Alvarez: It's 100 North Carolwood Drive, Los Angeles, California, 90077.

Operator: You said Carolwood?

Alvarez: Carolwood Drive, yes.

Operator: Okay, sir. What is the phone number that you're calling from?

Alvarez: [redacted]

Operator: And what exactly happened?

Alvarez: Sir, we have a gentleman here that needs help and he's not breathing yet. He's not breathing and we're trying to pump him, but he's not . . . he's not.

Operator: Okay, how old is he?

Alvarez: He's 50 years old, sir.

Operator: 50? Okay. He's not conscious, he's not breathing?

Alvarez: Yes, he's not breathing, sir. He's not conscious, sir.

Operator: Alright, is he on the floor? Where's he at right now?

Alvarez: He's on the bed, sir. He's on the bed.

Operator: Okay, let's get him on the floor. Let's get him down to the floor. I'm gonna help you with CPR right now.

Alvarez: We need him to get, we need a—

Operator: We're already on the way. I'm going to, as much as I can, help you on the phone. We're already on our way. Did anybody see him?

Alvarez: Yes, we have a personal doctor here with him, sir.

Operator: Oh, you have a doctor there?

Alvarez: Yes, but he's not responding to anything. He's not responding to CPR or anything.

Operator: Oh, okay. We're on our way there. If your guy is doing CPR and you're instructed by a doctor, he's a higher authority than me. And he's there on scene. Did anybody witness what happened?

Alvarez: No, just the doctor, sir. The doctor has been the only one here.

Operator: Okay, so the doctor saw what happened?

Alvarez: Doctor, did you see what happened, sir?

Dr. Murray [in the background]: I need an ambulance to come!

Alvarez: Sir, if you can please . . .

Operator: We're on our way, we're on our way. I'm just passing these questions on to my paramedics while they're on their way there.

Alvarez: Thank you, sir. He's pumping. He's pumping his chest, but he's not responding to anything. Please.

Operator: Okay, okay. We're on our way. We're less than a mile away and we'll be there shortly.

Paramedics from Los Angeles Fire Station 71 responded to the emergency. They walked through Michael's front door and up the stairs at 12:26 p.m. Michael was still in bed and very pale. The texture of his ribs was visible beneath his skin and his feet were a murky shade of blue.

"He looked like he had a chronic health problem," responding paramedic Richard Senneff confessed.

They lowered Michael's lifeless body to the floor and attempted CPR. He was unresponsive. His heart—the same one that had powered every iconic dance step since boyhood—was suddenly motionless.

Although Dr. Murray told the rescue workers that he was treating Michael for "dehydration and exhaustion," paramedic Marc Blount saw "three open vials of lidocaine" on the floor.

"Dr. Murray scooped all three of them up and put them into a black bag," Blount recalled.

After working for thirty minutes, the paramedics pronounced Michael Jackson dead at 12:57 p.m. But Dr. Murray overruled their decision.

He claimed that Michael still had a pulse and demanded they keep trying to save his patient. The paramedics fired off a defibrillator.

They tried inflating his lungs with an air pump.

They administered Michael a shot of adrenaline directly into his heart.

Each attempt was futile.

At 1:07 p.m., a stretcher carrying Michael's body was lifted into an ambulance.

The morbid news spread quickly.

During the brief ride to the UCLA medical center, Senneff saw "people running down the street taking pictures" and "random cars passing the ambulance."

Even though they knew it was too late to save the singer, emergency room doctors worked for another hour on the fallen star. His new official time of death became 2:26 p.m.

"It was madness at the hospital," Tohme said. "Police, fans, media . . . I saw Randy Phillips. He told me, 'We lost him.'"

Amidst the chaos, Tohme recalled being introduced to Dr. Murray.

"The first time I heard they hired a doctor for Michael was the first and only time I saw Dr. Murray," Tohme said. "He came in the [hospital] conference room with us and there was a conversation I can't talk about."

Dr. Murray likely confessed to playing a role in Michael's death. They also decided that Michael's older brother Jermaine would announce the tragedy to the press.

"This is hard," the fifty-four-year-old began. "My brother, the legendary King of Pop, Michael Jackson, passed away on Thursday, June 25, 2009, at 2:26 p.m. It is believed he suffered cardiac arrest in his home. However, the cause of death is unknown until the results of the autopsy are known."

Michael's battered body was immediately taken by helicopter to the Los Angeles County Coroner, where it rested on a metal gurney in the morgue. An external examination was conducted that day at 6 p.m. The medical report stated:

> The decedent was wearing a hospital gown. The body is that of an adult black male who appears to be approximately 50 years old. He has brown colored eyes, natural teeth and brown hair. The decedent's head hair is sparse and is connected to a wig. The decedent's overall skin has patches of light and dark pigmented areas. There was a dark black discoloration on the decedent's upper forehead near his hairline. Dark coloration was present on the decedent's eyebrows, eyelashes and lips. A small piece of gauze was found on the tip of his nose and an ETT (endotracheal tube), held in place with medical tape, was seen in his mouth. A red discoloration is prominent on the center of his chest.

An internal medical inspection of the body was performed the following day at 10 a.m. According to the toxicology report, Michael had six drugs in his system: Propofol, lorazepam, midazolam, lidocaine, diazepam, and nordiazepam. They listed his cause of death as "acute Propofol intoxication."

"The circumstances do not support self-administration of Propofol," the medical experts concluded. Meaning, someone must have assisted in Michael's demise.

The examiners also confirmed that Michael had nodular prostatic hyperplasia (a "moderately" enlarged prostate), vitiligo, tubular adenoma of colon (polyps that can eventually lead to cancer), osteoarthritis of the lower spine and several fingers, and both of his lungs were congested and partially hemorrhaged. Most shockingly, from his neck to his ankles, Michael had thirteen puncture wounds indicating he had recently been given injections.

Over sixty photos of Michael's body were taken before and during the autopsy, mostly documenting the numerous injuries he incurred during the several rescue attempts.

Adding to the tragedy, the doctors felt that, overall, Michael—and his heart— had been incredibly healthy.

Around the same time as the postmortem exam, police were conducting a lengthy interview with Dr. Murray.

Despite uncovering some alarming inconsistences in his story, the officers let the doctor go free. They were not yet prepared to press any charges.

Naturally, the world was stunned by the news of Michael's passing.

And, as he did many times in life, Michael broke records in the wake of his death. His albums sold out in stores and online and his singles burst back into the Top 100. Michael also became the first musician to have his songs downloaded over a million times in a week. The actual number was closer to two million.

On July 7, a public memorial was held for Michael at the Staples Center in downtown Los Angeles. In an eerie turn of events, it was the same venue where he had performed the night before his passing. The 17,000-seat arena was filled to capacity by ticket winners of an online lottery that attracted over a million submissions. Millions more around the world watched the event live on television and online.

Michael rested in a gold-plated casket lined with blue velvet. The lid was kept closed at the memorial. His family and a multitude of celebrities spoke about the late singer, and frequently to him.

"Daddy has been the best father you could ever imagine," eleven-year-old Paris said. "I just want to say I love him . . . so much."

On September 3, Michael was buried in a lavish granite and marble mausoleum at Forest Lawn Memorial Park in Glendale, California. His grieving children put a gold crown atop the flowers on the lid of his coffin.

Meanwhile, the police concluded their investigation into the late singer's death. They ruled it a homicide. Dr. Conrad Murray was officially charged with involuntary manslaughter, to which he emphatically pled "not guilty."

The matter of *People of the State of California v. Dr. Conrad Robert Murray* was held at the Los Angeles Superior Court in Los Angeles, with Judge Michael Pastor presiding.

"Your Honor, I am an innocent man," Dr. Murray told the judge at the hearing.

Dr. Murray's trial began on September 27, 2011, with prosecutors telling the jury that "misplaced trust in the hands of Murray cost Jackson his life."

Two months later, a jury agreed, and Murray was found guilty.

The doctor was given four years in prison and his medical license was either revoked or suspended in several states. He was released on parole on October 28, 2013, though he is no longer allowed to prescribe medication to patients.

CHAPTER THIRTY-FOUR

DIGGING UP DIRT

In the more than ten years since Michael's untimely passing, the singer's estate has worked feverishly to restore Michael's image and to settle his $500 million in debts. *This Is It* became the highest-grossing concert film and documentary in history, taking in over $250 million worldwide. A 10-track title became the singer's first posthumously released album. It featured all-new material recorded by Michael throughout his prolific career. Cirque du Soleil created two shows featuring Michael's music, *Michael Jackson: The Immortal World Tour* (2011) and *Michael Jackson: One* (2013). Both were hugely successful.

In 2014, Michael was controversially and somewhat grotesquely brought back to life in the form of a hologram for the Billboard Music Awards. He "performed" the song "Slave to the Rhythm," one of the singles from his second posthumously released album *Xscape*, which hit number two on the charts.

Through those ventures and more, Michael's debts have all been settled and his three children are well cared for. According to several insiders, Michael left "as many as 200 unpublished songs" as an insurance policy for his kids.

"The songs can't be touched by creditors," one source claims. "It's the only way to ensure that his kids will be properly taken care of."

But even in death, Michael's steadily rebounding musical legacy was once again overshadowed by his sordid legal history. Over the years, unsealed court documents containing startlingly explicit declarations from Michael's sexually abused accusers began to surface.

According to documents the author exclusively obtained in 2013, Wade Robson—for the first time—made a series of startling claims that would contradict his personal stance to date.

He said Michael allegedly made his move on the seven-year-old as the boy's sister Chantal slept just feet away at Neverland. The abuse allegedly continued unabated for a period of seven years.

"We can never tell anyone what we are doing," Michael told Robson, he said. "People are ignorant, and they would never understand that we love each other, and this is how we show it. If anyone were to ever find out, our lives and career would be over."

Robson recounted how on his first night at Neverland, he and Chantal both slept in Michael's bedroom—in the same bed as the adult singer. But the following night, Robson claimed, "Chantal expressed concern about sleeping in Michael's bed and elected instead to sleep in a separate bed on a different floor of his two-floor bedroom."

Robson, though, opted to sleep in Jackson's bed again. That's when Robson's lifelong nightmare was said to have begun.

"Michael began sexually abusing me on or about that night," Robson said. "The sexual abuse continued every night through the nearly two weeks that I spent at the ranch during that early 1990 visit, as well as at Michael's apartment in the Westwood section of Los Angeles."

Shedding light on their apparent and illicit bond, Robson said Michael "encouraged" him to call him "dad" and he would, in turn, call Robson his "son"—eerily familiar dialogue that matches Michael's scandalous home movies shot at Sun City in 1999.

Robson claimed that while his family was at Neverland, he continued sleeping with Michael in his bed and "the sexual abuse continued."

According to official documents, Michael's crude activity roster included:

- "Putting his hand over Wade Robson's clothed penis."
- "Putting his hand inside Wade Robson's underpants."
- "Taking Wade Robson's hand and putting it over Michael's clothed penis."
- "Taking Wade Robson's hand and putting it inside his underpants."
- "French kissing."
- "Rubbing Wade Robson's penis."
- "Having Wade Robson rub his penis."

- "Licking Wade Robson's anus while Michael masturbated using lotion."
- "The mutual fondling of genitals" with hands and mouths.
- "Mutual fellatio."
- "Lying on top of each other gyrating their genitals together."
- "Showering naked together."
- "Penetration of Wade Robson's anus with Michael's penis."

Michael requesting that Robson pose "naked, with his knees and palms extended like a dog on all fours."

The bombshell court documents also revealed that at age fourteen, when Robson began to show signs of puberty, "the sexual abuse by Decedent [Jackson] became less frequent."

Robson pledged to the hit-maker that he would never tell about what happened between them.

"I swore I would never tell a soul about what we did and did not until May 2012," Robson wrote in the seven-page, hand-signed declaration.

Robson has alleged that Michael "coached" him "every day" to provide certain statements against claims of molestation, beginning with the Chandler case in September 1993 and continuing through the criminal charges in 2005.

"He would tell me that our phones were tapped, and 'they' were listening to everything we said," Robson said of his private conversations with Michael. "He would role play with me and say to me, 'They are saying we did all of this disgusting sexual stuff. We never did any of that, right?' I would play along and answer, 'No way!' He would say, 'If they believed that we did any of this sexual stuff, you and I would go to jail for the rest of our lives. Our lives and careers would be over. We've got to fight this. We've got to beat them together.'"

Robson felt he had to make one aspect of the case very clear: he did not feel Michael's sexual desires were forced upon him.

"I believed that I was a consenting participant in the sexual acts that Michael and I engaged in," he stated of his juvenile mindset at the time. "I also believed that I was absolutely fine with what went on between us."

In the wake of the allegations, I approached Ron Zonen, the prosecutor who had grilled Robson during the 2005 child molestation trial—and who was met with Robson's steadfast denials in the courtroom that he wasn't sexually abused.

"It did not come as a surprise that Wade eventually acknowledged being a victim of years of sexual abuse," he told me.

"Try as we may to get victims to disclose what happened to them, they just don't do it on our schedule, they do it when they are ready. That often happens well into adulthood and often after a baby arrives. I wish Wade well; his disclosure is the first step to a complete recovery."

Interestingly, Zonen had specifically prodded Robson about the physical contact he had with Jackson.

Zonen: Mr. Jackson would periodically kiss you.

Robson: No

Zonen: Periodically hug you?

Robson: Yes

Zonen: Touch you?

Robson: Hug me.

Zonen: Did he ever kiss your lips?

Robson: No

Zonen: On occasions you stayed in bed with Mr. Jackson would you ever cuddle in bed?

Robson: No

Zonen: Would you lie next to one another?

Robson: No

Zonen: Would you touch?

Robson: No

At trial, Robson admitted to Zonen that his mother had given permission for him to sleep in Jackson's bedroom at Neverland Ranch, at his mother's apartment in Hollywood, in a Las Vegas hotel and at the pop star's condo in Century City, Calif., while his mother, Joy, stayed across the street at another hotel.

"Had you ever crawled into bed with a thirty-year-old man prior to that?" Zonen probed.

"My father," Robson said, defensively.

"Okay."

"But other than that, no," the witness said.

"Any person you had just met?"

"No."

But recently, Robson changed his opinion of the heinous events.

"I was psychologically unable and unwilling to understand that it was sexual abuse," Robson stated, further admitting that he "never forgot one moment" of what he went through with Michael.

Robson's attorney, Vince Finaldi, accused the singer of operating "the most sophisticated child sexual abuse procurement and facilitation operation the world has known."

"Neverland Ranch was nothing but a well-orchestrated trap," Finaldi stated. "It was custom-built to attract kids so he could groom them and decide which to sexually abuse."

And Michael wanted to ensure that his sexual saga remained secret.

According to members of the Jackson family, Michael once destroyed a hot-and-heavy romance between Robson and one of his nieces—Jackie's daughter Brandi.

Family members of Michael's then-teenage niece said that Brandi's breakup with Robson was so traumatic that the troubled teen was found babbling incoherently alongside a freeway.

Brandi was hospitalized and claimed it was "Michael's fault."

"Michael was the puppet master," a close relative revealed. "He did this, not Wade, and she nearly died because of it."

Michael allegedly put a stop to the relationship when he became scared that Robson would tell Brandi about her megastar uncle's perversions.

"Michael was insanely jealous because Wade was his property and knew all about the other molestations," the source said.

In the last few years, similar allegations of sexual deviancy began to surface about the singer's relationship with James Safechuck. The forty-one-year-old first made Jackson's acquaintance at age ten while shooting a Pepsi commercial promoting the *Bad* tour.

At Neverland, an employee saw Michael and Safechuck in a hot tub, at which time the singer had his hands "down the front of Jimmy's underpants and was manipulating the boy's genitalia."

A maid at Neverland also reported seeing her employer and Safechuck in bed together, with nothing on from the waist up. Safechuck admitted that Robson's testimony had inspired him to come clean about the scandal.

When criminal charges were brought against Michael in 2005, lie detection expert Michael Sylvestre decided to put Michael's innocence to the test—literally. Sylvestre—a reserve sheriff's deputy in Orange County, Florida—used a truth-detecting device to scrutinize Michael's claims regarding his sex abuse case. In his video recorded statement from January 30, the singer stated:

> In the last few weeks, a large amount of ugly, malicious information has been released into the media about me. Apparently, this information was leaked through transcripts in a grand jury proceeding, where neither my lawyers nor I ever appeared. The information is disgusting and false.
>
> Years ago, I allowed a family to visit and spend some time at Neverland. Neverland is my home. I allowed this family into my home because they told me their son was ill with cancer and needed my help. Throughout the years, I have helped thousands of children who are ill or in distress. These events have caused a nightmare for my family, my children, and me. I never intend to place myself in so vulnerable a position ever again.
>
> I love my community, and I have great faith in our justice system. Please keep an open mind and let me have my day in court. I deserve a

fair trial like every other American citizen. I will be acquitted and vindicated with the truth is told. Thank you.

Sylvestre ran the clips through the DecepTech Voice Stress Analysis Machine, a
computerized version of the Psychological Stress Evaluation, which is used by over
fifty law enforcement agencies in the US. The test is said to be superior to a conventional polygraph, though is not considered permissible as evidence in court.
The machine senses stress levels in the voice; frequent "peaks" on the readout indicate that the speaker is being dishonest.

"He was totally lying at several points," Sylvestre stated with certainty. "His
charts went through the roof."

The analyst concluded that Michael lied about why he befriended the accuser,
that he had no intention of repeating his actions, and that he would be found innocent. Bottom line? Michael flunked the test.

"It's true deception," Sylvestre said at the time. "He clearly believes that he will
be convicted."

In 2019, at this author's request, Sylvestre employed the same truth-seeking tactics on statements made by *Leaving Neverland* accusers Robson and Safechuck. It
is important to remember that, while law enforcement and intelligence agencies
might use tools such as the DecepTech Voice Stress Analysis Machine, for purposes of court procedures (like a lie detector test, absent a stipulation of the parties), the results are likely never admissible.

In the documentary, Safechuck claimed Michael held a mock ceremony and
even gifted him jewelry.

"I was really into jewelry at that time and he would reward me with jewelry for
doing sexual acts to him," Safechuck claimed. "He would say that I need to sell him
some so I could earn the gift."

The accuser alleged the mock wedding took place in Michael's bedroom.

"We filled out some vows like we would be bonded forever," he said. "It felt
good, and the ring is nice. It has a row of diamonds."

According to Sylvestre's analysis, Safechuck was probably being truthful about
the mock wedding, but levels of stress indicate he might not have been truthful
about the "rewards" for sexual favors. The DecepTech Voice Stress Analysis

Machine does not prove Safechuck's version of events, nor does it exonerate Michael. Like so much of the controversies surrounding the King of Pop, it leaves us to be the judge.

"That statement is truthful and is the least amount of deception he has, there is zero stress," the analyst said of the alleged event. "That is really good in the fact there is a lot of detail and it's truthful."

He claimed the vows portion of the interview has "a little bit of stress, but he's being truthful."

As for the two being bonded forever, the stress jumps at "forever."

"He had ninety percent stress in that response," he said. "They may have been bonding, but him talking today would break that bond."

As for receiving the ring and being into jewelry, "The statement yells out that I'm not sure he liked the ring. He wasn't necessarily being truthful. He would have been enamored by Michael more than jewelry."

Sylvestre also concluded Safechuck may not have been truthful about the reward for sexual acts.

"There may be embellishments here given it's the recollection of a ten-year-old and the sensitive nature of the claims," the analyst said, suggesting that Safechuck's testimony was tainted by the passage of time.

As for Robson, Sylvestre believes his statements also could have been "embellished."

"He looks away at times when he is speaking, which tells me he may not be truthful," he said. "Words like 'physical' and 'intertwined' may not be truthful. He goes back to being star struck and caught up in the moment."

It is hard to reconcile such analysis when individuals like Robson and Safechuck are so vociferous in their allegations against Michael. Additionally, as some media label the two men as "survivors" of Jackson, many are left to believe a conclusion to the case has already been formed. The question isn't whether one ought to believe "survivors"—of course one should. The question is whether everyone who alleges sexual abuse is, in fact, a survivor of sexual abuse.

There is no clear answer.

Armed with Sylvestre's conclusions, I sought more analysis from Ohio's Institute of BioAcoustic Biology. Here, Sharry Edwards uses a revolutionary computer algorithm to diagnose deception and behavior and spark "discussion and provid(e) insights".

Edwards used Robson and Safechuck's interviews with CBS *This Morning*'s Gayle King to provide the following analysis. First, Safechuck:

> Octaves are split indicating bipolar, split personality or untruthfulness.
>
> BioAcoustically there are indicators for a need to control here (-2 octave); that is a control-based octave. His note of C# (representing justice) and C (representing self and ego) are very high.
>
> Money issues usually show up in F, F# which this graph is missing. This leads me to surmise that Wade is leading the charge if money is involved.
>
> Fantasy indicators are off the scale with D# being 1404—an outrageously high indicator dealing with the use of information at a fantasy level. Wade has this same note as an extreme high. This is followed by a score of 471 in the note of E; indicating that the truth might come from him first also in a fantasy octave. D# represents the need to use information to help others even if that service may leave self-interests unresolved. Thinking is his first mode of action.

Edwards told me her BioAcoustic analysis of Robson was very similar to her analysis of Jerry Sandusky, the former Penn State assistant football coach who was convicted of rape and child sexual abuse. BioAcoustics evaluation showed that he was lying about the encounter when he spoke, she said. The Court convicted him of forty-five counts of child sexual abuse.

> There is some truth to what they are saying but their present versions are greatly embellished.
>
> This is a story based on facts that have been embellished. For Wade, something did happen that made him uncomfortable but whatever it was, it is not as he is reporting.
>
> Most of the information from both accusers is coming from a

fantasy perspective. This is a story that is far removed from actual events but a made-up story nevertheless.

They embellished much of what transpired or they have distorted memories that have only a bit of the truth involved.

An overview of both individual's motives indicates an emotional purpose for physical reasons is behind their behavior.

Put each of these men in a separate room and James will likely break first with the truth; especially with promised immunity. He will be happy to let someone else take the fall.

Wade is the more emotional of the two especially when it comes to the purpose of helping someone else. James has more of a "for a purpose" perspective. He wants a physical outcome that will bring him personal satisfaction.

Neither has thought this through logically. They seek a physically rewarding outcome.

Onlookers will need to realize that something did happen. I think Michael was very naïve as to how his actions could be perceived by adults.

The very large blank space between the octaves each vocal print indicates now that these men are not naïve, nor are they empathetic as to how this affects others long term.

James needs more control over his reputation about the outcomes of "story." Wade is more comfortable with expanding the story.

Although Robson and Safechuck are leading the renewed charge against the dissolute performer, in recent months up to a dozen new victims have come forward claiming they were molested and even raped by Michael when they were between the ages of seven and fourteen.

"He started far earlier than people think," one insider revealed, claiming Michael began sexually assaulting kids in his late teens. "His abuses go back more than thirty years and may involve thousands of victims."

Despite the flurry of new accusations against the deceased superstar, some of Michael's alleged victims prefer to leave their past behind.

Now in his late thirties, former accuser Jason Francia said he's shut out all news about the King of Pop. "I haven't followed anything regarding MJ," Francia told me, revealing that he only learned about Robson's latest claims when he was approached for comment by media outlets. "This is the first I'm hearing about all of this."

Francia's mother, Blanca, was a maid at the ranch from 1986 to 1991. She reportedly saw the pop star showering with another young boy. Both pairs of underwear remained on the floor outside the shower door. Michael denied any wrongdoing but gave the family $2 million to settle out-of-court. In court documents I reviewed, Robson's lawyers said Blanca told them:

> On one occasion, [she] entered Jackson's bedroom and heard sounds of laughter and playing around. At first, she thought the sounds might have been coming from the garden outside Jackson's bedroom, but then she peeked through open door to Jackson's personal bathroom and realized the sounds were coming from the shower in the bathroom. She saw two pairs of underwear laying on the floor next to the shower and recognized them as Jackson's and Robson's. The water was running in the shower and Francia heard the radio playing. Francia heard two voices for about a minute which she recognized as Jackson's and Robson's.

In the wake of the 2013 allegations, six years before *Leaving Neverland*, Robson reacted to my exclusive reporting, writing on Facebook:

> This article contains some of the details of my child sexual abuse. It was not the plan for this info to be made public, but now that it has, I am sharing it because it is important for these "uncomfortable" topics to be talked about in society. One in four girls and one in six boys are sexually abused before they are eighteen. We must face these facts and learn to prevent them in any way we can. Silence perpetuates abuse.

Even if supporters believed his claims, Jackson's estate vowed to fight the allegations—and they did successfully—to the finish. Weitzman told me:

> Twenty-five years after the fact and five years after Michael Jackson passed away Mr. Safechuck—who has many times over the years denied Michael Jackson did anything inappropriate to him—is now demanding money from Michael's Estate by claiming he suddenly recalls life differently. His new story is that Wade Robson's nearly identical lawsuit filed a year ago by the same attorney caused him to now recall certain events. Of course, Michael is not here to defend himself. Nonetheless, we believe these false and scurrilous allegations will not prevail. [Ultimately, in 2017, a judge dismissed the lawsuit brought by Robson. Judge Mitchell L. Beckloff's ruling against Robson found that the two Jackson-owned corporations, which were the remaining defendants in the case, were not liable for Robson's exposure to Jackson. He did not rule on the credibility of Robson's allegations themselves.]

But sexual assault allegations aren't the only reports that have denied Michael eternal peace.

A complete evidence list from the 2003 raid on Neverland conducted by the Santa Barbara County Sheriff's Department reveals more frightening details, as I uncovered. According to the official police inventory, a multitude of books found in the main residence contained photos of children and young adults in varying stages of undress, including some full-frontal nudity of boys.

Some of the titles in Michael's library included *The Fourth Sex: Adolescent Extreme*, *In Search of Young Beauty*, *Room to Play*, *The Boy: A Photographic Essay*, and *Boys Will Be Boys*, which was personally inscribed by Michael. Authorities believed materials like these could have been used by Michael to "desensitize" kids, making them more susceptible to sexual corruption.

Police also seized a plastic Disneyland bag from the premises that contained children's clothing and suspiciously bloodied bed linens. Officials could not match an identity to the DNA.

When the previously unreleased evidence list first appeared online, many people—including the police—questioned the authenticity of the reports. According to police protocol, case numbers must be present on all pages of an official report. That small detail was missing from some of the published pages of Michael's alleged case file.

"The photos that are interspersed appear to be some evidentiary photos taken by Sheriff's investigators and others are clearly obtained from the Internet or through unknown sources," the Sheriff's Department stated, at the time.

That assessment by police was enough for the Jackson estate to brush the documents off as Internet "click bait."

"Everything in these reports, including what the County of Santa Barbara calls content that appears to be obtained off the Internet or through 'unknown sources' is false," the Jacksons said in their follow-up statement, noting the June release date of the list was "no doubt timed to the anniversary of Michael's passing."

Although the files were not up to police standards, there's a very good reason why: the "interspersed" pages came from the confidential files of Michael's own private eye, Anthony Pellicano, who kept tabs on the singer and routinely kept him out of trouble.

During the 1993 Chandler scandal, Pellicano used a similar tactic when he advised Michael's camp to flood the media with "every single story that you could possibly imagine . . . so that when the trial comes out there is nothing left to talk about."

After spending over a decade as teammates, Pellicano and his high-profile client developed bad blood. The hot-tempered investigator—who recently finished a fifteen-year jail sentence for wiretapping, racketeering, identity theft, and destroying evidence—once threatened to "fire" Michael if he ever found out that the child abuse claims were true.

When Michael and Pellicano parted ways in the mid-2000s, it was because Pellicano discovered something "even darker" about his client.

"I quit because I found out some truths," the seventy-five-year-old sleuth recently confessed. "He did something far worse to young boys than molest them."

The tight-lipped private eye wouldn't go into detail about his shocking discovery, but his leaked intelligence (via a third party) regarding the contents of Michael's library seems tame by comparison.

Pellicano wasn't the only person who defended Michael and then had a major change of heart about the singer's innocence. In 2005, grandmother Eleanor Cook was a member of the jury that acquitted the superstar. The ninety-three-year-old now contends that she believed Michael was guilty, but other jurors pressured her into changing her mind.

"I definitely thought he was guilty with all my heart and soul," Eleanor stated. "In the end, it came down to two people—me and one man. We were the only ones that maintained he was guilty and we fought it to the end. I was bullied pretty badly into making the decision. We finally looked at each other and said, 'What the hell! These stupid people aren't budging!' You can only stick with it so long."

Eleanor blamed the other ten jurors of being so starstruck by the performer that they failed to properly evaluate the evidence presented in Santa Barbara County Superior Court. She also felt that Robson, who testified to Michael's innocence, was lying to protect him. She believed Michael "should have been sent to jail" and "punished" for his alleged crimes, but she also admitted she "felt sorry" for him because of his upbringing.

"Yes, he was guilty, and he did a lot of that stuff. But he had a hard life," she said. "His father mistreated him—and that came out in court."

If the jury had swung Eleanor's way and issued a guilty verdict, Michael would have spent several decades behind bars. However, he likely would have survived longer than the four years that ultimately remained in his life and would probably still be alive today.

CHAPTER THIRTY-FIVE

CAUSE FOR CONCERN

With more of Michael's assets being unearthed every year, including the unimaginable contents of numerous storage facilities and his seemingly endless trove of personal documents, insight into the legendary entertainer's private world is constantly developing. And the latest conclusions are chilling.

A newly discovered secret diary kept by Michael in the months before his tragic death show the performer still grappling with his desperation to be "the greatest ever." Several pages detail his blueprint to rebuilding his flagging career in the hope of eventually becoming "immortalized" like his idols Charlie Chaplin and Walt Disney.

"These men demanded perfection," he wrote, noting his potential to become the "first multi-billionaire entertainer-actor-director."

Michael envisioned himself making $20 million a week through various future enterprises, like Cirque De Soleil concerts, a "Nike deal," and through the hiring of a "merchandising guy." He was also eager to begin making films in Hollywood, including remakes of *Jack the Giant Killer*, *20,000 Leagues Under the Sea*, *The Seventh Voyage of Sinbad*, and a 3D version of *Aladdin*.

"Demand development of these movies," the singer scribbled. "If I don't concentrate [on] film, no immortalization."

The diary also shows Michael attempting to regain control of his exhausted assets.

"I want to sign all checks over $5000 now," he jotted down. "Hire accountant I trust now and lawyer. I want to meet him . . . I want inventory now on all auction items. No auction."

Michael also feared he was being taken advantage of by his manager Tohme.

"Tohmey (sic) away from my $ now," he blasted in one entry. "No Tohmey near me, No Tohmey on plane or in my house."

But the handwritten records also reveal how hopelessly addicted to drugs Michael was.

While flying to London for his doomed "This Is It" concerts, Michael was hankering for Dr. Murray to administer his sleep-inducing "drip" drugs.

"Conrad must practice now," Michael wrote. "I can't be tired."

In his final weeks, Michael was also convinced that his life was in jeopardy, but not due to his drug habit.

"I'm afraid someone is trying to kill me," Michael wrote in a 2009 note that he signed and dated. The singer feared he was being targeted for his $750 million song catalogue—ATV Music Publishing—and blamed a longtime entertainment lawyer for the murder plot.

"Evil people, everywhere," he alleged. "They want to destroy me and take my publishing company. The system wants to kill me for my catalogue. . . . ATV is my catalogue. I'm not selling it."

Were these the frightened thoughts of a man pushed to his limits or merely the ramblings of a paranoid drug user? Without a doubt, Paris believes her father was murdered.

"It's obvious," she said after her father's passing. "All arrows point to that . . . Everybody in the family knows it. It was a set up."

But some who were close to Michael in his final days feel the singer had a death wish.

Jason Pfeiffer, who worked for Michael's dermatologist Dr. Klein, intercepted a call from the singer on May 3, 2009.

Desperate to reach the doctor, Michael struggled to utter coherent sentences.

In the previously unheard voicemail, obtained during the yearlong investigation of *Bad*, a slurring Michael can be heard making a frantic call to Pfeiffer just seven weeks before his death in a desperate attempt to reach a doctor.

It proves the "Thriller" singer couldn't even properly utter a short sentence.

"It's Michael. Err, I can't find Klein," said Jackson. "Um, I have a problem in the groin area, and I don't want to say this on the phone . . . inflamed area there, um, on a private . . . I don't want to say this on the phone. Get him to call me please."

After a brief pause, the legendary King of Pop murmured, "Thank you. Right away. Bye bye."

"No one realized he was getting drugs from all these different places," Pfeiffer told me in an exclusive interview first published on RadarOnline.com. "It was inevitable something was going to go wrong. Michael was manipulative and overpowering when it came to getting what he wanted."

Toward the end of his life, Michael made several of these "out of it" phone calls to the office—even though Dr. Conrad Murray was in charge of him in his final months alive. Just eleven days before his death, Michael pleaded with Klein's assistant for propofol.

According to Pfeiffer, "Michael barely had time to say hello before he just asked for propofol. He asked me if I knew anyone that could supply him with that. Michael said, 'I do it all the time to sleep, and I wake up feeling refreshed. I have to be up for tomorrow.' When I said I couldn't help, Michael just shut me down and slammed the phone down on me."

Pfeiffer also knew of instances where Jackson faked medical issues so that he could receive Demerol, he said:

> My role [as Klein's clinic manager] was to monitor Michael after he had Demerol.
>
> He actually spent hours just lying on couches out flat or trying to sleep. The main reason he came into the surgery so often, was to get a fix of Demerol during his procedures. He begged everyone to give him it. He complained he couldn't sleep because his mind was racing constantly. By the end, it became like a fix for Michael; getting face fillers and Botox surgery was an easy way of getting Demerol.
>
> Michael was an addict. He always asked Klein to give him four times the regular amount even if it was for squeezing a spot or putting Botox into his skin. Michael felt he was immune to normal volumes and begged for extra quantities.
>
> Sometimes some of our patients were groggy after shots, but never like Michael.

Another insider has revealed that Michael was "at the end of his rope" and frequently contemplated taking his own life.

"Michael always talked about dying young," the insider said. "He wrote suicide notes, then tore them up. He kept one with him. He often read it."

In a chilling 1999 interview about the child sex–abuse allegations against him, the singer actually confessed that he had contemplated suicide.

"If it wasn't for the children I'd throw in the towel and I'd kill myself," he admitted.

And in 2003, Michael's former brother-in-law Jack Gordon even predicted that the singer would take his own life one day.

"I'm convinced that it's only a matter of time before he kills himself," said Gordon, who was married to La Toya from 1989 to 1997.

While the facts of Michael's demise don't add up to suicide, they certainly reveal an overburdened man who slowly killed himself through drug use. And those who surrounded him took advantage of his helplessness.

Shortly before his death, Michael's 182-piece collection of artworks—not art collected by him, but created by him, and valued at over $900 million—was simply given away, seemingly without the singer's permission. Tohme gifted all of Michael's sculptures, sketches, illustrations, and designs, and the rights "to keep, sell, copy, exhibit, and to use [the artwork] in whatever way," to Australian artist Brett-Livingstone Strong, who was Michael's art mentor and collaborator.

In a letter sent to Strong, Tohme expressed that "Michael wants you know he is truly grateful for the loyalty you have shown him over the years, and he views this as a small token of appreciation for your continued friendship and artistic partnership."

But trusted members of Michael's inner circle had their doubts about the veracity of the one-sided deal.

"Neither Michael's signature nor his initials are on the document," a source close to the Jackson family said. "It doesn't make sense that he would give up a collection worth hundreds of millions of dollars when he was swamped in debt. Michael's mother and his children were the dearest things in his life. He would have wanted them to benefit financially."

In 2011, an undisclosed international businessman bought the collection at auction for $87 million. Although Strong offered to compensate the Jackson family, Michael's mother Katherine felt her son's lifetime of illustrations shouldn't be kept in private hands.

"Michael was always drawing or doing art," the eighty-nine-year-old matriarch said.

"I think fans will want to see them, because it was a part of him."

Incredibly, the sale of the artwork was canceled. Plans to create an interactive Michael Jackson monument, where fans could buy prints of the artists' works, never materialized. Instead, Strong published a hardcover book in 2015 titled *Artworks by Michael Jackson: The Unknown Side of a World Star*. And Katherine wrote the foreword: a happy beginning after a tragic ending.

CHAPTER THIRTY-SIX

DOWN THE LINE

The latest round of allegations against the late Michael Jackson has taken a toll on the entire Jackson family, but perhaps none more severely than twenty-one-year-old Paris.

After their father's death, the Jackson children moved to Hayvenhurst, the sprawling Encino estate of their grandmother and official guardian. Hoping to counteract the children's tragic loss, other family members also took up residence at Katherine's home to create a family atmosphere.

"Paris writes letters to her dad in Heaven," La Toya once told me. "When Michael passed, the decision was made to unmask them, so they could have the liberty and freedom of normal children."

Michael's kids weren't the only members of the family given a new lease on life. Katherine restored Debbie's visitation rights and the children learned that she was their biological mother.

"They hadn't known," an insider revealed, claiming that Michael's kids believed "she was a family friend."

But Paris has admitted that the loss of her father set her on a downward spiral of drug use and self-injury.

"I was doing a lot of things that thirteen-, fourteen-, fifteen-year-olds shouldn't do," she confessed, calling her actions "self-hatred." Paris also claimed she was sexually assaulted at age fourteen by a "much older" person and that she "didn't tell anybody." That individual has never been named.

At age fifteen, the budding model was rushed to the hospital after cutting her wrists and swallowing twenty pain pills. She was later boarded at a school for troubled kids. In December 2018, Paris checked herself into rehab for alcohol abuse and mental health issues.

"Her family are concerned she'll die like her dad did," an insider sadly asserted.

Since childhood, Paris has been torn between loyalty for her beloved father and the sickening feeling that beneath it he was a scoundrel who did terrible things. The release of *Leaving Neverland* in late January 2019 officially shook Paris's confidence in Michael, and completely destabilized the recovering addict, according to a source close to the family. But she tried to put on a brave face.

"There's nothing I can say that hasn't already been said in regards to defense," Paris said on social media, wisely reminding the world "that's not my role."

That March, police and EMS responded to Paris' Los Angeles-based home at 7:28 a.m.

Michael's daughter was believed to have slashed her wrists. On the 911 tape, dispatch tells Rescue 827 the call is for "psychiatric problems." A short time later, the paramedics upgraded the status to "emergency." She denied it was a suicide attempt.

Paris was rushed to the hospital, where it was reportedly suggested she be put on "5150 hold," a seventy-two-hour involuntary psychiatric commitment.

Instead, she was released later that same day.

Adding further stress to her already strained situation, Paris is presently no longer certain that Michael is actually her biological father, a Jackson family source told me.

A recent DNA test revealed that her ancestry is predominantly Caucasian.

That result came as no surprise to her twenty-two-year-old brother Prince, who is well aware that he and his sister likely don't share the same father.

In fact, the latest reports suggest that it was scientifically impossible for Michael to procreate.

Paul Gohranson, a former live-in lover of Dr. Klein, claimed that the King of Pop was sterile. Gohranson also stated that the doctor donated his own sperm so that the superstar singer could be a father.

According to Gohranson, when Joe Jackson beat young Michael, on more than one occasion he savagely kicked him in the testicles. The injury likely prevented Michael from producing sperm.

"Michael said his testicle was never the same again," Gohranson revealed. "He said it was enlarged and was always painful."

Dr. Klein allegedly also confessed to Gohranson that he was the father of Michael's children. And their mother, Debbie, was kept in the dark about it.

She eventually learned the truth during her marriage to Michael.

Currently, Michael's kids are scattered in different homes around Los Angeles. The Hayvenhurst house sits empty while aging Katherine has moved in full-time with her sixty-eight-year-old daughter Rebbie. Michael Jr. recently graduated from Loyola Marymount University in Los Angeles.

"Honestly, I can't tell you if all of it was worth it yet, but I am proud of my degree as I believe it is a testament to my dedication and discipline," Michael's eldest child said.

Since his father's passing, Prince Michael "Blanket" Jackson II has kept a low profile. The seventeen-year-old is attending a private high school in Los Angeles. He is under the guardianship of his cousin, T. J. Jackson, for another year.

And Paris has been playing small music gigs around Hollywood with her band The Soundflowers.

Debbie is often proudly in attendance, as are several celebrities, including Chris Brown and Michael's old friend Macaulay Culkin. Paris is currently dating her bandmate Gabriel Glenn.

As Michael's children endeavor to move on with their lives, Michael's sisters Janet and La Toya have sensationally claimed that their late brother's ghost has visited them.

"Michael is still here," La Toya told me soon after his 2009 death. "I have had very significant experiences with Michael after death."

The sixty-three-year-old Jackson insisted her brother's spirit appeared to her at home, still dressed in the white pearl beads he wore when he was laid to rest. She said he made his presence felt in a typically theatrical fashion.

"The lights were out and Michael appeared in the curtains," she said. "It was just his face, and he began to move. His eyes were open and he appeared peaceful, but then he vanished."

According to La Toya, the late singer has appeared more than once. She once asked him to "flick the lights."

"The lights went on and off," she claimed. "Janet didn't see him, but she saw a shadow and she also said, 'I have to get out of the room, Michael is in that room.'"

La Toya's experiences were supported by her manager, Jeffre Phillips, who said he had also witnessed the star's spirit while packing up Michael's belongings.

"I saw Michael looking right at me," Jeffre said "He looked like Michael from the video "The Way You Make Me Feel" in 1987. He wasn't smiling or upset—and it wasn't evil—he was just looking through the window. I looked at him directly in the eyes and then I ran downstairs."

Reflecting on the loss of the world's most famous entertainer, seventy-five-year-old singer Diana Ross—the godmother to Michael's three kids—reassuringly stated, "I believe and trust that Michael Jackson was and is a magnificent and incredible force to me and to many others."

And weighing in on the factors that ultimately took him down, renowned healer Deepak Chopra believes that Michael was ultimately responsible for his own death.

"He would go to great lengths to get it," Chopra said of Michael's deadly desire for painkillers. "If one doctor didn't give it to him, he'd try another. It was an addiction."

In retrospect, producer Randy Phillips believed that Michael wasn't in it for the money. "It was just doing something greater than anyone else had ever done it before. That's what motivated him."

Dorian Holley, who went on tour with Michael for over twenty years and was the last person to hear him sing live, noted of the sacred experience, "We had the technology to isolate just his microphone and listen to his singing separate from everything else. I had no idea what a genius he was. The way he was able to use his voice as a percussion instrument, lyricist, and jazz singer all at the same time. I'm sure as people mine his works in years to come, they're going to discover how much is there."

Even saddled with how polarizing he had become late in his life, Michael Jackson is still arguably the most unifying artist to ever live—the likes of which we may never see again.

If you or someone you know is contemplating suicide, call the National Suicide Prevention Lifeline at 1-800-273-8255

APPENDICES

THE PEOPLE OF THE STATE OF CALIFORNIA
VERSUS MICHAEL JOE JACKSON

The People of the State of California versus Michael Joe Jackson

{A} Count 1: The Grand Jury of the County of Santa Barbara, State of California, by this Indictment, hereby accuses Michael Joe Jackson of a felony, to wit: a violation of Penal Code Section 182, subdivision (a), sub (1), conspiracy, in that on or about and between February 1, 2003, and March 31, 2003, in the County of Santa Barbara, State of California, he did conspire with Ronald Konitzer, Dieter Wiesner, and Frank Cascio, aka Frank Tyson, Vinnie Amen, Frederic Marc Schaffel, and other uncharged co-conspirators and co-conspirators whose identities are unknown, to commit the crime of a violation of Penal Code Section 278, child abduction, a felony; a violation of Penal Code Section 236, false imprisonment, a felony; a violation of Penal Code Section 518, extortion, a felony; and that pursuant to and for the purpose of carrying out the objectives and purposes of the aforesaid conspiracy, to wit: unlawfully controlling, withholding, isolating, concealing, enticing and threatening John Doe, James Doe, Judy Doe, all minor children, and Jane Doe, an adult, did commit one or more of the following overt acts in the State of California, at least one of them in the County of Santa Barbara:

{B} Overt Act Number 1: On or about February 4, 2003, Michael Joe Jackson told Jane Doe that the lives of her children, John, James and

Judy Doe, were in danger due to the recent broadcast on British television of the documentary *Living with Michael Jackson*, in which John Doe appears with Michael Joe Jackson. Michael Joe Jackson did tell Jane Doe that she and her three children would be flown to Miami to participate in a press conference, which press conference never took place.

{B} Overt Act Number 2: On and between February 4, 2003, and February 5, 2003, the documentary *Living with Michael Jackson*, in which John Doe appears, was broadcast in the United States. Michael Joe Jackson did personally prevent the Doe family from viewing the program, while at the Turnberry Resort Hotel in Miami, Florida.

{B} Overt Act Number 3: On and between February 7, 2003, and February 8, 2003, Michael Joe Jackson did return the Doe family to Santa Barbara in a private jet. On the flight, Michael Joe Jackson did sit with John Doe and did give him an alcoholic beverage, concealed in a soft drink can. Michael Joe Jackson did then present John Doe with a wristwatch. Michael Joe Jackson did tell John Doe that the watch was worth $75,000. Michael Joe Jackson did tell John Doe not to tell anyone about them drinking alcoholic beverages together.

{B} Overt Act Number 4: On or about February 8, 2003, Michael Joe Jackson brought the Doe family to Jackson's Neverland Ranch, where John, James, Judy, and Jane Doe remained for approximately five days.

{B} Overt Act Number 5: On and between February 6, 2003, and February 12th, 2003, in both Miami, Florida, and at Neverland Ranch in Santa Barbara County, Ronald Konitzer, and Dieter Wiesner did tell Jane Doe that there were death threats made against her and her children by unknown individuals. They did further tell Jane Doe that the only way to assure the safety of her family was for the Does to participate in the making of a "rebuttal" video favorable to Michael Joe Jackson.

{B} Overt Act Number 6: On and between February 12, 2003, and February 15, 2003, after the Doe family had departed Neverland Ranch in the night, Frank Cascio, aka Frank Tyson, did telephone Jane Doe and did urge her to return with her children to Neverland Ranch and did say, quote, "I know Michael would love for you to come back to the ranch, for the safety of all concerned," unquote; and, quote, "Now is not the time to be out there alone," unquote; and, quote, "Never turn your back on Michael," unquote; and, "Michael wants to see you and the family," that's in quotes; and, quote, "You need to go back up to the ranch and see Michael, because he's very concerned," unquote; and, quote, "Even staying another night alone is not safe," unquote. Frank Cascio, aka Frank Tyson, did tell Jane Doe that, "We would love for you to go on tape and just say something beautiful about Michael." Frank Cascio did assure Jane Doe and John Doe that Ronald Konitzer and Dieter Wiesner would no longer be present at the ranch if they returned. He did state, "They are not there; I know that for a fact."

{B} Overt Act Number 7: On and between February 2003 and March 2003, at Neverland Ranch, Frank Cascio, aka Frank Tyson, did threaten James Doe that Cascio did have ways to make James Doe's parents disappear. Frank Cascio did tell John Doe, "I could have your mother killed."

{B} Overt Act Number 8: On or about February 14, 2003, and February 15, 2003, Michael Joe Jackson's personal chauffeur, Gary Hearne, did drive to Jane Doe's Los Angeles residence and did transport her and her children back to the Neverland Ranch in Santa Barbara County.

{B} Overt Act Number 9: On and between February 14, 2003, and February 15, 2003, upon the Doe Family's return to Neverland Ranch, Ronald Konitzer and Dieter Wiesner were, in fact, present; whereupon Jane Doe asked to leave with her children. Ronald Konitzer and Dieter

Wiesner did tell Jane Doe that she was free to depart, however her children must remain at the ranch.

{B} Overt Act Number 10: During the month of February 2003, in Santa Barbara County, California, Michael Joe Jackson's personal security staff was directed in writing not to allow John Doe to leave Neverland Ranch.

{B} Over Act Number 11: During the month of February 2003, Frederic Marc Schaffel, Christian Robinson and an unknown attorney did prepare a script of questions to be asked of the Doe family during the filming of the "rebuttal" video by Hamid Moslehi, Michael Joe Jackson's personal videographer.

{B} Overt Act Number 12: On or about February 19, 2003, the Doe children were transported by Hamid Moslehi from Neverland Ranch to Moslehi's home in the San Fernando Valley, and on the same date, Vinnie Amen did transport Jane Doe to Hamid Moslehi's filming of the "rebuttal" video.

{B} Overt Act Number 13: On or about February 19, 2003, in Los Angeles County between 11:00 p.m. and 1:00 a.m., the employees and associates of Michael Joe Jackson did tape the "rebuttal" video, an interview of the Doe family, in the presence of Vinnie Amen and Bradley Miller, a licensed private investigator. During the taping, previously scripted questions were asked of the Doe family.

{B} Overt Act Number 14: On or about February 20, 2003, Vinnie Amen did transport Jane Doe to Norwalk, in Los Angeles County, to obtain birth certificates of the Doe family for the purpose of obtaining passports and visas to travel to Brazil.

{B} Overt Act Number 15: On and between February 25, 2003, and March 2, 2003, Vinnie Amen did take the Doe family from Neverland

Ranch to the Country Inn and Suites in Calabasas, Los Angeles County. Vinnie Amen did transport Jane Doe to public offices in Los Angeles County where passports showing the destinations of Italy and France and visas for entrance to Brazil for the Doe family were obtained. Frederic Marc Schaffel, business partner of Michael Joe Jackson and president of Neverland Valley Entertainment, did pay expenses in connection with this activity.

{B} Overt Act Number 16: On or about February 25, 2003, Frederic Marc Schaffel did make airline reservations for the Doe family to travel to Brazil on March, 2003.

{B} Overt Act Number 17: On or about February 26, 2003, Frederic Marc Schaffel and Frank Cascio, aka Frank Tyson. On or about February 26, 2003, Frederic Marc Schaffel paid Frank Cascio, aka Frank Tyson, $1,000 in connection with "vacation" expenses of the Doe family.

{B} Overt Act Number 18: On or about February 23, 2003, Frederic Marc Schaffel did pay Vinnie Amen the sum of $500 cash for costs related to the Brazilian visas of the Doe family.

{B} Overt Act Number 19: On and between February 2003 and March 2003, at the Neverland Ranch, Michael Joe Jackson did have John Doe sleep in his bedroom and in his bed.

{B} Overt Act Number 20: On and between February 2003 and March 2003, at Neverland Ranch, Michael Joe Jackson did house Jane and Judy Doe in a guest cottage on Neverland Ranch where Jane and Judy Doe slept.

{B} Overt Act Number 21: On and between February 2003 and March 2003, at Neverland Ranch, Michael Joe Jackson did show sexually explicit materials to John and James Doe.

{B} Overt Act Number 22: On and between February 2003 and March 2003, at Neverland Ranch, Michael Joe Jackson did drink alcoholic beverages in the presence of John and James Doe and provided alcoholic beverages to them.

{B} Overt Act Number 23: On and between February 2003 and March 2003, Michael Joe Jackson did monitor and maintain control over the activities at Neverland Ranch by means of multiple interior door locks, proximity sensor alarm devices, and a keypad combination lock, as well as video and telephone surveillance equipment. Michael Joe Jackson did personally monitor telephone conversations of Jane Doe, without her knowledge or permission.

{B} Overt Act Number 24: On or about March 1, 2003, Vinnie Amen did pay the rent on the residence of the Doe family in Los Angeles County and moved their belongings into storage.

{B} Overt Act Number 25: On or about March 6, 2003, Vinnie Amen did go to John Burroughs Middle School In Los Angeles County and he did withdraw John and James Doc from their enrollment there, telling school authorities that the children were relocating to Phoenix, Arizona.

{B} Overt Act Number 26: On or about March 9, 2003, Michael Joe Jackson was told by John Doe that John Doe had a medical appointment the following day, at which time he was to give his medical staff a 24-hour-long urine collection specimen for laboratory analysis. Michael Joe Jackson, in Santa Barbara County, did tell John Doe to cancel the appointment, because the sample would reveal that John Doe had been consuming alcoholic beverages while staying at the Neverland Ranch.

On or about March 10, 2003, in Los Angeles County, after Jane Doe refused to cancel the medical appointment and while on the way to the medical appointment, Vinnie Amen did destroy most of John Doe's collected urine specimen, intended for laboratory analysis in connection with John Doe's follow-up treatment for the disease of cancer.

{B} Overt Act Number 27: On and between February 2003 and March 2003, in Los Angeles County, and as revealed by a surveillance tape located on November 18, 2003, in the office of Private Investigator Bradley Miller, an unknown co-conspirator conducted video surveillance of John Doe and various members of John Doe's family, including his grandmother and grandfather, his mother, his mother's boyfriend, his brother and his sister, at and near their respective residences and elsewhere.

{B} Overt Act Number 28: On or about March 31, 2003, Michael Joe Jackson did direct Frederic Marc Schaffel to pay Frank Cascio, aka Frank Tyson, the sum of one million dollars, from "Petty Cash" of Neverland Valley Entertainment on behalf of Michael Joe Jackson.

{A} Count 2: The Grand Jury of the County of Santa Barbara, State of California, by this Indictment, hereby accuses Michael Joe Jackson of a felony, to wit: a violation of Penal Code Section 288, subdivision (a), lewd act upon a child, in that on or about and between February 20, 2003, and March 12, 2003, in the County of Santa Barbara, State of California, he did willfully, unlawfully, and lewdly commit a lewd and lascivious act upon and with the body and certain parts and members thereof of John Doe, a child under the age of 14—under the age of 14 years, with the intent of arousing, appealing to, and gratifying the lust, passions, and sexual desires of said defendant and the said child. The further allegation that in the circumstances of the crime alleged in this count the crime constituted substantial sexual conduct with a child under the age of 14 years, within the meaning of Penal Code Section 1203.066, subdivision (a)(8).

{A} Count 3: The Grand Jury of the County of Santa Barbara, State of

California, by this Indictment, hereby accuses Michael Joe Jackson of a felony, to wit: a violation of Penal Code Section 288, subdivision (a), lewd act upon a child, in that on or about and between February 20, 2003, and March 12, 2003, in the County of Santa Barbara, State of California, he did willfully, unlawfully and lewdly commit a lewd and lascivious act upon and with the body and certain parts and members thereof of John Doe, a child under the age of 14 years, with the intent of arousing, appealing to, and gratifying the lust, passions and sexual desires of said defendant and said child. The further allegation that in the 13 circumstances of the crime alleged in this count the crime constituted substantial sexual conduct with a child under the age of 14 years, within the meaning of Penal Code Section 1203.066, subdivision (a)(8).

{A} Count 4: The Grand Jury of the County of Santa Barbara, State of California, by this Indictment, hereby accuses Michael Joe Jackson of a felony, to wit: a violation of Penal Code Section 288, subdivision (a), lewd act upon a child, in that on or about and between February 20, 2003, and March 12, 2003, in the County of Santa Barbara, State of California, he did willfully, unlawfully and lewdly commit a lewd and lascivious act upon and with the body and certain parts and members thereof of John Doe, a child under the age of 14 years, with the intent of arousing, appealing to, and gratifying the lusts, passions, and sexual desires of said defendant and the said child. The further allegation that in the circumstances of this count, the crime constituted substantial sexual conduct with a child under the age of 14 years, within the meaning of Penal Code Section 1203.066 (a)(8).

{A} Count 5: The Grand Jury of the County of Santa Barbara, State of California, by this Indictment, hereby accuses Michael Joe Jackson of a felony, to wit: a violation of Penal Code Section 288, subdivision (a), lewd act upon a child, in that 14 on or about and between February 20, 2003, and March 12, 2003, in the County of Santa Barbara, State of

California, he did willfully and unlawfully and lewdly commit a lewd and lascivious act upon and with the body and certain parts and members thereof of John Doe, a child under the age of 14 years, with the intent of arousing, appealing to, and gratifying the lusts, passions, and sexual desires of said defendant and said child. The further allegation that in the circumstances of the crime alleged in this count the crime constituted substantial sexual conduct with a child under the age of 14 years, within the meaning of Penal Code Section 1203.066, subdivision (a)(8).

{A} Count 6: The Grand Jury of the County of Santa Barbara, State of California, by this Indictment, hereby accuses Michael Joe Jackson of a felony, to wit: a violation of Penal Code Sections 664 and 288, subdivision (a), attempt to commit a lewd act upon a child, in that on or about and between February 20, 2003, and March 12, 2003, in the County of Santa Barbara, State of California, he did willfully, unlawfully and lewdly attempt to have John Doe, a child under 14 years of age, commit a lewd and lascivious act upon and with Defendant Michael Joe Jackson's body and certain parts and members thereof, with the intent of arousing, appealing to, and gratifying the lust, passions, and sexual desires of the said defendant and the said child.

{A} Count 7: The Grand Jury of the County of Santa Barbara, State of California, by this Indictment, hereby accuses Michael Joe Jackson of a felony, to wit: a violation of Penal Code Section 222, administering an intoxicating agent to assist in the commission of a felony, in that on or about and between February 20, 2003, and March 12, 2003, in the County of Santa Barbara, State of California, he did unlawfully administer to John Doe an intoxicating agent, to wit: alcohol, with the intent thereby to enable and assist him to commit a felony, to wit: child molestation, in violation of Penal Code Section 288, subdivision (a).

{A} Count 8: The Grand Jury of the County of Santa Barbara, State of

California, by this Indictment, hereby accuses Michael Joe Jackson of a felony, to wit: a violation of Penal Code Section 222, administering an intoxicating agent to assist in the commission of a felony, in that on or about and between February 20, 2003, and March 12, 2003, in the County of Santa Barbara, State of California, he did unlawfully administer to John Doe an intoxicating agent, to wit: alcohol, and with the intent thereby to enable and assist himself to commit a felony, to wit: child molestation, in violation of Penal Code Section 288, subdivision 16 (a).

{A} Count 9: The Grand Jury of the County of Santa Barbara, State of California, by this Indictment, hereby accuses Michael Joe Jackson of a felony, to wit: a violation of Penal Code Section 222, administering an intoxicating agent to assist in the commission of a felony, in that on or about and between February 20, 2003, and March 12, 2003, in the County of Santa Barbara, State of California, he did unlawfully administer to John Doe an intoxicating agent, to wit: alcohol, with the intent thereby to enable and assist him to commit a felony, to wit: child molestation, in violation of Penal Code Section 288, subdivision (a).

{A} Count 10: The Grand Jury of the County of Santa Barbara, State of California, by this Indictment, hereby accuses Michael Joe Jackson of a crime, to wit: a violation of Penal Code Section 222, administering an intoxicating agent to assist in the commission of a felony, in that on or about between February 20, 2003, and March 12, 2003, in the County of Santa Barbara, State of California, he did unlawfully administer to John Doe an intoxicating agent, to wit: alcohol, with the intent hereby to enable and assist him to commit a felony, to wit: child molestation, in violation of Penal Code Section 288, subdivision (a).

It is further alleged that Counts 2 through 5 are serious felonies within the meaning of Penal Code Section 1192.7, subdivision (c)(6).

{A} As to Counts 2 through 5, it is further alleged, pursuant to Penal

Code Section 1203.066, subdivision (a)(8), that the victim in the above offense, John Doe, was under the age of 14 years and Michael Joe Jackson had substantial sexual conduct with John Doe. Pursuant to the provisions of Penal Code Section 293.5 the use of "John Doe" as it appears in the Indictment is for the purpose of protecting the privacy of the alleged victim.

THE PERSONAL DIARY OF MICHAEL JACKSON

Did a burning desire to be "the greatest ever" drive Michael Jackson to his tragic end?

This author has uncovered that haunting desperation in his never-before-seen diaries recorded in the months before his death, which also revealed Jackson's plans to rebuild his flagging career and the chilling decision to hire death doctor Conrad Murray.

Jackson grappled with his desperation to be more successful than others—a bigger star than Gene Kelly and Fred Astaire.

The twelve pages of the King of Pop's journal detail his blueprint to rebuild his flagging career in the hope of eventually becoming "immortalized"—like his idols Charlie Chaplin, Michelangelo, and Walt Disney.

But the notes, filed in a Los Angeles court as part of his wrongful death trial, also detail how a hopeless and drug-addicted Jackson wanted his personal physician, Conrad Murray, on the plane bound for London and his doomed "This Is It" tour to administer drugs.

The *Thriller* megastar wrote how he needed the death doctor—who administered Jackson's fateful dose of the powerful anesthetic proposal—to set-up a "drip" so he could get "Rim [sic] sleep," the handwritten notes reveal.

"Conrad must practice now," Jackson wrote. "I can't be tired after procedure to important Rim [sic] sleep."

He added, "Hire Conrad exclusive."

The diary is laced with a tortured Jackson's yearning to make his comeback series of fifty concerts a success, after years of sordid headlines, questionable behavior, and persistent child molestation allegations.

The "Billie Jean" hitmaker details his last-ditch attempt to begin earning $20 million income each week, by moving into movie production after the tour's end and ultimately becoming the "first multi-billionaire entertainer-actor-director."

"Better than Kelly and Astaire," wrote Jackson, who died at age fifty, a day after a rehearsal and three weeks before the first concert on what would have been his final tour.

"The greatest [ever] in the likes of Chaplin, Michelangelo and Disney—these men demanded perfection, innovation always."

The pop star remarked how he wanted AEG, the concert promoter, to help him develop and remake movies for such fantasy classics as *The 7th Voyage of Sinbad*, *Ali Baba and the Forty Thieves*, *Jack the Giant Killer*, and *20,000 Leagues Under the Sea*.

Jackson—who considered himself the real-life Peter Pan—also plotted to create a 3D version of *Aladdin*, the Disney animation mega-hit from 1992.

He scrawled, "If I don't concentrate [on] film, no immortalization."

The most celebrated entertainer the world has ever seen also wanted to take on "The Great White Way" with a musical about his life; as well as create his own merchandise lines of soda and cookies.

He noted his desire to meet with Simon Fuller, the man behind *American Idol* and the Spice Girls, whom he thought could help him resurrect his career.

While he had adulation for Fuller, Jackson couldn't say the same kind sentiments of Tohme Tohme, his ex-manager.

"Tohmey (sic) away from my $ now," he blasted in one entry. "No Tohmey near me, No Tohmey on plane or in my house," he added, in another.

The 13-Grammy Award winner—who was strapped for cash at the time and living like a vagabond, as a court has heard—noted how he needed to "hire an accountant I trust" and lawyer, but warned himself, "caution, caution."

In another note, he wrote: "Mother do you need $."

NO AEG unless Films are involved

Angelikson
Productions

Meeting peter lopez
Simon Fuller AEG Now.
Call Fuller myself.

MJ Musical Now

MMusgh Script
Should be in TUT
ned Musical.

ned Family Films

TOH mon Awkey Now
FROM my $ Now
No conTrcT.
witness my House
Phillips in conTract.
witness No money for
smells so stews

09/10/2013

Mother Do
You Need $

09/10/2013

Negociate $ 40 More Shows,
Movies when?
Randy philipps

Delio

Hollow een special

Ken Evrlikman

→ Delio peter Jackson

Randy philips Delio

MJ TV

MJ RADio London

MJ SODA can london Deal
Now

MJ Cookies Deal Now

games net vision
Now

that the giant killer

SinBAD = omar

AEG →

Demand Development Mysterious Isla

of these Movies

Aladin Cameron
u start to
now Familiar

3D Film
2 Hour Movie

SINBADS Seventh
Voyage

1001 nights part 2

Ali baba"
and forty thieves
set into four John Peter

1451 Diamond

Tot

More than human

Cash yellow
20,000 leagues under the

AEG Develop
now.

09/10/2013

RANDy
PHILLYPS
Need

representation
account
Lawyer
Manager
invest with phil

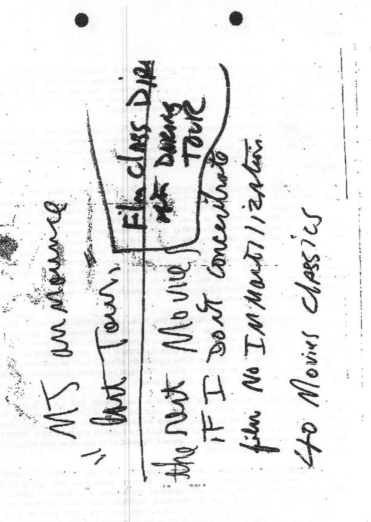

MJ's number
"that Tour,"

the next Movie
if I don't concentrate
film No Immortilization

40 Movie Classics

Film class Dur
not during
Tour

ConRAD on plane
DRip Rin sleep
NO TomMEY new
me no touvey on
plane was in my
House, Vegitarian Cook
Now Farm PRoduce →

Conrad MUST
practice now
I can't be tired after
procedure to important
Rim Sleep, for plane also
with Bed Hotel CONRAD exclusive

Cirque Du Soleil
10,000,000

AEG 250,000,000

Mike Deal.
Blue City
al Malik
Mino Farina

ALL Ray's gonna To TAX

Mirco House

Hire Much en disurgy gy

I want to sign all checks over 5,000,00 Now

Much end i Sing

CAUTION Opinions

Hire Accountant

I TRUST Now

will launch CAUTION

I want to MEET him

Auctions

I want investing now on all auction It has an No action.

09/10/2013.

MJ RADIO DAY
LONON

RANDy PHIlip

ORganize!

Weekly income
20 Million a week

First Multi

Billionais

Entertainer
actor

Better
than
{ Kelly &
Astaire

Director
100 Billion
the
greatest
MJ

in the likes of chaplin Michel aglo Disney
These men Demanded perFection innovation always